# **Mapping** Comprehensive Units to the **ELA Common Core Standards**

## K–5

*In memory of my beloved aunt, Selma Baum Abelson,*
*whose passion for education knew no bounds*

# Mapping Comprehensive Units to the **ELA Common Core Standards** K–5

## Kathy Tuchman Glass

Foreword by Cindy A. Strickland

**CORWIN**
A SAGE Company

**CORWIN**
A SAGE Company

FOR INFORMATION:

Corwin
A SAGE Company
2455 Teller Road
Thousand Oaks, California 91320
(800) 233-9936
www.corwin.com

SAGE Publications Ltd.
1 Oliver's Yard
55 City Road
London EC1Y 1SP
United Kingdom

SAGE Publications India Pvt. Ltd.
B 1/I 1 Mohan Cooperative Industrial Area
Mathura Road, New Delhi 110 044
India

SAGE Publications Asia-Pacific Pte. Ltd.
3 Church Street
#10-04 Samsung Hub
Singapore 049483

Acquisitions Editor:   Carol Chambers Collins
Associate Editor:   Megan Bedell
Editorial Assistant:   Sarah Bartlett
Project Editor:   Veronica Stapleton
Copy Editor:   Gretchen Treadwell
Typesetter:   C&M Digitals (P) Ltd.
Proofreader:   Scott Oney
Indexer:   Gloria Tierney
Cover Designer:   Janet Kiesel
Permissions Editor:   Adele Hutchinson

*Library of Congress Cataloging-in-Publication Data*

Glass, Kathy Tuchman.
Mapping comprehensive units to the ELA common core standards,
k-5/Foreword by Cindy A. Strickland; Kathy Tuchman Glass.

pages cm

Includes bibliographical references and index.
ISBN 978–1–4522–1730–7 (pbk.)

1. Language arts (Elementary)—United States. 2. Education,
Elementary—Standards—United States. 3. Curriculum planning.
I. Title.

LB1576.G4748 2012
372.6—dc23          2011048363

This book is printed on acid-free paper.

SUSTAINABLE FORESTRY INITIATIVE
Certified Chain of Custody
Promoting Sustainable Forestry
www.sfiprogram.org
SFI-01268
SFI label applies to text stock

12 13 14 15 16 10 9 8 7 6 5 4 3 2 1

# Contents

Additional materials and resources
related to *Mapping Comprehensive Units to
the ELA Common Core Standards, K–5* can be found at
http://www.corwin.com/mappingelaunits

# List of Figures

**Chapter 3: Unit Template With Examples**

**Chapter 4: Assessments**

**Chapter 5: Skills, Activities, Formative Assessments, and Resources**

**Chapter 6: Differentiated Instruction**

**Chapter 7: Lesson Design**

# Foreword

In cartoonist Mo Willems's (2003) book, *Don't Let the Pigeon Drive the Bus!*, we are introduced to a toddlerlike pigeon who, when the regular bus driver takes a break, tries every technique he can think of to convince the bus passengers to let him drive the bus. In spite of all the pigeon's wheedling, the passengers refuse to let him do so. They know that to get to where they are going safely and quickly, they need a cool-headed, professional driver with clear vision and a solid sense of direction.

In school, students are on an important journey, too. They are headed to their own futures! Along the way, students need a driver (teacher) with a clear vision of where the school bus is headed (standards), who makes use of the highest quality road map (curriculum) along the way, and who is unwavering in the commitment to get students to their destination as quickly and securely as possible.

The Common Core (CC) State Standards are designed to set a high bar for student accomplishment. They attempt to take the best of what we have learned over the years in working with individual state standards documents, consolidate and refine this information, and then make it accessible to all teachers and students no matter where students live or how many times they move from school to school. The CC Standards challenge teachers to help students meet 21st century learning goals, which include the ability to compete in an increasingly global economy that demands a high level of both critical and creative thinking skills. This is a complex goal for a complex society. And this complexity means the standards themselves are complex. Yet standards alone do not a curriculum make. While standards are a key component of determining where to take students, educators need to examine them, flesh them out, and play with them to ensure a depth of understanding that will allow curriculum to meet the needs of an increasingly diverse student population. Good teachers have always adapted *what* they teach to better match *whom* they teach. Some students take the expressway to standards; some take the scenic route. Some need rest stops or to take a few detours along the way. But they all must get there.

Author Kathy Glass and I share a love of writing good curriculum and a strong passion for helping teachers both write and use high-quality curriculum. In our 2009 book, *Staff Development Guide for the Parallel Curriculum*, Kathy and I provide step-by-step instruction on how to write conceptually based curriculum that challenges students with varied interests, learning profiles, and readiness levels to meet and move beyond standards as they work toward expertise in a discipline. This work begins with a teacher's clear articulation of unit or lesson goals, and then involves a constant vigilance in ensuring the degree to which the teaching and learning activities do the following:

- Build on key knowledge, understandings, and skills essential to the discipline of study.
- Organize and focus on essential outcomes (standards).

- Facilitate the use of knowledge and skills within a meaningful and engaging context.
- Require students to use both critical and creative thinking.
- Result in evidence of worthwhile student production.

*Mapping Comprehensive Units to the ELA Common Core Standards, K–5* echoes these themes as it helps teachers deconstruct and make sense of the new Common Core State Standards. Kathy's mission is to make teachers' labors easier and more streamlined without sacrificing quality or ignoring student differences.

What I particularly appreciate about Kathy's work is that she is not only clearly grounded in the disciplines related to the teaching of English language arts (ELA), but also highly practical in her support to teachers. In this book, she helps teachers first make sense of the ELA CC Standards for themselves, so that they can then devise appropriate sense-making activities for their students. She does this by helping teachers deconstruct, interpret, internalize, and even expand upon the ELA CC Standards. She then includes a cornucopia of meaningful ways to ensure that unit and lesson components are both rigorous in what they demand from students and relevant to individual students' current and future paths. The activities and strategies she suggests help ensure that students not only work with essential knowledge and skills, but also learn to ask and answer essential questions, helping them retain and transfer the knowledge and skills outlined in the common core documents. Moreover, Kathy integrates differentiation within many of these activities, reflecting her understanding of the increasingly diverse student body with which teachers work. Differentiating instruction makes sense and in fact is an imperative in a just society.

I'd be perfectly happy to get on any bus with Kathy in the driver's seat! I invite you to join her in the journey toward helping students meet the expected—and unexpected—challenges of the 21st century!

*Cindy A. Strickland*

# Acknowledgments

This book is a compilation of a great many years of practice, study, and effort made possible through my good fortune of working with innumerable educators near and far. Even though I've provided staff development to move *them* ahead on the professional continuum, I've learned enormously from them. Their insights, comments, and requests have enabled me to forge ahead to offer them more, which eventually set me on my way to write what I present here. As I rise to meet their continuous needs to reach their students, I learn and create new ways and tools to support their work. I particularly thank and appreciate teachers in the Portola Valley, Menlo Park, and Hillsborough school districts. These teachers know who they are.

Writing can be a solitary endeavor. As such, I am grateful to Cindy Strickland, who reviewed my manuscript offering sound suggestions and encouragement. In addition, I join Corwin in thanking the reviewers whose generous feedback helped me enormously. Gretchen Treadwell and Veronica Stapleton both deserve a big thank-you for powering through, providing key comments at a necessary juncture, and going to press in the nick of time. A huge debt of gratitude goes to my editor, Carol Collins, who made me see what was right before my eyes in figuring out this next book topic. Last but not least, I thank my supportive and nurturing husband, who is always available to lend a helping hand. Without him, this book would surely not be possible.

## PUBLISHER'S ACKNOWLEDGMENTS

Corwin gratefully acknowledges the contributions of the following reviewers:

Rochelle DeMuccio, Coordinator
English Language Arts/Reading, K–5
Half Hollow Hills School District
Dix Hills, NY

Arlene DeSiena, K–2 Literacy Supervisor
Assistant Principal of Bradt Primary School
Mohonasen Central School District
Schenectady, NY

Alesha M. Moreno-Ramirez, K–6 Literacy Consultant
Fresno, CA

# About the Author

**Kathy Tuchman Glass** consults nationally with schools and districts, presents at conferences, and teaches seminars for university and county programs delivering customized professional development. A former master teacher, she has been in education for over twenty years and works with administrators and teachers in groups of varying sizes from one-on-one to entire school districts, from kindergarten through high school. She leads and collaborates with educators to assist with strategic planning to determine school or district objectives; design standards-based differentiated curriculum; craft essential understandings and guiding questions; use compelling instructional strategies that engage all learners; incorporate effective pre-, formative, and summative assessments into curriculum; use six-trait writing instruction and assessment; create unit or yearlong curriculum maps using state or Common Core Standards; and more.

In addition to *Mapping Comprehensive Units to the ELA Common Core Standards, K–5*, she has written *Lesson Design for Differentiated Instruction, Grades 4–9* (2009), *Curriculum Mapping: A Step-by-Step Guide to Creating Curriculum Year Overviews* (2007), and *Curriculum Design for Writing Instruction: Creating Standards-Based Lesson Plans and Rubrics* (2005), and has coauthored the *Staff Development Guide for the Parellel Curriculum* (2009) with Cindy Strickland. In addition, she served as a differentiation consultant for Pearson Learning's social studies textbook series for K–5 (© 2013).

Originally from Indianapolis, Kathy resides in the San Francisco Bay Area. She can be reached through e-mail at kathy@kathyglassconsulting.com. Her website is www.kathy glassconsulting.com.

# Introduction

If you are an educator in one of the states that has adopted the Common Core State Standards, you are undoubtedly headed toward yet another change in our field. Like other educators in your same situation, you are embarking upon a new venture. This one is most likely here to stay, so do not assume this is a passing fancy! As stated in the Center on Education Policy's *Common Core State Standards: Progress and Challenges in School Districts' Implementation* (Kober & Renter, 2011), "Most of these states are expecting, rather than requiring, districts to undertake such activities as developing new curriculum materials and instructional practices, providing professional development to teachers and principals, and designing and implementing teacher induction programs and evaluations related to the standards" (p. 1). It is therefore not surprising that you probably need some support in navigating your way through these new standards and in using them to create curriculum. That's where I can help. I wrote this book for teachers, curriculum designers or directors, administrators, professors in teacher credentialing programs, or anyone who plans to use the Common Core Standards to write meaningful and effective curriculum that can make a lasting impression on our charges.

## ELA COMMON CORE

At the end of the book, a Resource section provides an overview of the new English language arts (ELA) Common Core (CC) Standards for K–5 titled "A Brief Primer on the ELA Common Core Standards." Most assuredly, you can plod through the voluminous material available on these standards yourself. Trust me, there is a daunting amount of resources surrounding them. However, I have combed the ELA Common Core Standards documents along with some key materials and share what I believe to be the highlights to save you some time. Those of you familiar with the organization and contents might choose to skim this section or skip it altogether. Or some of you might prefer to access the original source and read the Common Core "Introduction" and appendices in their entirety. If so, go to the Common Core State Standards Initiative website (www.corestandards.org) and navigate to locate pieces of information you want to read verbatim.

## WHAT TO EXPECT: UNIT MAP

Curriculum mapping allows educators to purposefully plan and outline what is taught in a given year. It allows for articulation across the grades and within each grade. As I state in my book *Curriculum Mapping: A Step-by-Step Guide for Creating Curriculum Year Overviews* (2007),

> A curriculum mapping document, as the name implies, maps everything—in all subject areas—that a teacher needs to cover in a given school year. The [map] accounts for all the content standards the district or state mandates, along with information that personalizes the document for each teacher. (p. 1)

Along with standards, curriculum maps can include key concepts, essential questions, skills, assessments, and more. Mapping a yearlong curriculum program allows educators to vertically and horizontally align their curriculum within a building and across the district. A map can uncover key learning that is repetitive, or missed entirely, so that educators become aware and accountable to students' learning.

Mapping the yearlong curriculum is advisable, and your school or district might be in the process of creating this kind of map or have plans to create one. However, teachers and curriculum designers need to understand the equally critical importance of creating a quality-driven unit map. That is the focus for this book: to guide readers to comprehensively map a unit of study using the ELA Common Core Standards. So whether or not schools or districts are in the process of a yearlong map, sooner or later teachers will need a comprehensive curriculum map for individual units. Doing so will clarify the outcomes for learners so that the curriculum and instruction aligned to these unit maps will emanate from quality.

The book not only introduces a process for developing your unit map but also includes a template with key components and thorough explanations for each one. Plus, the chapters feature many examples aligned to the ELA Common Core for these components, such as enduring understandings, guiding questions, culminating assessments with rubrics, differentiation ideas, skills, activity ideas, and so forth. There is also a lesson design template that is a natural subsequent step to the unit map along with several comprehensive lessons using this template. As you dive into the process of mapping a targeted unit, you will also become thoroughly knowledgeable about the Common Core Standards, because you will study them carefully to determine which ones to group together to form the basis for a unit. In addition, you will use these standards as a guide to identify the key conceptual understandings and skills that will drive quality curriculum and engaging instruction. Within the process, I walk you through the following steps that reflect the unit map template components:

- Grouping Common Core Standards
- Identifying what students should know
- Developing essential understandings
- Discerning between essential unit and lesson guiding questions and crafting them
- Identifying or creating culminating assessments for students to demonstrate learning
- Previewing prepared checklists and rubrics aligned to the Common Core Standards
- Considering ways to differentiate activities, assessments, and resources
- Distinguishing activities from skills and recording both
- Determining evidence of formative assessments
- Selecting appropriate resources

Truth be told, if you have done work with backward design, curriculum mapping, and differentiation, you will be familiar with much of what is presented here, but you should learn novel ideas or ways to approach what you have done in the past. My process for creating a map is akin to other methods and a compilation of successful work in the field from Heidi Hayes-Jacobs, Grant Wiggins, Jay McTighe, Lynn Erickson, Carol Ann Tomlinson, and a host of other revered academicians. Like my cohorts, I have my own twist on this work; my strategies have evolved from years of being in the trenches and consulting with teachers regularly. And I have found this process and the examples I share to resonate with them. As one New York City teacher commented, "You have an excellent ability to present material that can be 'overwhelming' into manageable chunks for success!" And from a teacher in Alaska, "Your ideas helped me see a new way of presenting information I didn't even realize. I was kind of 'stuck' in one way of thinking. Thank you!"

Before immersing yourself in these pages, I suggest you consider a targeted unit of study, print out the ELA Common Core Standards, gather a textbook and other resources for this unit, and begin to create a curriculum unit map with me. You can access my website at www.kathyglassconsulting.com for Microsoft Word formats of standards for each grade, K–8, by clicking on the appropriate links in the "Download Resources" section. That way you can download them onto your computer to cut and paste standards more easily for curriculum mapping and lesson design. For a PDF version of all the standards, go to the Common Core State Standards Initiative website, www.corestandards.org/, and for grade-specific ELA standards, www.corestandards.org/the-standards/english-language-arts-standards.

## COMPANION WEBSITE

This book provides a multitude of pertinent reproducibles to copy for classroom or professional use. Oftentimes, it is challenging to get a clear image of a page when copying from a book. For this reason, you can download all reproducibles and copy them from your printer through a companion website aligned to the book. Some reproducibles are in PDF format and others in a Microsoft Word version. The resources in Word are mostly handouts and activities for student use. You can download and adapt these figures to suit a particular grade level, or personalize or alter a specific assignment to meet students' needs. Throughout the book, you will see a mouse icon that indicates items that appear on this companion website. In some instances, a figure will be referenced in the book and appear in complete form in the companion website. To access this website, go to http://www.corwin.com/mappingelaunits.

# 1

# Standards and Knowledge

> *Standards are the foundation upon which almost everything else rests—or should rest. They should guide state assessments and accountability systems; inform teacher preparation, licensure, and professional development; and give shape to curricula, textbooks, software programs, and more. Choose your metaphor: Standards are targets, or blueprints, or roadmaps. They set the destination: what we want our students to know and be able to do by the end of their K–12 experience, and the benchmarks they should reach along the way.*
>
> —Chester E. Finn, Jr. and Michael J. Petrilli
> (as cited in Carmichael, Martino, Porter-Magee, & Wilson, 2010, p. 1)

Those new to the Common Core (CC) Standards or who wish to have a refresher might read the Resource section of this book, "A Brief Primer on the ELA Common Core Standards." Whether or not you read the primer for an overview of the CC Standards, this chapter is the starting point for the process of creating a curriculum map. It culminates with two exercises: grouping standards and using what you grouped to determine what you want students to know. These exercises are the launching pad for mapping an effective, concept-driven unit of instruction. To accomplish these tasks, the following is a snapshot of what this chapter includes that will familiarize you with these standards:

- A cursory overview of the role of standards
- Suggestions for comparing the Common Core Standards with your existing state standards (If you are not interested in the comparison of the two sets of standards or have already embarked upon this exercise, you might skip the section, "What to Look for When Aligning Existing Standards with the Common Core.")
- Specifics about what the genre of informational text entails, its distinguishing features, and how it differs from nonfiction; along with concrete examples of types of informational text and literature to help differentiate between them

- Definitions of the Common Core text types—opinion, informative/explanatory, narrative—along with ideas for writing prompts across content areas
- Insights gleaned from the Common Core and ways to group and use them to guide instruction and collaborate with colleagues, especially for standards relating to grammar and conventions

## THE PURPOSE OF STANDARDS

Standards get major attention in the world of education, and for good reason. They give teachers a starting point for teaching, for they are a guiding light to help them plan goals for students. Without standards driving curriculum, teachers could teach anything they wanted. That would probably wreak havoc for teachers as they would have no frame of reference to know what students have learned prior to entering their classroom. Therefore, September would be even more stressful than it already is because teachers would have difficulty planning instruction with no standards to guide them. In addition, any subject is quite expansive and covers a spectrum of teaching opportunities, so standards provide a direction for what teachers focus on in a given school year in a content area. If a school or district uses a curriculum guide for a particular unit, it likely bases this guide on standards so goals are embedded in the lessons teachers conduct. It is imperative to note that although standards provide a set of expectations, they do not diminish teachers' creative and professional capacity to plan curriculum and execute instruction, albeit instruction that is sound and based on research.

Standards alone will not guarantee that students will be successful. Using the blueprint metaphor from the beginning quote, an architect can design a detailed and magnificent building, but if the contractor cannot execute the plans, then how effective is the blueprint? Standards serve to guide expectations, but it takes insightful and skillful educators who make wise choices about what they teach and how they teach to really make an impact on students. You have probably heard of the powerful trio—know, understand, do (KUD)— that is repeatedly mentioned in educational literature as together the three form the basis for setting goals for effective teaching. Carol Tomlinson and Jay McTighe (2006) state what really matters in teaching:

> Central to teaching is *what* we ought to teach—what we want students to know, understand, and be able to do. To be an expert teacher is to continually seek a deeper understanding of the essence of a subject, to increasingly grasp its wisdom. That understanding is key to a teacher's role in curriculum planning. It is difficult to imagine someone becoming a great teacher without persistent attention to that element of the art of teaching. (p. 12)

Teachers use standards—like the Common Core—to help them identify what students should know, understand, and be able to do.

To become expert teachers, educators need to create a curriculum map that includes the KUDs along with other components (e.g., activities, differentiation, resources) to be sure that the unit is quality driven. Our journey on unit mapping begins by helping you familiarize yourself with the standards. The chapter then supports you in grouping standards and identifying what you want students to know from your selected standards. The subsequent chapter explains in detail the essential understandings and guiding questions that emanate from the work in this chapter. Later, we will tackle the other components in the curriculum unit map.

# WHAT TO LOOK FOR WHEN ALIGNING EXISTING STANDARDS WITH THE COMMON CORE

In terms of aligning existing state standards with Common Core Standards, many states are providing support to assist educators with the transition to the new standards by comparing the two documents. Some refer to this alignment and comparison between their state and the Common Core as *crosswalks.* Iowa, Massachusetts, North Carolina, Ohio, Utah, Washington, and California are just a handful of the many states that have produced such a document. Check out their websites or state departments of education for more information.

Because many states have already taken on the task of aligning state and Common Core Standards to see commonalities and differences, use the comparison or crosswalk documents as the basis for discussion and planning among colleagues. However, if your state has not produced such a document or you want more information about the relationship among the standards, the exercise can be a useful one. Comparative analysis can be helpful in assisting educators to adapt current curricula to new standards, consider different instructional strategies, obtain additional resources and materials, plan and create assessments, and so forth. Consider addressing these questions that can result from a careful analysis of cross-referencing these standards:

*Gaps and Overlap.* What knowledge, concepts, and skills are similar to existing standards that indicate overlap, and which are new expectations? Where are there gaps between the Common Core and the existing state standards? Where are specific inconsistencies with respect to cognitive expectations and rigor between the two sets of standards? What will need to be added to existing state standards? What will need to be eliminated?

*Formatting.* How is the structure and organization of the Common Core different than the existing standards? How is it the same? What are the strands between the two sets, and how do they overlap?

*Grade Alignment.* How do the two sets of standards compare with regard to concepts, knowledge, and skills associated with particular grade levels? Which Common Core Standards introduce concepts and skills in earlier or later grades than your state standards?

*Curriculum.* What revisions need to be made to curriculum (e.g., performance tasks, resources, materials, etc.) so it is focused on quality, differentiated, and aligned to the new standards? What are the plans to gather appropriate resources? Are textbooks aligned to the new standards? What are the policies and timeline in the district for adopting new textbooks?

*Assessments.* What pre-, formative, and summative assessments are needed that align to the new standards? Which ones need to be created, improved, or better aligned? Because administration of national assessments will be fully operational in the 2014 to 2015 school year, what assessments need to be in place to prepare students for these tests?

*Instructional Strategies.* Because some standards represent a change in cognitive demands, how can teachers adapt instruction accordingly? How does the increase of rigor of particular standards affect how teachers present content to assist students in grasping key concepts and skills?

*Professional Development.* Are some standards unfamiliar and/or daunting for teachers? Is there new vocabulary for teachers to learn? What professional development is needed to assist them in teaching to these particular standards effectively? What target areas of professional development are most pressing?

Yes, there is much to consider as you transition to the new Common Core. (I can visualize your heads bobbing in agreement.) By combing the comparative analysis, you will undoubtedly realize the work ahead to create an implementation plan for this transition process. However, do not get bogged down in the overlaps and gaps. Focus most critically on the particular grade level you teach: *What standards have remained the same? Where are the major changes?* The bottom line is that your state has adopted the Common Core Standards, and teachers are expected to implement them.

## UNDERSTANDING INFORMATIONAL TEXT AND HOW IT IS DIFFERENT FROM OTHER TEXT

With the CC Standards for the reading strand divided by literature and information text, it is worthwhile for educators to have a clear definition of informational text. Furthermore, categorizing the different types or genres of literature makes the distinction among them clear.

The terms *informational text* and *nonfiction* cannot be used interchangeably because not all nonfiction can be classified as informational text. Informational text is a type of nonfiction that is primarily used to convey factual information. In their book *Reading & Writing Informational Text in the Primary Grades*, Nell K. Duke and V. Susan Bennett-Armistead (2003) state that informational text has these distinctions:

- The primary purpose is to convey information about the natural and social world.
- It typically has characteristic features such as addressing whole classes of things in a timeless way that make these texts have a generalizing quality (e.g., sharks live in water).
- The text comes in many different formats, including books, magazines, handouts, brochures, CD-ROMs, and from the Internet.
- The text may include a repetition of a topic or theme; descriptions of attributes; a compare/contrast and classification structure; technical vocabulary; realistic illustrations or photographs; labels and captions; navigational aids such as indexes, page numbers, and headings; and graphical devices such as diagrams, tables, and charts.

As with any writing, in addition to distinctive features as shown in the prior list, the author's purpose is an important factor to consider when determining a text type. Therefore, some items on the previous list could apply to nonfiction, but the purpose of the piece helps to identify it as nonfiction or informational text. For example, an autobiography is a nonfiction account of one's life; however, the purpose is not to convey information about a general topic across time. Rather, an autobiography reveals information about one individual for a specified period, namely this person's lifetime or a period of the individual's life. Duke and Bennett-Armistead (2003) use the example of a procedural or how-to piece and do not classify it as informational. They assert that even though this type of text is nonfiction, its intended purpose is to relay to someone how to actually do something and not to convey information about something in the natural or social world (e.g., mammals, spiders, firefighters, cacti, snowflakes, plate tectonics, pilots, etc.). Finally, be aware that each example of informational text does not necessarily include all the features in the last bullet from the list (e.g., repetition of topic or theme, description of attributes, etc.). Each text will have specific features and emphasize some more than others based on the intent of the piece. For instance, a brochure about the Great Lakes may not rely heavily on technical vocabulary and diagrams, whereas a medical document about the digestive system surely might.

Literature can be in prose or poetry form. *Prose* is standard written literature (which encompasses both nonfiction and fiction) and plays. Literature in verse form is referred to as *poetry*. All literature can be classified into two types: fiction and nonfiction. Fictional literature or narrative literary works contain content that is produced by the imagination and is not necessarily based on fact. Nonfiction literature is opposite from fiction because it is informative and can include facts, details, anecdotes, and examples with analysis and illustrations. In addition, nonfiction can include text features, such as a table of contents, glossary, index, captions, bold and italicized type, charts, bibliographies, and so forth.

Figure 1.1 provides examples of each text type; however, do not consider these lists finite. As mentioned, because some forms of nonfiction can be informational text, you must

## Informational Text and Literature

| Informational Text | | |
|---|---|---|
| all-about books | handouts | newspaper articles |
| brochures | history textbooks | pamphlets |
| CD-ROMs | informational reports | research papers |
| encyclopedias | Internet websites | science textbooks |
| field guides | magazine articles | technical manuals |
| flyers | | |

| Types or Genres of Literature | |
|---|---|
| **Fictional Literature** (or Narrative Literature) | **Nonfiction Literature** (or Narrative Nonfiction or Literary Nonfiction) |
| children's literature | autobiography |
| contemporary realistic fiction | biography |
| drama/plays | diary |
| fantasy | essay (response to literature, persuasive, compare/contrast, etc.) |
| folklore (myths, legends, fables, trickster tales, fairy tales) | how-to paper |
| historical fiction | journal |
| mystery | magazine |
| novel | memoir |
| novella | newspaper |
| realistic fiction | personal narrative |
| science fiction | speech |
| short story | |
| tall tales | |

**FIGURE 1.1**

primarily consider the purpose of the text as well as the features when classifying the reading material. This mind-set can also help when you group standards so you can be aware to focus on reading for literature or informational text standards.

## DEFINITIONS OF THE COMMON CORE TEXT TYPES AND SAMPLE PROMPTS

Now let's move our attention from the reading strand to writing. Before grouping the standards, it is important to be familiar with the three different writing types so you can plan curriculum using them: (1) opinion/argument, (2) informative/explanatory, and (3) narrative. What follows is an explanation of these genres and some ideas for assignments tied to them that can help you get a better handle on these writing standards. But I forewarn you that they can be a bit confusing, so discuss and collaborate with colleagues to get consensus on clear expectations for students. As the authors of Fordham Institute's "The State of State Standards—and the Common Core—in 2010" (Carmichael et al., 2010) assert, "One troublesome aspect of the writing standards is the persistently blurry line between an 'argument' and an 'informational/explanatory essay'" (p. 26). The authors admit that appended materials might provide some clarity but, in the end, state that "these new definitions are likely to confuse teachers, curriculum developers, and publishers" (p. 26). Appendix A of the Common Core Standards (National Governors Association [NGA], 2010, pp. 23–24) provides a brief explanation of each genre, which I will share in this chapter and on which I will provide further elaboration. The student writing examples in the Common Core's Appendix C are also helpful as they include not only the student work across the grades and genres, but also an annotation that highlights the criteria according to the Common Core Standards. However, the designers of Appendix C do not evaluate each example of student work; they merely highlight specific writing excerpts that align with the criteria. In addition to these appendices, I will help you distinguish one text type from another.

There are instances in which text types are combined in a particular writing exercise, so when you group standards, you need to be mindful of this overlap. For example, a short story assignment would largely fall under the narrative realm. However, within the short story, students might create paragraphs that inform or explain to readers about a character's personality or physical appearance. Such a paragraph can begin with a topic sentence—*Mr. Hudson is a selfish man who cares only for himself*—and continue with details to support this impression. Or, for example, a paragraph might begin with *My mother is a beautiful woman. She has blue eyes that are the color of the sky. Her hands are soft rose petals* . . . In this regard, elements of informative or explanatory text are woven into the narrative. In fact, the Common Core raises this point and states that skilled writers oftentimes do blend the three text genres for a particular purpose, so it is important to be aware of this as you read further about the writing applications.

To begin, take a look at Figure 1.2, ELA Common Core State Standards for Writing K–6, which is a condensed version of the writing and research standards (NGA, 2010) and can also be viewed and downloaded from the companion website. It includes the exact research and writing standards formatted by text type in linear fashion, so you can see the progression from grade to grade for each isolated genre. Grade 6 is included so that fifth-grade teachers know the expectations for their students as they enter the middle grades. The research standards should be considered for opinion/argument and informative/explanatory as students conduct research to provide evidence for these papers.

*(Text continued on page 17)*

# ELA Common Core State Standards for Writing K–6

## Text Types and Purposes

### 1. Opinion Pieces and Arguments

|  | | |
|---|---|---|
| **K** | • Use a combination of drawing, dictating, and writing.<br>• Tell reader the topic or name of the book as the basis for writing. | • State an opinion or preference about the topic or book (e.g., *My favorite book is . . .*). |
| **Grade 1** | • Introduce the topic or name of the book as the basis for writing.<br>• State an opinion. | • Supply a reason for the opinion.<br>• Provide sense of closure. |
| **Grade 2** | • Introduce the topic or book as the basis for writing.<br>• State an opinion.<br>• Supply reasons that support the opinion. | • Use linking words (e.g., *because, and, also*) to connect opinion and reasons.<br>• Provide concluding statement or section. |
| **Grade 3** | Write opinion pieces on topics or texts, supporting a point of view with reasons.<br><br>a. Introduce topic or text, state an opinion, and create an organizational structure that lists reasons. | b. Provide reasons that support the opinion.<br>c. Use linking words and phrases to connect opinion and reasons.<br>d. Provide concluding statement or section. |
| **Grade 4** | Write opinion pieces on topics or texts, supporting a point of view with reasons and information.<br><br>a. Introduce topic or text clearly, state an opinion, and create an organizational structure in which related ideas are grouped to support the writer's purpose. | b. Provide reasons that are supported by facts and details.<br>c. Link opinion and reasons using words and phrases.<br>d. Provide a concluding statement or section related to the opinion presented. |
| **Grade 5** | Write opinion pieces on topics or texts, supporting a point of view with reasons and information.<br><br>a. Introduce topic or text clearly, state an opinion, and create an organizational structure in which related ideas are logically grouped to support the writer's purpose. | b. Provide logically ordered reasons that are supported by facts and details.<br>c. Link opinion and reasons using words, phrases, and clauses.<br>d. Provide a concluding statement or section related to the opinion presented. |
| **Grade 6** | Write arguments to support claims with clear reasons and relevant evidence.<br><br>a. Introduce claim(s) and organize the reasons and evidence clearly.<br>b. Support claim(s) with clear reasons and relevant evidence, using credible sources and demonstrating an understanding of the topic or text. | c. Use words, phrases, and clauses to clarify the relationships among claim(s) and reasons.<br>d. Establish and maintain a formal style.<br>e. Provide a concluding statement or section that follows from the argument presented. |

**FIGURE 1.2** *(Continued)*

## 2. Informative/Explanatory Texts

|  |  |
|---|---|
| **K** | • Use a combination of drawing, dictating, and writing. • Name what they are writing about. • State and supply some information about the topic. |
| **Grade 1** | • Write. • Name a topic. • Supply some facts about the topic. • Provide a sense of closure. |
| **Grade 2** | • Introduce a topic • Use facts and definitions to develop points. • Provide a concluding statement or section. |
| **Grade 3** | Write to examine a topic and convey ideas and information clearly. a. Introduce a topic and group related information together; include illustrations when useful to aiding comprehension. b. Develop the topic with facts, definitions, and details. c. Use linking words and phrases to connect ideas within categories of information. d. Provide a concluding statement or section. |
| **Grade 4** | Write to examine a topic and convey ideas and information clearly. a. Introduce topic clearly and group related information in paragraphs and sections; include formatting (e.g., headings), illustrations, and multimedia when useful to aiding comprehension. b. Develop the topic with facts, definitions, concrete details, quotations, or other information and examples related to the topic. c. Link ideas within categories of information using words and phrases. d. Use precise language and domain-specific vocabulary to inform about or explain the topic. e. Provide a concluding statement or section related to the information or explanation presented. |
| **Grade 5** | Write to examine a topic and convey ideas and information clearly. a. Introduce a topic clearly, provide a general observation and focus, and group related information logically; include formatting (e.g., headings), illustrations, and multimedia when useful to aiding comprehension. b. Develop a topic with facts, definitions, concrete details, quotations, or other information and examples related to the topic. c. Link ideas within and across categories of information using words, phrases, and clauses. d. Use precise language and domain-specific vocabulary to inform about or explain the topic. e. Provide a concluding statement or section related to the information or explanation presented. |

|  | | |
|---|---|---|
| **Grade 6** | Write informative/explanatory texts to examine a topic and convey ideas, concepts, and information through the selection, organization, and analysis of relevant content.<br><br>a. Introduce a topic; organize ideas, concepts, and information, using strategies such as definition, classification, comparison/contrast, and cause/effect; include formatting (e.g., headings), graphics (e.g., charts, tables), and multimedia when useful to aiding comprehension.<br><br>b. Develop the topic with relevant facts, definitions, concrete details, quotations, or other information and examples. | c. Use appropriate transitions to clarify the relationships among ideas and concepts.<br><br>d. Use precise language and domain-specific vocabulary to inform about or explain the topic.<br><br>e. Establish and maintain a formal style.<br><br>f. Provide a concluding statement or section that follows from the information or explanation presented. |

**3. Narratives**

|  | | |
|---|---|---|
| **K** | • Use a combination of drawing, dictating, and writing to narrate a single event or several loosely linked events. | • Tell about the events in the order in which they occurred<br>• Provide a reaction to what happened. |
| **Grade 1** | • Write narratives to recount two or more sequenced events.<br>• Include some details regarding what happened. | • Use temporal words to signal event order.<br>• Provide sense of closure. |
| **Grade 2** | • Write narratives to recount a well-elaborated event or short sequence of events.<br>• Include details to describe actions, thoughts, and feelings. | • Use temporal words to signal event order.<br>• Provide a sense of closure. |
| **Grade 3** | Write narrative to develop real or imagined experiences or events using effective technique, descriptive details, and clear event sequences.<br><br>a. Establish a situation and introduce a narrator and/or characters; organize an event sequence that unfolds naturally. | b. Use dialogue and descriptions of actions, thoughts, and feelings to develop experiences and events or show the response of characters to situations.<br><br>c. Use temporal words and phrases to signal event order.<br>d. Provide a sense of closure. |

**FIGURE 1.2** *(Continued)*

**13**

| | |
|---|---|
| **Grade 4** | Write narratives to develop real or imagined experiences or events using effective technique, descriptive details, and clear event sequences.<br><br>a. Orient the reader by establishing a situation and introducing a narrator and/or characters; organize an event sequence that unfolds naturally.<br><br>b. Use dialogue and description to develop experiences and events or show the responses of characters to situations.<br><br>c. Use a variety of transitional words and phrases to manage the sequence of events.<br><br>d. Use concrete words and phrases and sensory details to convey experiences and events precisely.<br><br>e. Provide a conclusion that follows from the narrated experiences or events. |
| **Grade 5** | Write narratives to develop real or imagined experiences or events using effective technique, descriptive details, and clear event sequences.<br><br>a. Orient the reader by establishing a situation and introducing a narrator and/or characters; organize an event sequence that unfolds naturally.<br><br>b. Use narrative techniques, such as dialogue, description, and pacing, to develop experiences and events or show the responses of characters to situations.<br><br>c. Use a variety of transitional words, phrases, and clauses to manage the sequence of events.<br><br>d. Use concrete words and phrases and sensory details to convey experiences and events precisely.<br><br>e. Provide a conclusion that follows from the narrated experiences or events. |
| **Grade 6** | Write narratives to develop real or imagined experiences or events using effective technique, relevant descriptive details, and well-structured event sequences.<br><br>a. Engage and orient the reader by establishing a context and introducing a narrator and/or characters; organize an event sequence that unfolds naturally and logically.<br><br>b. Use narrative techniques, such as dialogue, pacing, and description, to develop experiences, events, and/or characters.<br><br>c. Use a variety of transition words, phrases, and clauses to convey sequence and signal shifts from one time frame or setting to another.<br><br>d. Use precise words and phrases, relevant descriptive details, and sensory language to convey experiences and events.<br><br>e. Provide a conclusion that follows from the narrated experiences or events. |

**Research to Build and Present Knowledge**

| | 4. Research Projects/Writing |
|---|---|
| **K** | 1. Participate in shared research and writing projects (e.g., explore a number of books by a favorite author and express opinions about them). |
| | 2. With guidance and support from adults, recall information from experiences or gather information from provided sources to answer a question. |
| **Grade 1** | 1. Participate in shared research and writing projects (e.g., explore a number of "how-to" books on a given topic and use them to write a sequence of instructions). |
| | 2. With guidance and support from adults, recall information from experiences or gather information from provided sources to answer a question. |
| **Grade 2** | 1. Participate in shared research and writing projects (e.g., read a number of books on a single topic to produce a report; record science observations). |
| | 2. Recall information from experiences or gather information from provided sources to answer a question. |
| **Grade 3** | 1. Conduct short research projects that build knowledge about a topic. |
| | 2. Recall information from experiences or gather information from print and digital sources; take brief notes on sources and sort evidence into provided categories. |
| **Grade 4** | 1. Conduct short research projects that build knowledge through investigation of different aspects of a topic. |
| | 2. Recall relevant information from experiences or gather relevant information from print and digital sources; take notes and categorize information, and provide a list of sources. |
| | 3. Draw evidence from literary or informational texts to support analysis, reflection, and research. |
| |   a. Apply Grade 4 Reading Standards to literature (e.g., Describe in depth a character, setting, or event in a story or drama, drawing on specific details in the text.). |
| |   b. Apply Grade 4 Reading Standards to informational texts (e.g., Explain how an author uses reasons and evidence to support particular points in a text.). |

**FIGURE 1.2** *(Continued)*

15

| Grade 5 | 1. Conduct short research projects that use several sources to build knowledge through investigation of different aspects of a topic. |
|---|---|
| | 2. Recall relevant information from experiences or gather relevant information from print and digital sources; summarize or paraphrase information in notes and finished work, and provide a list of sources. |
| | 3. Draw evidence from literary or informational texts to support analysis, reflection, and research. |
| | a. Apply Grade 5 Reading Standards to literature (e.g., *Compare and contrast two or more characters, settings, or events in a story or a drama, drawing on specific details in the text.*). |
| | b. Apply Grade 5 Reading Standards to informational texts (e.g., *Explain how an author uses reasons and evidence to support particular points in a text, identifying which reasons and evidence support which point[s].*). |
| **Grade 6** | 1. Conduct short research projects to answer a question, drawing on several sources and refocusing the inquiry when appropriate. |
| | 2. Gather relevant information from multiple print and digital sources; assess the credibility of each source; and quote or paraphrase the data and conclusions of others while avoiding plagiarism and providing basic bibliographic information for sources. |
| | 3. Draw evidence from literary or informational texts to support analysis, reflection, and research. |
| | a. Apply Grade 6 Reading Standards to literature (e.g., *Compare and contrast texts in different forms or genres [e.g., stories and poems; historical novels and fantasy stories] in terms of their approaches to similar themes and topics.*). |
| | b. Apply Grade 6 Reading Standards to literary nonfiction (e.g., *Trace and evaluate the argument and specific claims in a text, distinguishing claims that are supported by reasons and evidence from claims that are not.*). |

**FIGURE 1.2**

## What Do Opinion Piece/Argument Texts Entail?

Many of you are familiar with persuasive writing, which is akin to the Common Core's opinion piece in K–5 that prepares students for argument writing in Grades 6 to 12. Unlike some state standards, where persuasive writing is not expected until third grade or later, the Common Core includes opinion pieces as early as kindergarten. To gain a better understanding of this text type, read the following:

- The "Opinion Pieces and Arguments" section of Figure 1.2, which shows a progression of these standards from grade to grade
- "Research Projects/Writing" in Figure 1.2, because students can gather research for their evidence in an opinion piece
- Figure 1.3, Definition and Application of Text Type: Argument, an excerpt from Appendix A of the Common Core that features a snapshot of the text type

# Definition and Application of Text Type: Argument

| Definition |
| --- |
| Arguments are used for many purposes—to change the reader's point of view, to bring about some action on the reader's part, or to ask the reader to accept the writer's explanation or evaluation of a concept, issue, or problem. An argument is a reasoned, logical way of demonstrating that the writer's position, belief, or conclusion is valid. |
| **Grades K–5 Writing Applications** |
| Although young children are not able to produce fully developed logical arguments, they develop a variety of methods to extend and elaborate their work by providing examples, offering reasons for their assertions, and explaining cause and effect. These kinds of expository structures are steps on the road to argument. In Grades K–5, the term "opinion" is used to refer to this developing form of argument. |
| **Grades 6–12 Writing Applications** |
| <ul><li>In English language arts (ELA), students make claims about the worth or meaning of a literary work or works. They defend their interpretations or judgments with evidence from the text(s) they are writing about.</li><li>In history/social studies, students analyze evidence from multiple primary and secondary sources to advance a claim that is best supported by the evidence, and they argue for a historically or empirically situated interpretation.</li><li>In science, students make claims in the form of statements or conclusions that answer questions or address problems. Using data in a scientifically acceptable form, students marshal evidence and draw on their understanding of scientific concepts to argue in support of their claims.</li></ul> |

**FIGURE 1.3**

In primary grades, opinion pieces involve students stating their opinion or preference about a book or topic, such as *I like dogs because . . .* or *My favorite book is . . .* and then offering a reason for their assertion. Students progress through the grades refining their skills so that in upper elementary they are expected to write opinion pieces on a particular topic or text with reasons that are supported by facts and details requiring research or textual evidence. To offer support, Appendix C of the Common Core document includes these student writing samples: for kindergarten and second grade, opinions about works of literature (i.e., *Do You Want to Be My Friend?* by Eric Carle and *Owl Moon* by Jane Yolen, respectively) and for fourth grade, an opinion letter to persuade readers about going on a field trip. In the fourth-grade sample, students include a counterargument in addition to the grade-level standards.

This text type has opportunities for several options that might be familiar from your state standards, such as response to literature, opinion about or response to a nonfiction topic, or persuasive letter or essay. When I taught or collaborated with others on response to literature, I didn't necessarily emphasize the opinion aspect of the writing. Rather, the focus was primarily on students demonstrating understanding of the literary work, providing an interpretation, and supporting it with clear textual evidence (e.g., characters' actions or traits, theme, etc.). If you choose to maintain this focus, then response to literature can be aligned to the informative/explanatory text type. If, however, you would like to invite students to write a literary response aligned to opinion/argument, merely make opinion central to the writing focus. Because this type of writing begins in kindergarten as students might tell about a book they like and why, it would be a natural progression in the upper grades.

As stated earlier, persuasive writing is very similar to the Common Core's opinion/argument writing. In teaching persuasive writing, many teachers—especially in upper elementary or beyond—expect students to include a call to action in the conclusion after they present their viewpoint or position, provide reasons and supporting evidence (e.g., facts, details, examples), and even address reader concerns. Note that a call to action is absent in the opinion writing standards, which is a characteristic of persuasive writing, but you can still expect students to include this component.

As students further advance into middle and high school, the emphasis of this Common Core text type moves from opinion pieces to argument so they are more aptly prepared for college and careers. Appendix A devotes a full page subtitled "The Special Place of Argument in the Standards" (NGA, 2010, p. 24) so educators are well aware of the research that states the critical value of argument not only in writing, but also in oral communication. After quoting many sources that deem argument as paramount to college and career success, the Common Core designers conclude the section with this statement: "The value of effective argument extends well beyond the classroom or workplace. . . . Such capacities are broadly important for the literate, educated person living in the diverse, information-rich environment of the twenty-first century" (p. 25).

To determine which writing unit you will conduct to align with this standard, consider these factors: *content area* (e.g., science, social studies, literature), the *topic* or *text* (e.g., literary or informational text) students will use as the basis for the writing, the *resources* students will use to gather evidence (e.g., secondary and primary sources, literary work, prior knowledge), and above all, the critical element—the *purpose* for writing: to persuade, to inform, or to explain. Chapters 3 and 4 include opinion writing rubrics and checklists, plus an assignment and brainstorming sheet that align to the Common Core text type so you can see criteria you might expect. Select the appropriate assessments for the grade level and student population you teach or mentor, or adapt as needed. It is critical for educators to use rubrics to be clear minded about expectations for students in association with the standards to ensure there is no ambiguity.

Literacy is expected across the curriculum, so consider the types of writing assessments across subject areas for opinion writing in Figure 1.4 and be mindful to use them to support your opinion writing unit. As such, it would behoove you to incorporate any of these prompts within your curriculum or within your unit on this text type as opposed to issuing prompts in isolation. For example, if you are teaching about community service workers in social studies, use the appropriate prompt idea in Figure 1.4 to check for understanding of this particular content. Or feature a story within your unit that lends itself to opinion and include an appropriate guiding question geared to this text type, such as *How do characters' viewpoints shape the plot?* Then, when you instruct students to respond to a prompt, it is folded into your unit goals. You might even use some of these prompts as oral exercises as a precursor to writing that focuses on an element of opinion. Use this same concept of avoiding assigning prompts in isolation to the other text types, as well.

## Writing Prompts for Opinions/Arguments

| | |
|---|---|
| **Social Studies** | Create a classroom rule or a law that your community should vote to adopt. Give reasons why you think this rule or law should be adopted. |
| | Choose a community service job that is your favorite or you think is most important. (Many people work in our community to provide services, such as police officers, librarians, and street sweepers.) Read about it, and then write a thank-you letter giving your opinion about why it is the best or most important job. |
| | Identify someone that you think is an American hero from the past or today. Provide reasons for your opinion using informational text. |
| | For a unit on the causes of the American Revolution, write an opinion piece from the point of view of a Tory, Loyalist, or Neutralist persuading others to adopt this position. |
| | Write a letter from the viewpoint of Native Americans to the president or settlers. In the letter, use evidence from informational texts to explain how you have been treated by the settlers who have tried to force you from your land. Or write a letter stating your cultural perspective on land usage and rights. In other words, is land meant to be owned? |
| **Science** | After reading a book about seasons, identify your favorite season and provide reasons for your opinion. |
| | Choose a renewable resource that you think is the most valuable. Using informational text about this resource, give your opinion about why it is the most important one. |
| | For a unit on food and nutrition, write an opinion piece in response to these guiding questions: *Should students be mandated to bring nutritious lunches to school? Should schools be expected to provide nutritious lunches to students?* |
| | Select a plant or animal and the environment in which it lives. Write an opinion piece from the plant's or animal's point of view in response to this guiding question: *How is this plant or animal well suited to live in its environment?* In your response, discuss other environments and explain how they would not be appropriate environments for your selected plant or animal. (Example: *Some might think this animal could live in . . . , but the problem with this environment is that . . .* ) |

| | |
|---|---|
| **Language Arts** | Consider any of these questions as the basis for an opinion paper. Use informational text to gather evidence: *Should sports figures be allowed to use steroids? Should there be a ban on using animals for testing chemicals and drugs? Is it okay to modify the environment for our benefit? Should the government spend money on space exploration? Why should schools include physical education and recess as part of the school day?* |
| | In response to reading *The Great Kapok Tree: A Tale of the Amazon Rain Forest* by Lynne Cherry, write an opinion piece about why saving the tree is so imperative. |
| | Read Emma Lazarus's poem "The New Colossus" or Mildred Taylor's *Roll of Thunder, Hear My Cry* and related informational text (e.g., immigration, civil rights). State a claim about the theme of the text, and defend interpretations and judgments through evidence from the text while also acknowledging and addressing alternate or opposing claims. |
| | Write a persuasive letter from the point of view of a character in one story to another character in the same story (or a character in another book) about something controversial that you did. Persuade this character that your actions were wise, and defend this position. |
| | Choose an antagonist from any fairy tale, such as the wolf from *Little Red Riding Hood* or the stepmother from *Cinderella*. Write from this character's point of view defending his or her actions and feelings. As a precursor to this exercise, read *The True Story of the 3 Little Pigs!* by Jon Scieszka. |
| | Choose an issue such as school uniforms, curfews, longer school days, wearing bike helmets, mandatory community service hours, or field trips and defend your position with strong reasons and evidence. |

**FIGURE 1.4**

## What Do Informative/Explanatory Texts Entail?

This writing type seems quite broad and can encompass myriad possibilities as students write to inform and explain. For an overview, see the following excerpt in Figure 1.5, reprinted from Appendix A of the Common Core Standards, plus the grade-to-grade progressive view in the "Informative/Explanatory Texts" section of Figure 1.2. Also look at "Research Projects/Writing" from Figure 1.2, because this writing calls upon students to research primary and secondary sources to cull examples, facts, definitions, and details depending upon the grade.

To clarify this writing type, the following provides a brief overview of the student writing samples from the Common Core Appendix C (NGA, 2010):

- In the kindergarten sample, the student begins by explaining that the teacher reads a story about frogs in reading groups, and that the class is expected to write about frogs. The student then writes an observation about the tadpole that is in the classroom's science center by describing its appearance (e.g., *It has 2 bac ligs*) and its behavior (e.g., *Wen it has 2 frunt ligs its tal disupirs and it can not eat* and *Saum of the frogs bloo baubools*). (p. 7)
- The first-grade student writes a straightforward informative report about Spain aptly titled "My Big Book About Spain." (p. 11)

# Definition and Application of Text Type: Informative/Explanatory

| Definition |
| --- |
| Informational/explanatory writing conveys information accurately. This kind of writing serves one or more closely related purposes: to increase readers' knowledge of a subject, to help readers better understand a procedure or process, or to provide readers with an enhanced comprehension of a concept. To produce this kind of writing, students draw from what they already know and from primary and secondary sources. With practice, students become better able to develop a controlling idea and a coherent focus on a topic and more skilled at selecting and incorporating relevant examples, facts, and details into their writing. They are also able to use a variety of techniques to convey information, such as naming, defining, describing, or differentiating different types or parts; comparing or contrasting ideas or concepts; and citing an anecdote or a scenario to illustrate a point. |

| Writing Applications |
| --- |
| Informational/explanatory writing addresses matters such as the following:<br><br>• **Types** (What are the different types of poetry?)<br>• **Components** (What are the parts of a motor?)<br>• **Size, function, or behavior** (How big is the United States? What is an X-ray used for? How do penguins find food?)<br>• **How things work** (How does the legislative branch of government function?)<br>• **Why things happen** (Why do some authors blend genres?)<br><br>Informational/explanatory writing includes a wide array of genres, including academic genres such as literary analyses, scientific and historical reports, summaries, and précis writing as well as forms of workplace and functional writing such as instructions, manuals, memos, reports, applications, and resumes. As students advance through the grades, they expand their repertoire of informational/explanatory genres and use them effectively in a variety of disciplines and domains. |

**FIGURE 1.5**

• The third-grade student sample is about horses, and the writer divides her paper into sections, such as *why I chose this animal, horse families, markings, breeds and color coats, breeds I like, friendly horses, horse survival,* and so on. As I read this student sample, I paused to pay attention to some elements of opinion in this informative/explanatory piece: *I chose horses because I like to ride them. I also like to pet them. I like Icelandic and Shetland ponies because they are so very cute, pretty and small* (p. 18). The conclusion also includes preferences: *I like horses and I know a lot about them. I like to ride them and they're so beautiful!* (p. 20). Even though the writer does include opinions, her overriding purpose was made clear: to inform readers about horses.

- The fifth-grade paper is a literary response about Roald Dahl's works as it informs readers about Dahl's similar plots and writing style across his books. It is not focused on an opinion or claim that the writer defends about a particular story (pp. 29–30).

There can be confusion between the two genres, which the designers of the Common Core seem to have anticipated. Therefore, they provide the synopsis in Figure 1.6 to help make the distinction between the two easier to understand.

---

## Argument and Explanation Text Types

Although information is provided in both arguments and explanations, the two types of writing have different aims.

- Arguments seek to make people believe that something is true or to persuade people to change their beliefs or behavior. Explanations, on the other hand, start with the assumption of truthfulness and answer questions about why or how. Their aim is to make the reader understand rather than to persuade him or her to accept a certain point of view. In short, arguments are used for persuasion and explanations for clarification.
- Like arguments, explanations provide information about causes, contexts, and consequences of processes, phenomena, states of affairs, objects, terminology, and so on. However, in an argument, the writer not only gives information but also presents a case with the "pros" (supporting ideas) and "cons" (opposing ideas) on a debatable issue. Because an argument deals with whether the main claim is true, it demands empirical descriptive evidence, statistics, or definitions for support. When writing an argument, the writer supports his or her claim(s) with sound reasoning and relevant and sufficient evidence.

---

**FIGURE 1.6**

In addition to including literary analysis, scientific and historical reports, and so on, this writing genre can also include compare/contrast, all-about writing (e.g., all about me, all about animals, etc.), information or research reports, problem/solution, and cause/effect. Process papers can fall under narrative writing in the Common Core: "In science, students write narrative descriptions of the step-by-step procedures they follow in their investigations so that others can replicate their procedures and (perhaps) reach the same results" (NGA, 2010, Appendix A, p. 24). When I read the narrative standards, they seem more suited to telling a story with the explicit expectations of incorporating characters and dialogue in some grades. However, a narrative account of science procedures would make interesting reading and allow student writers to articulate and creatively apply what they learned. If you want students to write in a more formal or conventional manner for a scientific procedure, though, then follow the informative/explanatory standards. Again, it's all about the purpose for writing. Whichever approach you choose, make sure you communicate to students the purpose for their writing and present a checklist or rubric for clear expectations. The following list provides some other examples that address informative/explanatory writing across content areas:

- **Types.** What are the different types of governments? Communities? Habitats? Rocks? Renewable energy?
- **Components.** What are the parts of a plant? Cell? Government?
- **Size, function, or behavior.** What is the size of our state? Oceans? Molecule? House of Representatives? What is a compass used for? Telescope? Microscope? How do an animal's physical traits help it to survive? How does sound enable us to hear? How do the different forms of matter change from one form to another? How can people practice good citizenship? How do people use and adapt to the environment to survive?
- **How things work.** How does the system of checks and balances work? How do simple machines help us move heavy or difficult objects? How does a law get passed?
- **Why things happen.** Why do animals adapt to their environment? Why do natural events occur (e.g., floods, earthquakes, tornadoes)? Why do communities change over time? Why do groups enter into conflict? Why do people persecute or take advantage of others?

Some categories could prove worthwhile for a thought-provoking response to literature assignment as well. How do settings impact characters? How are most fairy tales structured in a similar way? *How do characters behave who are selfish, compassionate, or humble? How does a character's behavior impact the plot (or other characters)? How and why do characters change over time? How does a narrator's point of view influence readers?* The possibilities are vast. You might have students cite a particular character and identify what caused that character to behave in a certain way. They can compare and contrast characters (i.e., protagonists and antagonists) in various fairy tales and discuss how they share common traits. You could extract a salient quote from the text and have students interpret or respond to it. Or you might ask students to change or invent a new setting and describe how the story would be different. Whichever writing you assign, students should use their schema—their own background knowledge—and textual references to support their responses. Clearly articulate writing expectations because students can respond to literature through an informational text lens, as this section defines, or an opinion lens as discussed earlier.

## What Do Narrative Texts Entail?

Figure 1.7, which provides an overview of this writing type, is reprinted in an excerpt from Appendix A (pp. 23–24) of the Common Core document. Also, see the grade-to-grade progressive view in the "Narratives" section of Figure 1.2. The Common Core authors state that they do not include all forms of creative writing, such as poetry, in the text types. They leave it up to educators to determine other creative expressions besides narrative writing.

The student samples represented in Appendix C of the Common Core (NGA, 2010) are all autobiographical except for the fourth-grade piece. The kindergartner writes about a vacation to Disneyland; the first grader focuses on a hamster that he bought and returned; the second grader writes about a first visit from the tooth fairy; the third grader relays a sad tale about her lost puppies that never returned home; and the fifth grader recalls a suspenseful tale of waiting for, and then receiving, a dreaded shot from the doctor. The only sample that diverts from the autobiographical category is the on-demand assessment in fourth grade in which the writer responds to a prompt about waking up and finding a strange pair

# Definition and Application of Text Type: Narrative

| Definition |
| --- |
| Narrative writing conveys experience, either real or imaginary, and uses time as its deep structure. It can be used for many purposes, such as to inform, instruct, persuade, or entertain. |
| **Writing Applications** |
| <ul><li>In ELA, students produce narratives that take the form of creative fictional stories, memoirs, anecdotes, and autobiographies. Over time, they learn to provide visual details of scenes, objects, or people; to depict specific actions (for example, movements, gestures, postures, and expressions); to use dialogue and interior monologue that provide insight into the narrator's and characters' personalities and motives; and to manipulate pace to highlight the significance of events and create tension and suspense. With practice, students expand their repertoire and control of different narrative strategies.</li><li>In history/social studies, students write narrative accounts about individuals. They also construct event models of what happened, selecting from their sources only the most relevant information.</li><li>In science, students write narrative descriptions of the step-by-step procedures they follow in their investigations so that others can replicate their procedures and (perhaps) reach the same results.</li></ul> |

**FIGURE 1.7**

of glowing shoes that are left by the bed. In this sample, the student tells a story about what happens when these special shoes are discovered.

Typically, the purpose of narrative writing—which can be found in novels, biographies, autobiographies, essays, and short stories—is to entertain or describe. As shown in Figure 1.7, narratives can also inform, instruct, or persuade. The following are some possibilities to get your creative energy flowing for these other purposes for narrative options you might assign. When using any of these ideas, remember to include the tenets of narrative, such as sensory details, description, dialogue, pacing, or suspense.

*Entertain.* (1) Students write a short story about a realistic or an imagined character to entertain readers. This story could even be a mystery, science fiction, or fantasy. (2) If the short story is tied to social studies, students can base the story on a historical setting and invent characters who behave, dress, and speak in a manner true to the chosen time period. (3) Students create an autobiography based on one meaningful event that serves as the central conflict or climax of the story so that they have an intact plotline.

*Inform.* (1) Students write an eyewitness account of an event in history to inform readers of what happened during a past noteworthy incident. The writer assumes the role of someone at the actual event watching it transpire. (2) Students write a biography of an American hero, a leader, or a scientist to inform others about this person's accomplishments, influences, aspirations, and so forth. (3) Students write an autobiography about several events in their lives. This type of writing does not necessarily follow the basic plot diagram of a problem and solution, but rather recounts milestones and detailed information about their lives.

(4) Students write a personal journal or letter from the perspective of a historical character, for example, a pioneer who travels west, explaining to others who stayed home about the adventures experienced. (5) Students craft a detailed and descriptive invitation communicating to parents about an upcoming school or classroom function (e.g., open house, party, social, field trip, etc.) that includes creatively written information about the event and its logistics.

*Instruct.* (1) Students write a procedural account of a science experiment as mentioned previously. (2) Students write detailed descriptions to instruct readers how to do something, such as make a peanut butter and jelly sandwich, play a game, bake a cake, construct a device to allow a raw egg to drop without breaking from a balcony, and so forth. Students are encouraged to use sensory details and transitional words and phrases to provide narrative focus. (3) Students write a descriptive letter to a character in a story giving advice about what this character should do about a problem the character faces.

*Persuade.* (1) Students write an autobiography about a significant event in their lives and include a persuasive element along with narrative features. For example, if a student recounts an experience of riding a bike without a helmet and falling down and getting injured, he can persuade readers about bike safety in addition to using sensory details to describe the event and emotions associated with it. Or a student can write about a personal topic such as the death of a loved one, persuading others to appreciate those close to us more and describing the personal bonds. (2) After reading a story in which a character misbehaves or shows poor judgment, students can craft a convincing letter to the character to act more appropriately (e.g., Peter Rabbit in Beatrix Potter's books; Harriet in Marla Frazee's *Harriet, You'll Drive Me Wild!*; Arthur in Bernard Waber's *An Anteater Named Arthur*; classmates of Chrysanthemum in *Chrysanthemum*).

## IDENTIFYING AND ARTICULATING THE LANGUAGE STANDARDS ACROSS GRADES

The language strand includes conventions (i.e., English grammar and usage, capitalization, punctuation, and spelling), knowledge of language, and vocabulary acquisition and use. The Common Core designers make a point to state that even though language standards are relegated to their own strand, these skills are interwoven throughout the other strands of reading, writing, speaking, and listening. Indeed, language skills are part and parcel of formal spoken English as well as formal written English. Therefore, when you group standards, it is imperative to consider which language standards complement a unit of instruction you are teaching. For example, if you are teaching a short story writing unit, you would want students to include dialogue. As such, it is important to include language standards for punctuating dialogue correctly along with verb usage for the speaker tags.

In Figure 1.8, Common Core State Standards Language Progressive Skills, by Grade, you will see selected, key Common Core Standards for this strand written in a continuum: "While all of the Standards are cumulative, certain Language skills and understandings are more likely than others to need to be retaught and relearned as students advance through the grades" (NGA, 2010, Appendix A, p. 29). I couldn't agree more. However, in looking at this table of progression and also at the comprehensive grade-by-grade standard expectations for this strand, I realize that teachers might have the same struggles as I did when I taught ELA and that my clients also share: They might need more support. Allow me to explain.

# Common Core State Standards Language Progressive Skills, by Grade

The following skills, marked with an asterisk (*) in Language standards 1–3, are particularly likely to require continued attention in higher grades as they are applied to increasingly sophisticated writing and speaking.

| Standard | Grade(s) | | | | | | | |
|---|---|---|---|---|---|---|---|---|
| | 3 | 4 | 5 | 6 | 7 | 8 | 9–10 | 11–12 |
| **L.3.1f.** Ensure subject-verb and pronoun-antecedent agreement. | ■ | ■ | ■ | ■ | ■ | ■ | ■ | ■ |
| **L.3.3a.** Choose words and phrases for effect. | ■ | ■ | ■ | ■ | ■ | ■ | ■ | ■ |
| **L.4.1f.** Produce complete sentences, recognizing and correcting inappropriate fragments and run-ons. | | ■ | ■ | ■ | ■ | ■ | ■ | ■ |
| **L.4.1g.** Correctly use frequently confused words (e.g., to/too/two; there/their). | | ■ | ■ | ■ | ■ | ■ | ■ | ■ |
| **L.4.3a.** Choose words and phrases to convey ideas precisely.* | | ■ | ■ | ■ | | | | |
| **L.4.3b.** Choose punctuation for effect. | | ■ | ■ | ■ | ■ | ■ | ■ | ■ |
| **L.5.1d.** Recognize and correct inappropriate shifts in verb tense. | | | ■ | ■ | ■ | ■ | ■ | ■ |
| **L.5.2a.** Use punctuation to separate items in a series.† | | | ■ | ■ | ■ | ■ | | |
| **L.6.1c.** Recognize and correct inappropriate shifts in pronoun number and person. | | | | ■ | ■ | ■ | ■ | ■ |
| **L.6.1d.** Recognize and correct vague pronouns (i.e., ones with unclear or ambiguous antecedents). | | | | ■ | ■ | ■ | ■ | ■ |
| **L.6.1e.** Recognize variations from standard English in their own and others' writing and speaking, and identify and use strategies to improve expression in conventional language. | | | | ■ | ■ | ■ | ■ | ■ |
| **L.6.2a.** Use punctuation (commas, parentheses, dashes) to set off nonrestrictive/parenthetical elements. | | | | ■ | ■ | ■ | ■ | ■ |
| **L.6.3a.** Vary sentence patterns for meaning, reader/listener interest, and style.‡ | | | | ■ | ■ | ■ | ■ | |
| **L.6.3b.** Maintain consistency in style and tone. | | | | ■ | ■ | ■ | ■ | ■ |
| **L.7.1c.** Place phrases and clauses within a sentence, recognizing and correcting misplaced and dangling modifiers. | | | | | ■ | ■ | ■ | ■ |
| **L.7.3a.** Choose language that expresses ideas precisely and concisely, recognizing and eliminating wordiness and redundancy. | | | | | ■ | ■ | ■ | ■ |
| **L.8.1d.** Recognize and correct inappropriate shifts in verb voice and mood. | | | | | | ■ | ■ | ■ |
| **L.9–10.1a.** Use parallel structure. | | | | | | | ■ | ■ |

*Subsumed by L.7.3a
†Subsumed by L.9–10.1a
‡Subsumed by L.11–12.3a

**FIGURE 1.8**

When I taught, standards guided me in determining what I was to teach. Like the Common Core, each standard was relegated to a particular grade level with the expectation that it would be taught and mastered in an appointed school year. Invariably, there were particular grammar and convention standards that seemed developmentally challenging or too intense for students to master all in one year. For some standards, on the other hand, I could say with conviction that most of my students could achieve proficiency within the school year. It is true that the Common Core includes gradual progression for some standards, but not necessarily a complete flow of support from grade to grade. So for the more challenging and lofty ones where there is no indication of preparation, teamwork in the school might be advantageous; therefore, teachers in the grade level prior might introduce them. That way, when students come into a classroom, they might be familiar with the vocabulary of a standard even if they are unclear or forgot how to actually demonstrate clear understanding. For example, teaching complex sentences requires knowledge of subordinating conjunctions, independent and dependent clauses, and also commas if the sentence begins with the dependent clause. It would be helpful if students were exposed to examples and the terminology in the year prior. A teacher would then repeat and formally teach complex sentences so students could identify and write them with proficiency, but the teacher would know that students had some introductory lessons and familiarity with the skill in the previous grade. So for the more rigorous and complicated standards that teachers and students find daunting to learn, you might welcome the support of colleagues.

To address the issue of teaching challenging standards, it occurred to me in consulting and working with teachers who had the same issues that a continuum to show progression and teamwork for introducing and mastering grammar and conventions would be needed. The Common Core "Language Progressive Skills, by Grade" attempts to accomplish this goal, but I went a bit further in my Language Continuum in Figure 1.10 so teachers could see exactly what is incumbent upon them to teach in a particular grade to help achieve proficiency in a grade-level standard. This figure includes every Common Core Standard for the language strand K–5 plus additional standards I thought should be added. I reference the expectations I include with shaded rows that can complement the Common Core Standards, which are identified by unshaded rows and with the reference to the CC Standard in parentheses next to them. In augmenting the Common Core with standards that I think are noteworthy and important to teach, I have followed the suggestions of the Common Core designers to use their standards as a framework and my professional judgment for additions. I have organized Figure 1.10 into these straightforward categories; the Common Core Language Standards are embedded within. The complete figure is located in the companion website; two pages are printed in this chapter so you can see the format and what to expect of the entire document.

- Print concepts
- Capitalization
- Spelling/penmanship
- Punctuation
- Sentence structure
- Knowledge of language
- Vocabulary acquisition

With the help of many teachers along the way, we created the key in Figure 1.9 to accompany Figure 1.10. As shown, a symbol—introduction (bullet), ongoing instruction (arrow), proficiency (asterisk)—is assigned to each grade-level standard. Each standard will have no more than a three-year stint. Those with a three-year learning span are for the more complicated standards, and instruction would follow this process:

- A *bullet* signifies an introductory year and would mean teachers realize it is the first exposure students will have to this standard. They will teach the academic vocabulary associated with the standard, show examples of it in writing, and ask students to practice the skill.
- If an *arrow* is shown in a particular grade level, teachers will be aware that students have had some instruction in the year prior and will continue to hone this skill or concept in the next grade. Therefore, this teacher continues instruction to help students learn terminology, identify the standard in published and student work, and practice writing according to this standard.
- In the final phase, indicated by an *asterisk*, teachers are aware it is their responsibility to have students gain proficiency.

---

**SYMBOL KEY:**

- ● introduce skill, strategy, concept, etc.
- → continue to teach knowing students received an introduction previous year
- ✳ seek to gain proficiency at an intermediate level for 90% of students

---

**FIGURE 1.9** Symbol Key

As stated, each standard will have no more than a three-year stint; therefore, you will not find the same symbol two straight years in a row. My rationale is that if a standard needs four years, then it is too sophisticated and should be introduced in a later grade, or the standard might need to be separated into chunks and listed as two or more standards. For example, Language Standard 1.j. for first grade reads: "Produce and expand complete simple and compound declarative, interrogative, imperative, and exclamatory sentences in response to prompts" (NGA, 2010). This standard can be addressed on different days and even within different units of study at different times of the school year. The same principle applies with Language Standard 1.i. in third grade: "Produce simple, compound, and complex sentences" (NGA, 2010).

You will also see standards on the continuum where there is a bullet and asterisk in the same grade level because a standard could be introduced and mastered in a given school year. It is important to note that I was mindful to use an asterisk to indicate proficiency where the Common Core Standards show them at a particular grade level. I then used my professional judgment to determine if I thought the standard could be mastered in a given school year, needed two years to learn, or was a more challenging standard that required three years. If you use this continuum, consider your student population and feel free to alter where the symbols are while still being cognizant of the target year for Common Core Standards. After all, students will be assessed against these standards in the appointed grade level.

Even though I am consistent with the Common Core Standards timeline, you—like me—might have reservations that some standards are not necessarily assigned to the appropriate grade levels. You may have had this discussion with your colleagues. I realize being bound to their developmental dictates might prove to be challenging because where the authors put some conventions and grammar standards in some grades and not others is confounding. For example, in California, students learn how to use a colon to introduce a list in fifth grade. In the Common Core, this standard is stated in Grades 9 and 10. However, students "use commas to separate single words in a series" (NGA, 2010, L.1.2c) in first grade and "use punctuation to separate items in a series" (L.5.2a) in fifth grade, so introducing a colon to precede this list might not be too difficult to learn in fifth grade. Another example pertains to compound sentences. Since students are expected to produce compound sentences in the primary grades (see L.1.1j, L.2.1f, L.3.1i), why not teach the semicolon in fourth grade along with the comma to connect two independent clauses: "Use a comma before a coordinating conjunction in a compound sentence" (L.4.2c)? Instead, the Common Core waits until Grades 9 and 10 to teach the semicolon: "Use the semicolon to link two or more closely related independent clauses" (L.9–10.2a). It seems natural to show that a semicolon is one option to use between two independent clauses in a simple compound sentence, but I guess you can save that one for high school. You might also consider using these examples, and other similar ones, to differentiate for advanced learners.

By the same token, where the Common Core designers put some standards seems too aggressive, in my opinion. For instance, "Produce simple, compound, and complex sentences" (NGA, 2010, L.3.1i) is a third-grade standard. The part that seems daunting is for all third graders to produce complex sentences. I believe, though, that they can begin to understand the formula for a complex sentence and identify examples in reading in third grade. They could surely experiment with writing compound sentences in this grade; however, actually mastering producing complex sentences I would save for fourth grade. Therefore, I broke this standard and put it on two different line items in the continuum in case readers want to treat it separately. The same applies to the standard "Ensure subject-verb and pronoun-antecedent agreement" (L.3.1f). Subject-verb agreement in third grade seems just fine, but pronoun-antecedent agreement? That seems a bit overreaching. I see many adults make this mistake frequently. Take these common examples from a typical teacher letter: "Each student should bring their homework folders home to review." Or "Everyone must come tomorrow with their signed papers." And I bet some of you read these and wondered, "What's wrong with those sentences?" The answer is pronoun-antecedent agreement. *Each student* is singular, but *their* is plural. To make it correct, it should read *Each student* should bring *his or her* homework folder home to review, or *students* should bring *their* homework folders home to review. In the second example, *everyone* is singular, so *their* should be replaced by *his or her*, or *students* must come tomorrow with *their* signed papers. Even though I cite these two examples of precociousness, you must be mindful that the Common Core Standards do expect third graders to produce complex sentences and ensure pronoun-antecedent agreement.

# Language Continuum

| | K | 1 | 2 | 3 | 4 | 5 |
|---|---|---|---|---|---|---|
| **Print Concepts** | | | | | | |
| Identify letters of the alphabet. | ●/* | | | | | |
| Write using a left to right, top to bottom progression. | ● | * | | | | |
| Recognize word boundaries. | ● | * | NOT APPLICABLE | | | |
| Recognize line boundaries. | ● | * | | | | |
| Know the concept of a letter and a word. | ● | * | | | | |
| **Capitalization** | | | | | | |
| Capitalize the first word in a sentence and the pronoun I (L.K.2a). | ● | * | | | | |
| Capitalize names of people (L.1.2a). | ● | * | | | | |
| Capitalize dates [i.e., months and days of the week] (L.1.2a). | | ●/* | | | | |
| Capitalize holidays, product names, and geographic names (L.2.2a). | | | ● | * | | |
| Capitalize the first word in quotations. | | ● | ● | * | | |
| Capitalize all proper nouns, words at the beginning of sentences and in greetings, and titles (Mr./Mrs./Ms.) and initials of people. | | ● | ↑ | * | | |
| Capitalize appropriate words in titles (L.3.2a). | | | ● | * | | |
| Capitalize holidays, historical periods, and special events. | | | | ●/* | | |
| Capitalize names of magazines, newspapers, artwork, musical compositions, and organizations. | | | | ● | ↑ | * |
| Apply capitalization rules correctly. | | | | | ● | * |

**SYMBOL KEY:**

● introduce skill, strategy, concept, etc.

↑ continue to teach knowing students received an introduction previous year

* seek to gain proficiency at an intermediate level for 90% of students

## Sentence Structure

| | Grade(s) | | | | | |
|---|---|---|---|---|---|---|
| | K | 1 | 2 | 3 | 4 | 5 |
| **SENTENCE TYPES AND STRUCTURE** | | | | | | |
| Produce and expand complete sentences in shared language activities (L.K.1f). | ●/* | | | | | |
| Recognize and use coherent sentences when speaking. | ● | * | | | | |
| Produce and expand complete simple and compound declarative, interrogative, imperative, and exclamatory sentences in response to prompts (L.1.1j). | | ●/* | | | | |
| Use singular and plural nouns with matching verbs in basic sentences (e.g., He hops. We hop.) (L.1.1c). | ● | * | | | | |
| Recognize and use the correct word order in written sentences. | | ● | * | | | |
| Produce, expand, and rearrange complete simple and compound sentences (e.g., The boy watched the movie. The little boy watched the movie. The action movie was watched by the little boy.) (L.2.1f). | | ● | * | | | |
| Ensure subject-verb agreement (L.3.1f). | | | ● | * | | |
| Ensure pronoun-antecedent agreement (L.3.1f). | | | ● | * | | |
| Identify the subject and predicate of simple sentences. | | | ● | * | | |
| Produce simple and compound sentences (L.3.1i). | | ● | ↑ | * | | |
| Define independent clause (i.e., complete sentence with a subject and verb). | | | ● | * | | |
| Identify subject and predicate of compound sentences. | | | ● | * | | |
| Produce complex sentences (L.3.1i). | | | ● | * | | |
| Identify the structure of dependent clauses and their role in complex sentences. | | | ● | * | | |
| Distinguish between sentences and fragments. | | ● | ↑ | * | | |
| Produce complete sentences, recognize and correct inappropriate fragments and run-ons (L.4.1f). | | | ● | ↑ | * | |
| Use sentence beginning variety (e.g., start with dependent clause; prepositional phrase, adverbs [softly/quickly]; subjects [noun, proncun, proper noun]; etc.). | | | | ● | ↑ | * |
| Expand, combine, and reduce sentences for meaning, reader/listener interest, and style (L.5.3a). | | | | ● | ↑ | * |

**SYMBOL KEY:**

●  introduce skill, strategy, concept, etc.

↑  continue to teach knowing students received an introduction previous year

*  seek to gain proficiency at an intermediate level for 90% of students

**FIGURE 1.10**

And then there are standards that are absent altogether. For example, these comma standards are omitted from the Common Core, but I added them to my continuum: *Use commas to keep numbers clear, use commas between city and state, use commas to set off interjections,* and *use commas to set off appositives.* Although similes and metaphors are part of the language and reading standards as students "determine the meaning . . . explain the meaning . . . interpret figurative language" (see NGA, 2010, RL.5.4, L.4.5a, and L.5.5a, respectively), there is no reference that students write their own similes or metaphors. I think this would be a reasonable expectation, so I include that students write these forms of figurative language in the Figure 1.10 continuum. Appositives are also not in the Common Core, but I think they are worth teaching, for example, *Mrs. Fisher,* **my second-grade teacher**, *was always patient and helpful.* They are included in the California fourth- and fifth-grade standards, so they might be in your existing standards as well.

To find standards that you feel are worthy of instruction from your existing standards but you're not sure if they are in the Common Core, conduct a search of the Common Core using the Adobe tool search engine. I wondered where appositives were listed in the CC Standards because I couldn't find them in the language strand where I thought they might logically be. So I right-clicked and the Adobe Reader toolbar appeared on the left-hand side of my screen. I then clicked on the binoculars icon and typed both "appositive" and "appositives" so the computer could search for those words. The outcome showed no results, but if it had been there, you would see the list of entries and could click on each one to see the full standards associated with your search word(s). If you decide to revise this continuum or add standards, pay attention to verb usage. I found that *use* repeatedly offset many expectations in the language strand, so I assume that *identify* and *understand* is implied. However, you might want to be particularly clear for certain standards and consider other verbs, such as *write, produce, distinguish,* and so forth.

I am not advocating that you overhaul the language strand, but that you possibly add standards to the continuum you feel are necessary to student growth. As mentioned earlier, the Common Core advocates using professional expertise in making additions. Nevertheless, talk with your administrators about augmenting standards because of the 15 percent guideline mentioned in "A Brief Primer on the ELA Common Core Standards" in the Resource section. It might be overreacting to bring it up if you are minimally supplementing this strand, but I would be remiss if I did not reference this guideline.

The continuum can be a very useful document to hold teachers accountable to teaching particular language standards and also to avoid repetition. Honestly, not all teachers look at the standards in the grade before and after theirs because they access the Common Core Standards for their grade level only. Therefore, teachers plan their year based on standards in that grade level. If, however, teachers in a building and district use this continuum as a guide to plan language instruction, it would assist them in targeting their instruction more narrowly to be clearer about their responsibilities. By using the continuum to guide planning, along with results from pre- and formative assessments, teachers will be more apt to improve student achievement. Have this continuum—or a similar one you create—easily accessible so when you prepare curriculum for your year, you will be aware that this is your school's document and can plan accordingly.

## EXERCISE 1: What Is the Best Way to Group Standards?

With an overview of the standards and what they entail, this section now walks you through the first task in creating a unit map. At the end of this upcoming exercise on grouping standards, you will have a compilation of standards recorded for a targeted unit of study. Chapter 3 provides completed examples of unit maps, so you can review the standards portion to see the final goal of this exercise. Note that the standards are clustered by strand.

### Unit Focus and Template

At this juncture, you should have a unit in mind to use for this first exercise and also as you continue reading this book, as the best way to learn this process is to actually dive in and do the work. Think of a unit that involves the ELA CC Standards. You can focus on language arts, of course, but you can also choose a social studies or science unit as long as it involves reading and culminates in a writing piece or some kind of project that has a writing component. The previous section, "Definitions of the Common Core Text Types and Sample Prompts," provides examples that you can use or that might foster ideas. You will complete the top part of the unit template that is reprinted in the following example for easy reference (see Figure 1.11). Ultimately, you will complete the entire unit template as you respond to exercises in this book, so now is the time to retrieve it in hard copy, as a downloaded document, or both. To do so, you have several options: (1) print out a hard copy from Figure 3.1 in Chapter 3, (2) access it through the companion website (http://www.corwin.com/mappingelaunits) and print or download it onto your computer, (3) access it from my website (www.kathyglassconsulting.com) by clicking "Unit Template" on the right-hand side of the home page and print or download it onto your computer, or (4) use Figure 3.1 as a guide to create your own table in Microsoft Word or another program.

## Unit Template Excerpt 1

Unit: _____

Grade: _____  Timing: _____

| Standards | |
|---|---|
| | |
| Know | |
| | |

**FIGURE 1.11**

## Considerations for Grouping Standards

When you teach a writing domain, it isn't just a writing unit. Because the two are intertwined, reading is embedded in any writing unit. Students need to be deluged with reading student and published samples of a particular genre to be immersed in the components of the writing type and be clear on the ultimate expectations for the unit. If reading drives your unit because students are studying content knowledge in social studies or science or because they are focusing on reading strategies (e.g., inference, clarifying, questioning, etc.), you will also expect some writing throughout the unit so students can demonstrate what they learn. Speaking and listening are also a part of any unit as students engage in discussion and stay on topic, invent stories orally before writing, identify the main idea and supporting details, and so forth. In the Common Core Standards, technology and media are embedded throughout, so make sure to include these key expectations as appropriate for your unit. Standards are interconnected no matter which strand drives your unit. So when you record the standards on your template, although they are organized by strand, don't lose sight of the fact that the unit as a whole incorporates aspects of selected strands.

Be aware that you will need to naturally group some standards together when teaching certain skills or concepts. See the language strand examples in Figure 1.12 for compound sentences, complex sentences, and sentence beginnings. The Common Core Standards are referenced in parentheses; those without a reference are my own. Each sentence structure skill requires several standards to teach it thoroughly and appropriately as shown in the figure. Note that for compound sentences, there is not much difference between the coordinating conjunctions standard in first grade (NGA, 2010, L.1.1g) and third grade (L.3.1h) except that in third grade, you'll probably review what was taught previously and teach the rest of the complete set of coordinating conjunctions: *for, nor, yet*. However, I frankly don't think *nor* or *yet* are altogether appropriate for third graders.

You will also need to group some reading, writing, and speaking and listening skills together. If my targeted unit involves students reading informational text and eventually

## Sentence Structure

| Compound Sentences |
| --- |
| **Compound Sentence** |
| • Produce simple and compound sentences (NGA, 2010, L.3.1i). |
| **Independent Clause** |
| • Define independent clause (i.e., complete sentence with a subject and verb). |
| **Coordinating Conjunctions** |
| • Use frequently occurring conjunctions (e.g., *and, but, or so, because*; L.1.1g).<br>• Use coordinating conjunctions (L.3.1h). |
| **Comma to Separate the Independent Clauses** |
| • Use a comma before a coordinating conjunction in a compound sentence (L.4.2c). |

| Complex Sentences |
| --- |
| **Complex Sentence** |
| • Produce complex sentences (L.3.1i). |
| **Dependent Clauses** |
| • Identify the structure of dependent clauses and their role in complex sentences.<br>• Use subordinating conjunctions (L.3.1h). |
| **Independent Clauses** |
| • Define independent clause (i.e., complete sentence with a subject and verb). |
| **Subordinating Conjunctions** |
| • Use subordinating conjunctions (L.3.1h). |
| **Commas After a Dependent Clause That Begins a Sentence** |
| • Use a comma to separate an introductory element from the rest of the sentence (L.5.2b). |
| Sentence Beginnings |
| **Dependent Clauses (complex sentence)** |
| • Identify the structure of dependent clauses and their role in complex sentences.<br>• Use subordinating conjunctions (L.3.1h).<br>• Use a comma to separate an introductory element from the rest of the sentence (L.5.2b). |
| **Adjectives or Adverbs** |
| • Use adjectives and adverbs, and choose between them depending on what is to be modified (L.2.1e). |
| **Prepositional Phrases** |
| • Explain the function of prepositions in general and their function in particular sentences (L.5.1a).<br>• Form and use prepositional phrases (L.4.1d). |
| **Subjects (common, proper noun, personal pronoun)** |
| • Identify and correctly use singular possessive pronouns (e.g., my/mine, his/her).<br>• Explain the function of nouns and their function in particular sentences (L.3.1a).<br>• Form and use regular and irregular plural nouns (L.3.1b).<br>• Use abstract nouns (e.g., childhood; L.3.1c). |

**FIGURE 1.12**

writing an informative/explanatory piece, then these standards shown in Figure 1.13—among others—would have to be grouped together in this second-grade example. Of course, there are some other standards that could be added depending on the direction you want the unit to go, but the following are non-negotiable as they are essential to producing an informative/explanatory piece.

Refrain from entering standards on your unit map that you are not going to assess. For example, reading with fluency and accuracy is a fine standard; however, if you are not going to specifically assess (not to mention instruct!) this standard, do not enter it on your map. You might very well have students read aloud text from time to time, but unless it is a targeted standard where you specifically teach and assess it, leave it for another time.

# Possible Standards for Informative/Explanatory Unit

| Writing Standard |
|---|
| • Write informative/explanatory texts in which they introduce a topic, use facts and definitions to develop points, and provide a concluding statement or section (NGA, 2010, W.2.2).<br>• With guidance and support from adults and peers, focus on a topic and strengthen writing as needed by revising and editing (W.2.5). |
| **Reading Standards for Informational Text** |
| • Identify the main topic of a multiparagraph text as well as the focus of specific paragraphs within the text (RI.2.2).<br>• Know and use various text features (e.g., captions, bold print, subheadings, glossaries, indexes, electronic menus, icons) to locate key facts or information in a text efficiently (RI.2.6).<br>• Identify the main purpose of a text, including what the author wants to answer, explain, or describe (RI.2.7).<br>• Describe how reasons support specific points the author makes in a text (RI.2.8). |
| **Speaking and Listening** |
| • Recount or describe key ideas or details from a text read aloud or information presented orally or through other media (SL.2.2). |

**FIGURE 1.13**

## Two Approaches

There are a couple of ways to approach the task of grouping standards for your targeted unit. To choose the best method, it depends on your comfort level with the unit content you're about to map and on your personality style. If the unit is relatively new for you and you've not taught it before, the first option might be to go directly to the standards to group them from the start. Reading the various standards from the different strands and selecting ones that make sense to pull together can help you get a better idea of the whole unit. You might conduct this exercise with a textbook or other resources in front of you to use as a guide for content knowledge. If, however, you are comfortable with the content and are already thinking of a culminating assessment, have taught the unit before but are thinking of a new direction, or feel the need to discuss the overarching expectations with colleagues so you are all on the same page, the second option is to perform a pseudo stream of consciousness routine prior to grouping specific standards. Because the standards are organized by strands, grouping them might seem a bit compartmentalized. It is true that you probably teach in a similar fashion in which you have students read or listen and then practice writing. However, the entirety of the unit should be a holistic piece with interweaving strands, so before grouping standards, you might want to experience the interconnectedness of the standards that might seem more natural and work better for you.

For the approach explained in the second option, let's say that your targeted unit is narrative reading and writing. You want students to ultimately produce a narrative writing piece, specifically a short story, by the end of the unit. Think about your expectations for students in this short story unit and your ideas for a culminating product even if it's a rough idea. Jot down some ideas, mull it over in your head, or have a conversation with a colleague. I imagine your notes, monologue, or conversation would include something like the following for a third-grade class:

> *For a short story, I want kids to include the elements of literature in their writing: character, setting, plot, and point of view. In reading, I want them to identify all of these elements including theme. I don't think they necessarily need to state the theme prior to writing their own stories, but they surely would need to brainstorm a plot diagram that has the problem and solution along with the events, plus include the characters and setting. I want them to describe in detail at least one character. I want to know what that character looks like and also a personality trait for this character. They should be able to support their trait instead of just writing that so-and-so is mean. I want to know what this character does to show he's mean. So reading and writing are interconnected as they read and analyze stories from various authors and identify these elements in the literature. When they write their own stories, I want them to use the writing process, so I'll teach and support them through the steps. They should include sensory details, different kinds of sentence structures—I don't want every sentence starting the same way—and proper grammar and conventions.*

And so on. After this list or conversation, begin identifying and grouping appropriate standards. You could also have this type of conversation with colleagues or yourself and concurrently find standards to group as you hit on each point. As you review the standards, you will probably realize you have missed criteria that you want to add that wasn't on your list or part of your conversation.

Whether you go right to grouping standards or first stop to think or talk about your expectations, enter the standards on the unit template and group them by strands. You can do this by cutting and pasting standards from the Common Core website (www.corestandards.org/the-standards), which is in PDF format; from a Word version of the standards found on my website (www.kathyglassconsulting.com) under the link "ELA Common Core Standards Grades K–5 (Word)"; or by writing down the letters and numbers associated with each standard and entering them on the unit template (e.g., W.2.1 = writing strand, Grade 2, Standard 1).

## EXERCISE 2: HOW ARE STANDARDS USED TO DETERMINE WHAT STUDENTS SHOULD KNOW?

When educators design a unit of instruction, identifying what students should know, understand, and be able to do helps professionals focus on the unit outcomes. In this exercise, we will focus on what students should know for your targeted unit. Knowledge encompasses the factual information that students use as the foundation for gleaning overarching concepts, such as facts, dates, people, places, examples, and terms or definitions.

Besides using standards to compile your list, you can access a textbook, other resources, colleagues, and professional judgment to help generate knowledge items. See Figure 1.14 for examples of how to use standards to identify what students should know. For example, the fourth-grade literature standard focuses on point of view: "Compare and contrast the point

# Identifying What Students Should Know

| Standards | Knowledge |
|---|---|
| **Reading Standards for Literature (Grade 1)**<br><br>• Ask and answer questions about key details in a text (NGA, 2010, RL.1.1).<br>• Retell stories, including key details, and demonstrate understanding of their central message or lesson (RL.1.2).<br>• Describe characters, settings, and major events in a story, using key details (RL.1.3). | • Reading strategies—questioning, retelling<br>• Key details<br>• Elements of literature—characters, setting, events, theme (central message) |
| **Reading Standards for Literature (Grade 4)**<br><br>• Determine the meaning of words and phrases as they are used in a text, including those that allude to significant characters found in mythology (e.g., *Herculean*) (RL.4.4).<br>• Explain major differences between poems, drama, and prose, and refer to the structural elements of poems (e.g., verse, rhythm, meter) and drama (e.g., casts of characters, settings, descriptions, dialogue, stage directions) when writing or speaking about a text (RL.4.5).<br>• Compare and contrast the point of view from which different stories are narrated, including the difference between first- and third-person narrations (RL.4.6). | • Allusion: A reference within a literary work to another work of fiction, a film, artwork, or a real event.<br>• Mythology: Stories of a particular culture focusing on its origin (e.g., creation myths), history, deities, ancestors, and heroes.<br>• Mythological characters<br>• Genres and their structures—poems, drama, prose<br>• Point of view—first and third person<br>• Pronouns—first- and third-person pronouns<br>• Narrator: Who is telling the story.<br>• First-person (or personal) point of view: Uses the pronoun *I* since the narrator is a character within the story; the narrator can reveal his or her own thoughts and feelings and what he or she is told by others; first-person pronouns are used (*I, we, our,* etc.)<br>• Third-person omniscient point of view: The narrator is an all-knowing outsider who can enter the minds of several characters and can reveal the thoughts and feelings of these characters; third-person pronouns are used (*him, her, they, them,* etc.)<br>• Third-person limited point of view: The narrator is an outsider, like in third-person omniscient point of view, but in limited point of view; the narrator can only reveal the thoughts and feelings of a single character; third-person pronouns are used (*him, her, they, them,* etc.) |

**History (Mid-Continent Research for Education and Learning [McREL] Grades K–2)** (Kendall, 2011)

**Standard 1.** Understands family life now and in the past, and family life in various places long ago.

1. Knows a family history through two generations (e.g., various family members and their connections).

2. Understands family life today and how it compares with family life in the recent past and family life long ago (e.g., roles, jobs, schooling experiences).

3. Knows the cultural similarities and differences in clothes, homes, food, communication, technology, and cultural traditions between families now and in the past.

4. Understands family life in a community of the past and life in a community of the present (e.g., roles, jobs, communication, technology, style of homes, transportation, schools, religious observances, cultural traditions).

5. Understands personal family or cultural heritage through stories, songs, and celebrations.

6. Knows ways in which people share family beliefs and values (e.g., oral traditions, literature, songs, art, religion, community celebrations, mementos, food, language).

- Terms/vocabulary—family, generation, ancestor, community, culture, communication, technology, traditions, transportation, religion, celebration
- People can collect photographs and interview others to learn about family members of the past.
- Culture is a way of life that includes clothing, food, religion, music, language, and homes.
- Stories, songs, and celebrations are ways people can learn about family and culture.
- Countries of origin for ancestors
- Historical time—yesterday; today; tomorrow; long ago; long, long ago
- Family structures (e.g., adoptive parents, stepparents and stepsiblings, foster parents, other relatives)

**FIGURE 1.14**

of view from which different stories are narrated, including the difference between first- and third-person narrations" (NGA, 2010, RL.4.6). In dissecting this standard and thinking about what it means, I would want students to know the definitions of first- and third-person point of view and the associated pronouns. That information is not explicitly stated in the CC Standards, but I know that is what I would teach, so I write it down.

When entering your work on the unit template—such as this knowledge list—consider your audience. If it is just for your own personal use, you may prefer to be brief. For instance, if you want students to know the writing process, you can merely write *writing process*. However, if colleagues will view this document, I suggest being more detailed and entering *planning, drafting, editing, revising, publishing,* or even a definition of each step. In some districts, teachers put their work on a district server or share with a number of colleagues, so adding detail is important for everyone to be clear about what your unit entails so they have the necessary information to devise effective curriculum from it. Another reason to add detail is to ensure all who devise curriculum from this outline to teach are operating from the same definitions. To this end, I have defined certain terms—*allusion, mythology, first- and third-person points of view*—instead of merely listing them in the fourth-grade example in Figure 1.14. In addition, I include some basic facts in the first-grade unit that I would want my colleagues to know about for planning purposes and that ultimately should be communicated to students (e.g., *People can collect photographs and interview others to learn about family members of the past. Culture is a way of life that includes . . .* ).

Using your standards as a guide, along with other resources that can help you identify factual information for your targeted unit, record what you want students to know onto the unit template. Remember that knowledge is very straightforward and includes facts, dates, people, places, examples, and terms/definitions. Make sure to see additional examples of knowledge that are listed in the unit map examples in Chapter 3.

## CLOSING

This chapter has focused extensively on the standards, how to group them, and how to list what students should know for a particular unit of study. Specifically, a case is stated for why standards are so important in guiding curriculum and instruction. Also, the chapter focuses on the cross-referencing between the Common Core and state standards. Some states have alignment documents that compare the Common Core with existing state standards that might be useful for educators to preview. There are also some questions presented to use in discussing these comparative documents; however, educators should be cognizant to spend time wisely studying the gaps and overlaps because the hard work is on implementation. The chapter continues with a thorough explanation of the writing types and offers suggestions for assignments aligned to them. For the language strand, a continuum can be used to support progression from grade to grade and foster collegiality to help teach grammar and conventions.

At the end of this chapter, readers should have targeted a unit of study as the basis for a curriculum map, grouped standards for this unit, and identified what students should know with regard to this unit. The standards and knowledge should be entered on the template. The next chapter provides a comprehensive treatment of essential understandings and guiding questions so you can add these to your unit template.

# 2

# Essential Understandings and Guiding Questions

> When curriculum and instruction require students to process factual information through the conceptual levels of thinking, the students demonstrate greater retention of factual information, deeper levels of understanding, and increased motivation for learning.
>
> —H. Lynn Erickson (2007, p. 2)

We often say to ourselves, "If only I knew then what I know now." How true. I think back to when I had my own classroom and wish I had the knowledge base then that I do now. People ask me if I miss having my own classroom. In some respects, I surely do. I miss the rapport with the kids, the ah-ha moments students have when they get something they struggled to understand, the creating and delivering of instruction, and much more. But I am passionate about what I do now and feel that when I train teachers or others in the field and they embrace what is cutting edge and research based in education, I'm touching more than just the classrooms of students I've been fortunate to teach. I'm touching a multitude of students indirectly by passing on what I have learned to educators. And I am still teaching; I'm just teaching to a more mature audience. The cascading implications of my work will be felt by my students' students!

Essential understandings and guiding questions represent a pivotal shift in my teaching and tangible evidence of growth for my students and my clients' students. Therefore, I believe what I share in this chapter is a significant gift that educators can give students that yields enormous benefits in critical thinking and problem solving. Teaching by using essential understandings and questions is wildly impactful for students to connect knowledge across grades, and sometimes subjects, and to apply what they have learned to their immediate world and the greater world at large. If you follow what I suggest here, I guarantee it will transform your teaching or the way those you mentor teach. The obvious by-product is a more meaningful learning experience for students. It is not easy, but once you bear with me and grasp the overall *why* and then delve into the *how,* you'll see what I mean.

Many academic experts have espoused the virtues and efficacy of using understandings and guiding questions as a driving force in instruction. There are too many to name here; however, those that stand out for me are Lynn Erickson, who popularized concept-based instruction; Grant Wiggins and Jay McTighe, for their work in backward design; and Carol Tomlinson, who is at the forefront of differentiation. Erickson crystallized the relationships between concepts and facts for me, as well as featured a novel way to fashion essential understandings in a provocative and insightful manner that will raise the bar for students. In her work, she talks about the "synergistic interplay between the factual and conceptual levels of thinking" (Erickson, 2007, p. 2) as a pathway to intellectual growth. Most people don't remember a litany of facts; however, if you tie them to concepts so there is a home base, then people are much more likely to recall these facts. It is imperative that teachers present and teach the factual information (know) and skills (do), but the end goal is to have students use them to make sense of a greater realization. As mentioned in Chapter 1, KUDs—what we want students to know, understand, and do—form the basis for a unit of instruction and emanate from standards. This chapter addresses the unit map components of essential understandings and guiding questions.

## THE NATURE AND CRITICAL IMPORTANCE OF ESSENTIAL (OR ENDURING) UNDERSTANDINGS

You might have heard the term *enduring understandings* from Wiggins and McTighe's (1998) prominent work *Understanding by Design.* These men also use the phrase *big ideas,* which is also a term that appears in many textbooks. Others (including me) call them *essential understandings* (Erickson, 2007). But no matter the terminology, these understandings or big ideas share a common denominator: They are conceptually based statements that teachers invent or borrow and use to design curriculum and instruction that emanate from standards. As Wiggins and McTighe (1998) state, "*Enduring* refers to the big ideas, the important understandings, that we want students to 'get inside of' and retain after they've forgotten many of the details. . . . Enduring understandings go beyond discrete facts or skills to focus on larger concepts, principles, or processes" (p. 10).

So why should teachers spend the time to create essential understandings? I can explain it best by giving you an example. Let's say you are teaching the American Revolution in fifth grade. As a guide about what to teach, you look to the standards, which might look like the California standards shown in Figure 2.1 (California Department of Education, 2000).

There is a lot of factual material included in these standards, such as the dreaded acts the colonists abhorred (e.g., Stamp Act, Townshend Acts, Coercive Acts, etc.), the government committees (e.g., second Continental Congress, Committees of Correspondence), the Declaration of Independence, and the people (e.g., King George III, Patrick Henry, Thomas Jefferson, George Washington, etc.). The California standards omitted the following; however, this factual information is implied and will probably appear in the student textbook and should be covered: other people (e.g., Benjamin Franklin, Sam Adams, Abigail Adams, Crispus Attucks, Patrick Henry, Thomas Paine, etc.), groups (e.g., Sons of Liberty, Tories, Loyalists, Neutralists, etc.), events (e.g., Boston Tea Party, Boston Massacre, tar and feathering, etc.), famous quotes ("Give me liberty, or give me death." "No taxation without representation."), and some key facts. All of this is critically important to teach this period in history and, as such, should be included in the knowledge piece explained in Chapter 1, but it still is a litany of factual information. To help students make sense of it all, we need to

## 5.5 Students Explain the Causes of the American Revolution

1. Understand how political, religious, and economic ideas and interests brought about the Revolution (e.g., resistance to imperial policy, the Stamp Act, the Townshend Acts, taxes on tea, Coercive Acts).

2. Know the significance of the first and second Continental Congresses and of the Committees of Correspondence.

3. Understand the people and events associated with the drafting and signing of the Declaration of Independence and the document's significance, including the key political concepts it embodies, the origins of those concepts, and its role in severing ties with Great Britain.

4. Describe the views, lives, and impact of key individuals during this period (e.g., King George III, Patrick Henry, Thomas Jefferson, George Washington, Benjamin Franklin, John Adams).

**FIGURE 2.1**   Fifth-Grade California History–Social Studies Content Standard

create conceptual statements that embody this knowledge so students can couch these facts in some greater understanding. And as educators, it is important that we study these standards carefully and consider what we really want students to leave a particular unit of study understanding. It is by creating essential understandings that we discern what the standards mean and what we really want our students to take away. Consider the essential understandings, shown in Figure 2.2, tied to the social studies standards cited earlier.

You undoubtedly noticed that Figure 2.2 includes more than one essential understanding for each standard. This is intentional as you can see that some contain subtle differences,

## Possible Essential Understandings Aligned to Social Studies Standards

| California Standards | Possible Essential Understandings |
|---|---|
| **Standard 5.5:1** Understand how political, religious, and economic ideas and interests brought about the Revolution (e.g., resistance to imperial policy, the Stamp Act, the Townshend Acts, taxes on tea, Coercive Acts) (California Department of Education, 2000). | • Control for power and desire for independence and economic gain can cause nations to engage in conflict and persecute one another. |
| | • Differences in political and economic ideals and interests may foster acrimony that results in conflict. |
| **Standard 5.5:2** Know the significance of the first and second Continental Congresses and of the Committees of Correspondence. | • People who share a common interest may be more powerful and successful in confronting an adversary as a unified group than if they work alone. |
| | • Political representatives forge alliances and debate issues to arrive at decisions and compromises that serve the best interest of their constituencies. |

**FIGURE 2.2** *(Continued)*

| **Standard 5.5:3** Understand the people and events associated with the drafting and signing of the Declaration of Independence and the document's significance, including the key political concepts it embodies, the origins of those concepts, and its role in severing ties with Great Britain. | • Framers of political documents incorporate key concepts as an embodiment of ideals and a system of government. |
| | • Documents can serve as a catalyst for changing people's views on issues. |
| | • Politicians use preceding government systems and key concepts to create new systems that address the needs and ideals of the current society. |
| | • Political independence produces risks and rewards. |
| **Standard 5.5:4** Describe the views, lives, and impact of key individuals during this period (e.g., King George III, Patrick Henry, Thomas Jefferson, George Washington, Benjamin Franklin, John Adams). | • Individuals can make powerful contributions for targeted groups of people that might lead to change, growth, and survival. |
| | • Effective leaders help unite disparate groups to achieve a unified goal. |
| | • Leaders' perspectives, personality traits, and actions can help shape and impact others' political opinions and involvement thereby generating change. |

**FIGURE 2.2**

in which case you would choose the one that clearly indicates the direction for your teaching. You don't want overlap; this is because each essential understanding should stand alone. Other times, however, you might have two understandings aligned to a particular standard because they represent two directions that a standard can take, and you might teach to both. Since teachers use the understandings to write, find, or revise curriculum, it's imperative to be clear in your goals for the unit as these statements form the basis for teaching. The exercise of creating or finding the right essential understanding allows educators to be altogether focused in what they want students to understand as indicated by the standard, so it serves as a kind of statement of conceptual intent.

Why isn't there one universal, associated essential understanding or two for each standard? There are many reasons for teachers to craft a different essential understanding to the same standard. As mentioned before, the standard might be hefty and require two essential understandings to cover different aspects of it. In addition, it might be that teachers interpret the same standard slightly differently because they view it through their own individual lens, want to go beyond the standard, have various rich resources at their disposal to use, teach multiple subjects so they are incorporating history or another subject to teach the standard, are using a particular novel in language arts that emphasizes some elements of literature or literary devices more than others, work on an interdisciplinary team and have colleagues who will touch on other aspects of the standards, use different textbooks than another school or district, and so forth. To aid them in their endeavor, teachers can find or create essential understandings to address these types of questions: *What do you want your students to really remember long after they have forgotten the discrete facts? What is your goal for student understanding based on the standards? What is the essence of this particular unit of study? What differentiated resources will you use to illuminate the standards? What textbook is at your disposal? Are you team teaching with other staff members who will address standards? How can you help students transfer the knowledge they learn across subjects and grades? How can you help students make various connections: text-to-self, text-to-text, and text-to-world?*

Essential understandings are for educators to gain clarity on the direction of a unit and its outcomes based on standards so they are keenly focused on their goals prior to teaching. They are written in adult language, so not all students can decipher them. Some teachers, though, like to translate them into "kid language." Unit guiding questions, which are addressed in detail later in the chapter, should be posted for students of all ages to see throughout the whole unit because they focus students on the purpose for their learning. Unlike the essential understandings, teachers purposefully write these questions in language suitable for their students' age and readiness. The essential unit guiding questions are pointed, succinct, and provocative; they guide instruction and promote self-discovery.

The essential understandings basically reveal the answers to the guiding questions and give away what you want all students to realize, so if you show or read them, this is most effective near the end of the unit. Consider the pairing of essential understandings and unit guiding questions in Figure 2.3. You can see that the language for essential understandings is not only sophisticated, but also reveals the answers to the guiding questions that form the basis for teaching.

## Possible Essential Understandings and Unit Questions

| Essential Understandings | Essential Unit Questions |
|---|---|
| To determine the central message, lesson, or moral and to demonstrate understanding of key text details, readers can recount stories and ask and answer various literal and inferential questions. | Why do readers ask and answer questions? |
| | How do readers figure out the central message of a story? (Or, how do readers identify the theme of a story?) |
| Characters can change over time through events, setting, or interaction with other characters, which can, in turn, shape the plot. | How and why do characters change over time? |
| To explain what the text explicitly says and to draw inferences about characters, setting, or events, readers need to select and cite specific quotes from the text as concrete evidence for opinions. | How does textual evidence support a reader's interpretation of a story? |

**FIGURE 2.3**

So should teachers share essential understandings with students? Again, I don't necessarily recommend sharing them with students prior to the unit. It is, however, imperative that students see the unit guiding questions throughout the unit of study because they are an expression of the essential understandings. To share essential understandings, substitute difficult vocabulary for age-appropriate language and show the connections between the questions they explored throughout the unit and the associated essential understandings. Or you can conduct one of the following exercises through discussion or writing, as you wish. Any would help to further foster the goal of having students engage in thinking critically and making connections.

- Have students brainstorm a list of lessons and activities they have completed during the unit in small groups or as a class. Then ask them to work in pairs or trios to create general statements about what they learned based on the list they generated. You can help guide them to take the factual information from the lessons and see if they can arrive at a larger understanding. Promote conversation through these kinds of questions: *Why did we learn about this? Can you make any connections between this unit and other units we have studied? Can you make connections about life based on what you learned? Did you learn how to solve any problems through our work in this unit? How so? Can you think of a theme based on what we studied much like you would consider the theme or central message of a story?*

- Write each factual piece of information that was presented in the unit on a separate card. Have groups of students categorize the cards in a way that makes sense. Then ask them to carefully study all the cards in one category at a time. At the top of each category, have them write a general statement on a blank card that does not include any of the proper nouns that are on the teacher-prepared cards they grouped. Each group can share with the whole class and discuss these generalizations. You can then reveal the essential understandings and see if any are similar to what they created as the springboard for discussion.

- As a class, generate a list of the different lessons and activities students completed in the unit. Then distribute concept cards to small groups, for example, *diversity, patterns, conflict, friendship,* and so on. Instruct groups to identify the concept cards that are associated with what they learned, and use these concepts to create general statements to share with the class.

## EXAMPLES OF ESSENTIAL UNDERSTANDINGS ALIGNED TO THE COMMON CORE READING STANDARDS FOR LITERATURE

Although standards serve as a guide, they can be interpreted in slightly different ways as mentioned earlier. It is incumbent upon curriculum designers, teachers, and other educators to critically examine them to discover the concepts and foundational core that is the basis for a particular unit. Once you undergo the exercise to target standards and grapple with finding, revising, or creating essential understandings for them, you will be meeting a higher level of professionalism as you clearly identify what matters most in a unit that you want to impart to students.

Before learning a suggested process to follow in creating essential understandings, it will be helpful to peruse many examples that I wrote to align with the Reading Standards for Literature K–5 (see Figure 2.4). You might tweak what I've written because not all educators will create the same exact essential understanding for the same standard. These are merely my interpretations. Pay attention to the following as you read my understandings in Figure 2.4. Note that only a portion of Figure 2.4 is included in this chapter. Access the companion website and download the entire figure, and then go on a scavenger hunt alone or with colleagues to find examples of the following:

- *Concepts.* Concepts are "a mental construct that frames a set of examples sharing common attributes . . . concepts are timeless, universal, abstract, and broad" (Erickson, 2002, p. 164). They are expressed as nouns and can be one or two words, such as *theme, writing process, figurative language,* and *persuasion.* Look for concepts in some of my essential understandings in Figure 2.4. Note that because concepts are defined as timeless, universal, abstract, and broad, you won't find any proper nouns. To help you identify concepts, they are capitalized in the following examples; also see Figure 2.5, English Language Arts Concepts.

   o CHARACTERS can *change* over time through EVENTS, SETTING, or INTERACTION with other characters, which can, in turn, *shape* the PLOT.
   o WRITERS *experiment* with various DIALOGUE TAGS to *enhance* the spoken words of CHARACTERS through *illustrating* TONE and GESTURES.

- *Number of concepts.* Each essential understanding forges a relationship between at least two concepts. Make sure you find more than one concept per statement. Oftentimes there are more than two.

## Essential Understandings Aligned to the Common Core for Literature K–5

| I./2./3. Key Ideas and Details | |
|---|---|
| **Common Core Standards** | **Essential Understandings** |
| **Kindergarten/Grade I**<br><br>• With prompting and support, retell familiar stories, including key details (NGA, 2010, RL.K.2).<br>• With prompting and support, identify characters, settings, and major events in a story (RL.K.3).<br>• Describe characters, settings, and major events in a story, using key details (RL.1.3). | To facilitate deeper discussion and engagement with the text, proficient readers or listeners can retell a story and identify and describe the characters, setting, and plot. |
| **Kindergarten/Grades I & 2**<br><br>• With prompting and support, ask and answer questions about key details in a text (RL.K.1).<br>• Ask and answer questions about key details in a text (RL.1.1).<br>• Ask and answer such questions as who, what, where, when, why, and how to demonstrate understanding of key details in a text (RL.2.1). | To improve overall comprehension, proficient readers ask and answer various literal and inferential questions to clarify meaning and engage more deeply with the text. |

**FIGURE 2.4** *(Continued)*

| **Grades 1, 2, & 3**<br><br>• Retell stories, including key details, and demonstrate understanding of their central message or lesson (RL.1.2).<br>• Recount stories, including fables and folktales from diverse cultures, and determine their central message, lesson, or moral (RL.2.2).<br>• Recount stories, including fables, folktales, and myths from diverse cultures; determine the central message, lesson, or moral and explain how it is conveyed through key details in the text (RL.3.2). | To determine a central message, lesson, or moral, readers can retell the story and discuss key details about characters, settings, and plot. |
| | Stories from diverse cultures can share common themes and provide insights about their way of life. |
| **Grade 2**<br><br>• Describe how characters in a story respond to major events and challenges (RL.2.3). | Characters respond to major events and challenges as the author develops a plot and works to resolve the central conflict. |
| **Grade 3**<br><br>• Ask and answer questions to demonstrate understanding of a text, referring explicitly to the text as the basis for the answers (RL.3.1). | To demonstrate understanding, readers can engage in questioning and explicitly reference the text to support their answers. |
| **Grade 3**<br><br>• Describe characters in a story (e.g., their traits, motivations, or feelings) and explain how their actions contribute to the sequence of events (RL.3.3). | Characters' traits, motivations, or feelings drive their actions and contribute to plot development. |
| **Grade 4**<br><br>• Refer to details and examples in a text when explaining what the text says explicitly and when drawing inferences from the text (RL.4.1).<br><br>• Describe in depth a character, setting, or event in a story or drama, drawing on specific details in the text (e.g., a character's thoughts, words, or actions) (RL.4.3). | To explain what the text explicitly states and to draw inferences about characters, setting, or events, readers refer to specific details and examples from the text as evidence. |
| **Grade 5**<br><br>• Quote accurately from a text when explaining what the text says explicitly and when drawing inferences from the text (RL.5.1). | To explain what the text explicitly states and to draw inferences about characters, setting, or events, readers select and cite specific quotes from the text as concrete evidence for their assertions. |

**FIGURE 2.4**

# English Language Arts Concepts

| Reading for Literature | Reading for Informational Text | |
|---|---|---|
| • reading strategies (e.g., questioning, inference, retelling, summarizing, prediction, monitoring and clarifying, visualization, connection) <br> • metacognition <br> • genres (e.g., fables, folktales, drama, story, poem, myth, mystery, adventure, graphic novel) <br> • elements of literature (i.e., character, plot, setting, theme, point of view) <br> • heroes <br> • protagonist/antagonist <br> • problem/solution <br> • interactions <br> • relationships <br> • transformation <br> • motivation <br> • cause/effect <br> • conflict <br> • central message/moral/theme <br> • literary devices (e.g., allusion, suspense, dialogue, dialect, mood, symbolism) | • words/phrases/language <br> • sounds of language (e.g., rhythm, rhyme, meter, repetition, alliteration, onomatopoeia) <br> • figurative language (e.g., simile, metaphor, personification, sensory detail/imagery) <br> • culture <br> • diversity <br> • pattern <br> • structure <br> • sequence <br> • narrator/narration <br> • persuasion <br> • author/writer <br> • reader <br> • purpose <br> • audience <br> • perspective <br> • perception <br> • illustrations/visuals <br> • writer's style <br> • voice | • reading strategies (see "Reading for Literature") <br> • main topic/key details <br> • ideas/concepts <br> • evidence/reasons/support <br> • thesis/topic sentence <br> • structure <br> • comparison/contrast <br> • similarities/differences <br> • procedure <br> • chronology <br> • sequence/time <br> • cause/effect <br> • problem/solution <br> • relationships <br> • interactions <br> • interpretations <br> • integration <br> • research <br><br> • fact/opinion <br> • illustrations/visuals/images <br> • author's purpose <br> • perspective/point of view <br> • words/phrases/language <br> • text features (e.g., table of contents, captions, bold print, subheadings, icons, electronic menus, diagrams, illustrations, glossary, index) <br> • search tools (e.g., key words, sidebars, hyperlinks) <br> • print concepts (e.g., front cover, back cover, title page, text direction) <br> • author <br> • purpose <br> • writer's style <br> • voice |

**FIGURE 2.5** *(Continued)*

49

| Writing | Speaking and Listening | Language |
|---|---|---|
| • text types (e.g., opinion pieces, informative/explanatory, narrative)<br>• purpose (e.g., to persuade, narrate, describe, inform, etc.)<br>• bias<br>• perspective<br>• perception<br>• beliefs<br>• elements of literature (see "Reading for Literature")<br>• evidence/reasons/support<br>• thesis/topic sentence<br>• organizational structure<br>• sequence/logical order<br>• transitions<br>• fact/opinion<br>• writing process (e.g., prewriting, drafting, editing, revising, publishing)<br>• research/resources<br>• bibliography<br>• investigation<br>• audience<br>• analysis/reflection/interpretation<br>• summarizing/paraphrasing<br>• word choice/language<br>• writer's style | • collaborative conversations<br>• collaborative discussions<br>• communication<br>• main ideas/supporting details<br>• facts/details<br>• formal vs. informal discourse<br>• comprehension (e.g., questioning, clarifying, retelling, summarizing, paraphrasing)<br>• active listening<br>• oral communication (e.g., volume, pitch, intonation, phrasing, pace, modulation, facial expressions, verbal cues, gestures)<br>• visual displays | • language<br>• grammar and usage<br>• sentence structure<br>• conventions (i.e., capitalization, punctuation, spelling)<br>• vocabulary acquisition<br>• word relationships<br>• word nuances<br>• words/phrases<br>• figurative language<br>• idioms/adages/proverbs<br>• references (e.g., thesaurus, dictionary, etc.)<br><br>**Foundational Skills for Reading**<br>• phonics<br>• word recognition<br>• word analysis<br>• print features (e.g., follow words on a page, spacing in letters and words, upper- and lowercase letters, etc.)<br>• reading accuracy<br>• reading fluency |

**Macroconcepts (broad, interdisciplinary concepts)**

| | | | |
|---|---|---|---|
| change | function | order | reflection |
| community | identity | pattern | structure |
| connection | interdependence | perspective | system |
| form | movement | | |

**FIGURE 2.5**

- *Verbs.* Look at the verbs used to connect the concepts in each essential understanding in the previous examples. The verbs are underlined for easy reference. None will include forms of the verb *to be,* such as *is, are, was, were.* I learned this trick from Erickson's book *Concept-Based Curriculum and Instruction for the Thinking Classroom* (2007). I pervasively see essential understandings written with forms of the verb *to be.* When I engage in a mental exercise of rewriting them using stronger verbs, they are invariably more sophisticated. Also note that the verbs are expressed as present tense, supporting timelessness. (See the weak and strong examples for comparison in Figure 2.6.)

| Weak Essential Understandings | Stronger Essential Understandings |
| --- | --- |
| Paragraphs are organized in a logical order in an informative paper. | Logically organizing paragraphs in a sequential fashion facilitates comprehension. |
| Context clues are what readers use to help understand unfamiliar words. | Readers use context clues as a means for deciphering unknown words, which ultimately aids in overall comprehension. |
| It is important for writers to be aware of purpose and audience when they begin their writing project. | Knowing the purpose and audience at the outset of writing guides authors to produce a piece that incorporates the appropriate elements for a specific genre and focus writing on a target audience. |

**FIGURE 2.6**   Strong Versus Weak Essential Understandings I

- *Importance factor.* Not only are the examples in the left column of Figure 2.6 weak because of the verbs *to be;* they also seem incomplete in terms of what teachers want students to really understand and viscerally grasp. To merely state that *paragraphs are organized in a logical order in an informative paper* begs the questions *Who cares? Why should students know this? So what?* Plus, it is more a statement of fact than an essential understanding. If, however, I write *why* organization matters, then I've written a stronger essential understanding. So to answer the question *Why is it worth knowing that paragraphs are organized logically?* I can respond, *Logically organizing paragraphs in a sequential fashion facilitates comprehension.* Know that a significant factor in creating and teaching around essential understandings is to have students come to realize an enduring truth. Let's try the second example: *Why is it worth knowing that context clues are what readers use to help understand words?* Because *using context clues provides readers with a means for deciphering unknown words, which supports overall comprehension.*

- *Transfer value.* A significant goal of teaching is to help students make connections, transfer knowledge, problem solve, and think critically. When teachers write or find profound and worthwhile essential understandings to represent what is important for students to retain, and they stay on course with using these statements to guide their instruction, they prime students to reach this goal. When students say something like the following, they have arrived, and teachers have aided them on their journey:

> *This character is like the one from the novel I'm reading at home because both show that selfishness leads to loneliness.*

*That's cool how the theme of this story and the one we just read are the same, but the characters and settings are completely different.*

*The situation this character is facing is like what we are studying in history with the Native Americans: Both are being treated unfairly.*

*When I write this research paper, it follows the same format that I learned about in other expository writing. Now I get it!*

*I didn't realize there are so many different groups of people who have moved to different places like I have. The Pilgrims moved here from Europe, the Native Americans were even forced to move, and people decided to move west long ago. I guess I'm not alone.*

As adults, we make connections and transfer knowledge repeatedly when we watch the news or encounter new situations. It actually helps us make sense of the world or gain deeper insights. For students, we need to help them along to do this work so they become more global, broader thinkers, and even productive individuals. Look at a few examples of my essential understandings in Figure 2.4 and think about or discuss with colleagues how they can transfer to different units of instruction across grades and subjects.

## EXERCISE 3: HOW DO EDUCATORS CREATE (OR REVISE) ESSENTIAL UNDERSTANDINGS?

Chapter 1 guided you in two exercises: (1) What Is the Best Way to Group Standards? and (2) How Are Standards Used to Determine What Students Should Know? At this juncture, you will embark upon Exercise 3: How Do Educators Create (or Revise) Essential Understandings? In the unit template, you will see that there is a spot for essential understandings at the top. After this exercise and the next one for essential unit and guiding questions, you will have completed three components as circled in Figure 2.7, Unit Template Excerpt 2. Note that each page of the template is devoted to one essential understanding and associated guiding questions. This allows space to write a comprehensive and organized unit map.

## Unit Template Excerpt 2

| **Essential Understanding:** | | | | |
| **Essential Unit Guiding Question:** | | | | |
| **Lesson Guiding Questions** | **Skills** | **Activities** | **Resources** | **Formative Assessment Evidence** |
| | | | | |

**FIGURE 2.7**

Essentially, I use a formula to create essential understandings. However, I must admit it is challenging work, so I'm not going to pretend it is easy. There is a process to follow, and I find that those who abort the process and jump ahead do not necessarily create the most enriching essential understandings. Invariably, they end up forging ahead only to find that if they had started with step one, they would have had a stronger end result.

It is important to know the time you have available to teach your targeted unit and find or craft essential understandings that take this factor into consideration. If you have three weeks for a unit, you wouldn't want five statements because you would not get to explore them all thoroughly. By the same token, you don't want more than six essential understandings for a comprehensive unit because that is probably about the maximum you can aptly cover for six to eight weeks. So, as you do the following exercise, keep in mind how many understandings you will create based on the time you have available to teach your targeted unit.

When you build or revise essential understandings, be aware that as students advance through the grades, the essential understandings should be commensurate with their growth and development and serve to continuously challenge them. You know that essential understandings are expressly written to form a relationship between at least two concepts that emanate from standards to articulate what students should understand. You will undoubtedly see some of the same concepts from grade to grade, and it is important to determine what you want students to glean as they become more adept learners. Therefore, note that there are many different ways that an essential understanding can be written using the same concepts. For example, *character* and *setting* are concepts that students will be exposed to repeatedly throughout their schooling. As students learn and apply more sophisticated reading strategies with more complex text, it is critical that they should be required and challenged to apply and synthesize these concepts at a higher level.

In addition to creating essential understandings to meet the demands of students as they advance through the grades and become more capable learners, you must take into consideration the text and the content matter that is used as the basis for writing these statements. With regard to text, even though reading can be grouped as informational text or literature, each selection is unique, so you need to write essential understandings specific to each work (e.g., research materials, textbook, literary work, informational text, etc.). In general, keep these factors top of mind when crafting or finding understandings: the specific text, more complex text, more sophisticated standards, content matter or topic, grade level, the purpose for the task, the insight you want students to glean, and so forth. After all, if teachers were to create the same understandings from the elementary years into high school using the same concepts, then the bar for students would be set too low for them to demonstrate higher learning and growth as they mature. Following are several understandings that can be used with the two concepts *character* and *setting* for various grades and literary units of study. Some clearly overlap so teachers can choose the language they prefer; others are more sophisticated for older and advanced students. But the point is that given two concepts, there are myriad ways to write essential understandings, so be sure to scaffold them accordingly and match them to appropriate groups of students and their characteristics.

- Settings can change characters.
- Settings can shape and transform characters' thoughts, feelings, and actions.
- Characters evolve and behave differently as they encounter various settings.
- Settings can facilitate growth and change for characters, thereby impacting the plot.
- Authors suggest settings through characters' dialectical and speech patterns.
- Settings can create a mood or atmosphere that impacts characters' motivations and actions.

- Authors can incorporate symbolism into settings and characters to enhance meaning and lead readers to alternate, underlying interpretations.
- Historical settings can influence the interactions between main and subordinate characters, which can ultimately impact the plot.

As mentioned previously, essential understandings serve to foster critical thinking and problem solving and help students make connections and transfer knowledge. To support this goal, consider essential understandings that span two or three grade levels. As students approach different and more complex subject matter, topics, and texts, encourage them to see the relationships. For example, your understandings can serve grade clusters (e.g., K–1, 2–3, 4–5, or K–2, 3–5) focusing on specific concepts as shown in Figure 2.8 for the Common Core Reading Literature Standard 5, Craft and Structure (NGA, 2010). Teaching with this type of mind-set also supports the notion of curriculum mapping as educators build upon prior knowledge, scaffold learning, introduce appropriately challenging material, and avoid repetition. When essential understandings guide instruction and when there is an intentional fluid progression of skill building and conceptual focus, students can more easily see connections and transfer knowledge from grade to grade and subject to subject (i.e., text-to-text, text-to-self, and text-to-world)

*STEP 1: Assemble materials.* Before beginning, lay out the tools you'll need for your targeted unit: English language arts (ELA) Common Core Standards that you grouped (Chapter 1, Exercise 1) that should be entered on the unit template; the knowledge list you created (Chapter 1, Exercise 2) that should also be on the unit template; textbook, materials, and resources tied to the unit; laptop or paper and pencil; and a little chocolate wouldn't hurt.

*STEP 2: Find and make a list of concepts embedded in the standards.* Review the standards on your unit template and systematically make a list of all the concepts that are in each standard on a separate sheet of paper. Use Figure 2.5, English Language Arts Concepts, to assist with this task. These concepts are categorized based on the ELA Common Core headings (e.g., Reading Standards for Literature, Reading Standards for Informational Text, etc.). Plus, I added other concepts that should be beneficial in crafting your essential understandings along with larger macroconcepts. Basically, these are overarching megaconcepts that can be used across subjects and grades. Because they are broad and encompass many concepts, they are certainly used for crafting interdisciplinary units. Figure 2.5 also provides some concepts in more than one category since there is a great deal of overlap, for example, those you find in the reading and writing strands. Also, you might find concepts that you listed in the *knowledge* component; it is fine to record these again on your concept list. If you see concepts in Figure 2.5 that are related to your standards but are not stated in the standards verbatim, feel free to include them. You will need this list of concepts that you generate for the next step, so keep it handy. If you typed the list on a computer, I suggest you print it out.

*STEP 3: Brainstorm statements.* To create your essential understandings, keep your tools out for reference: the standards you grouped, your list of knowledge (factual information), and the textbook. In addition, consider the age and readiness level of your students, rich materials and resources at your disposal, and above all, the essence of what you want students to glean from this unit. You might look at the completed unit templates in Chapter 3 and the companion website to see other examples of essential understandings that are not in this chapter. Now look at the concept list you generated, and begin brainstorming statements that include relationships between at least two concepts. Truly brainstorm by avoiding any conversation or critiquing as you list statements; know that in the next step you will edit and revise to find just the right verb or collapse statements that appear too similar. If you are having trouble getting started, have

| Common Core Standards | Essential Understandings | Possible Activities |
|---|---|---|
| **Kindergarten and Grade 1**<br><br>• Recognize common types of texts (e.g., storybooks, poems) (NGA, 2010, RL.K.5).<br>• Explain major differences between books that tell stories and books that give information, drawing on a wide reading of a range of text types (RL.1.5). | Types of reading materials share commonalities and differences, and each has a specific purpose and structure. | Compare and contrast different types of reading materials and their purposes and structures. To do so, read stories, poems, and informational text. Discuss the purpose for each text type as well as the structure, and physically sort each into an appropriate pile. |
| **Grade 2**<br><br>• Describe the overall structure of a story, including describing how the beginning introduces the story and the ending concludes the action (RL.2.5). | Plot forms the basic structure of a story with a central conflict setting the story in motion followed by a series of actions that lead to conflict resolution. | Bridge previous learning by recalling the structure of stories, poems, and informational text. Focus specifically on the purpose for a story and emphasize its structure. Recall several familiar story examples. Introduce new stories as well. Compare these story examples using a graphic organizer that features the problem-solution structure. |
| **Grades 3, 4, & 5**<br><br>• Refer to parts of stories, dramas, and poems when writing or speaking about a text, using terms such as chapter, scene, and stanza; describe how each successive part builds on earlier sections (RL.3.5).<br>• Explain major differences between poems, drama, and prose, and refer to the structural elements of poems (e.g., verse, rhythm, meter) and drama (e.g., casts of characters, settings, descriptions, dialogue, stage directions) when writing or speaking about a text (RL.4.5).<br>• Explain how a series of chapters, scenes, or stanzas fits together to provide the overall structure of a particular story, drama, or poem (RL.5.5). | Poems, dramas, and prose works each contain unique structural elements that build upon earlier sections to create an overall fluid and organized piece. | Expand knowledge of story structure beyond problem-solution to include other plot elements (e.g., central conflict, rising action, climax, etc.) as well as features of a story (e.g., character, setting, theme, etc.). Compare a story's structural format and specific features to dramas by reading and analyzing examples. Then read and identify the structural format (e.g., lines, stanzas) and characteristics of poems (e.g., rhythm, rhyme, meter). Complete an ongoing chart that shows the structural elements and specific characteristics of these text types, using genre-specific terms. Refer to this chart often while reading text and making entries. |

**FIGURE 2.8**  Essential Understandings by Grade Cluster

a conversation with colleagues (or yourself) about the key takeaways from this unit using this beginning frame: *Students will understand that. . . .* The sentence that follows is the rough statement that you should write down for your brainstorming. Avoid fragments because essential understandings are expressed in complete sentences. Again, don't be concerned about the right verb or statements that are too similar; just brainstorm, brainstorm, brainstorm.

   *STEP 4: Edit and revise the brainstormed statements.* Edit and revise your statement for these four purposes:

1. **Wordsmith.** Combine similar statements and/or wordsmith them to arrive at one essential understanding that can stand alone. If some statements subsume others, then merge them or just keep one statement that is the strongest. Here are examples of similar statements to think about or discuss with colleagues. You could select, merge, or rewrite to arrive at the one that best represents what you want students to understand about the literary work:

   - Settings impact characters' actions.
   - Settings shape and transform characters.
   - Settings can change characters.
   - Characters evolve as they encounter various settings.
   - Settings can facilitate growth and change for characters, thereby impacting the plot.

2. **Verb usage.** Use Figure 2.9, Verbs That Show Relationships, to revise your statements so that there are no forms of the verb *to be* to connect concepts. In addition, make sure you write present tense verbs. Once you write past tense verbs, you have associated your statement with an event, situation, or person from the past. You want your statement to be current so it has the ability to be used in different situations across time.

3. **Transfer value.** Besides using present tense verbs to allow your statement to apply to different situations, make sure your essential understandings are void of proper nouns. Replace any proper nouns, such as the name of a specific character or references to a period in history, with general concepts. I can't impress upon you enough the importance of creating conceptually based, general statements that can span across time and situations as shown in Figure 2.10. When you create your lesson guiding questions, you will address the nitty-gritty of the unit and include the specific factual knowledge. But the glory of essential understandings is that they are enduring, so do not include those proper nouns or past tense verbs. Your goal is for kids to have discovery moments of making connections, and they can't do this if you have inserted Apache and Navajo, Concord and Lexington, Declaration of Independence, a character's name, or the Mississippi River in your statements.

   - Strong Example 1. *Fables use animals with good and evil traits to demonstrate moralistic lessons about life.*
   - Weak Example 1. *The lion and the mouse show that enemies may prove to be great friends.*
   - Strong Example 2. *Different cultures adapt to their physical environment to survive.*
   - Weak Example 2. *The Native American Ohlone tribe used the natural resources of northern California to survive.*

4. **The why factor.** Make sure your essential understandings answer the question of why the content is important to learn. *Everyone has work to do* is a weak essential understanding for primary students because it doesn't explain why everyone has work. What's the point of work? The following is stronger: *Everyone contributes to the*

# Verbs That Show Relationships

| | | | |
|---|---|---|---|
| construct | encourage | introduce | reduce |
| contrast | establish | invent | reinforce |
| contribute | estimate | lead to | regulate |
| control | evolve | manage | relate |
| convert | examine | manipulate | resolve |
| cooperate | expand | map | respond |
| correspond | explain | model | restore |
| create | expound | modify | revitalize |
| define | express | motivate | separate |
| demonstrate | facilitate | offer | sequence |
| describe | formulate | organize | shape |
| design | generate | originate | share |
| determine | guide | perform | show |
| develop | identify | persuade | simplify |
| devise | illustrate | point to | solve |
| differentiate | impact | precipitate | stimulate |
| direct | improve | prevent | structure |
| discriminate | incorporate | produce | suggest |
| display | increase | promote | support |
| disseminate | infer | prompt | transfer |
| distinguish | influence | propel | transform |
| distribute | initiate | propose | transition |
| elicit | institute | provide | translate |
| employ | integrate | provoke | transmit |
| enable | interact | recommend | uncover |
| enhance | interpret | reconcile | use |
| | | | utilize |

**FIGURE 2.9**

*well-being and functionality of a community by working in some capacity.* Another weak example is *People can learn from stories about the past.* Why do people listen to stories? What can they learn? A stronger essential understanding would be *People learn about cultural practices and beliefs through storytelling and pictures.*

*STEP 5: Record your essential understandings.* Once you have crafted each essential understanding, logically sequence them based on how you will teach the unit if you haven't done so already. Then enter one understanding per page on your unit template. In the next exercise, you will create and enter guiding questions.

| Weak Essential Understandings | Red Flags | Stronger Essential Understandings |
|---|---|---|
| New York communities have a long history and have changed greatly from the time of early explorers to today. | • *New York* is a proper noun and shouldn't be used since the statement would only work for this state and couldn't transfer.<br>• The verbs could be stronger.<br>• Although there are concepts—*community, history, explorers*—there are other concepts that should be included that contribute to change. So what is really worth knowing is why communities change, a question which isn't fully addressed. | Communities change and grow throughout time by the cultural and religious contributions of the people who live there. |
| In *The Hundred Dresses*, Maddie realizes that standing by while Wanda was bullied made her an accomplice and just as guilty of bullying as the other girls who taunted her. | • The essential understandings should be void of proper nouns: *The Hundred Dresses*, Maddie, Wanda.<br>• The statement is specific to a work of literature even though it contains global concepts. | Those who witness an act of bullying and fail to take action perpetuate cruel and unacceptable behavior, thereby serving as accomplices in persecuting others. |

**FIGURE 2.10**  Strong Versus Weak Essential Understandings 2

## THE NATURE AND IMPORTANCE OF ESSENTIAL UNIT AND LESSON GUIDING QUESTIONS

As mentioned earlier in the chapter, guiding questions should be clearly visible for students when teaching every unit. The essential understandings are written in more adult language, so some teachers might not post them, but students should have the essential questions at the center of their learning and see them regularly. *Each activity, each lesson, each reading assignment, each assessment should be focused around a guiding question so teachers have a commitment to what they are teaching and students have a purpose for what they are expected to accomplish.* I know for me, I was great at finding activities and assessments from colleagues, on the Internet, or in a textbook. And I would spend time creating, revising, finding, and then finally teaching them. Even though I knew the materials were engaging and purposeful, I sometimes forgot to tell students the purpose of what they were doing. If I had, what I was teaching would have been much more meaningful. It's a winning combination to not only deliver compelling instruction, but also alert students to the overriding goal of each learning opportunity so they are clear about the outcomes and intent. Through essential guiding questions, you can do this.

Following are two scenarios. In which way—through the first or second—would students be more likely to remember the facts, people, characters, and events?

1. Students are studying the concept of movement both literally and figuratively. From a literal vantage point, students learn about the history of their communities by focusing

on the explorers who discovered their region and settlers who moved there. Students are exposed to a variety of photographs and video excerpts, along with differentiated reading materials, and engage in many activities tied to them. From a figurative angle, they select a literary work from a collection that centers on characters' movement as they change and mature throughout the story. Examples of activities students will engage in include a jigsaw in groups, graphic organizers, games, and oral and written responses to essays and journal prompts.

2. In addition to Scenario 1, students focus on these questions that are tied to everything they do throughout the thematic unit on movement:

   - How can movement lead to positive growth and change?
   - Why do people avoid movement?
   - How can movement create conflict?

Sure, the obvious answer is Scenario 2. When students know why they are completing an activity, reading an excerpt, watching a video clip, working with a computer software program, or listening to a lecture, they are apt to glean more. This Scenario includes a list of essential unit guiding questions that students would be exposed to throughout the unit and would then need to answer at the end of the unit to demonstrate understanding.

I worked with teachers from Oak Knoll School in Menlo Park, California, to create a map for a mini-unit based on the theme of movement that included similar questions to those in the previous example. These essential understandings are linked to the guiding questions:

   - Movement provides an opportunity for individuals to experience new situations and ideas that cause them to grow and change emotionally and intellectually.
   - Movement can create discontent and conflict, which can lead to negative consequences for individuals or groups.
   - People who avoid change might become stagnant and miss valuable opportunities.
   - With movement, people usually discover or encounter something unfamiliar which makes some individuals uncomfortable.

In June, teachers conduct a book talk, and students in their multi-age class of third, fourth, and fifth graders select a book tied to the theme of movement to read over the summer. Title choices include *The Lightning Thief*, by Rick Riordan; *Pedro's Journal*, by Pam Conrad; *A Lion to Guard Us*, by Clyde Robert Bulla; *In the Year of the Boar and Jackie Robinson*, by Bette Bao Lord; *So Far From Home*, by Barry Denenberg; and *Night Journeys*, by Avi. When students return in the fall, they meet in groups according to their summer book selections. In these groups, leaders—comprised of teachers and administrators—conduct a discussion based on the guiding questions. They explain that this launch activity serves as a model template for the school year as it sets the stage for their ongoing, interdisciplinary study about literal and figurative movement. Specifically, students are told that everything they do in their classrooms— activities, reading, assessments, and so on—all have a greater purpose, which is to answer the conceptually based guiding questions. They will be encouraged to make connections across units and grades and apply what they learn to their own lives. This beginning mini-unit not only primes students for how teachers will use questions (and the associated essential understandings) to guide instruction, but also plants the seed for making connections and transferring knowledge. For instance, teachers will help students see how physical movement applies to the unit on exploration or immigration to the New World and how movement of thought is necessary to convince others to join in the fight for American independence. In language arts, characters experience change and movement both physically and mentally, a change that contributes to maturity. The guiding questions serve as a constant reminder of the purpose for learning.

## THE DIFFERENCES BETWEEN ESSENTIAL UNIT AND LESSON GUIDING QUESTIONS

There are two sets of guiding questions. What has been introduced thus far are what I call *essential unit guiding questions.* They are overarching, derived from the essential understandings, and are transferrable. Many of the questions can apply to other units of study and even provide commentary about life because they are written in general terms that can be interpreted in different ways. For example, the essential unit guiding question *How can movement create conflict?* can apply to the following:

- When Pilgrims immigrated and settled colonies, they experienced conflict with each other as they worked to survive, with Native Americans whose land they wanted, and within themselves as they struggled emotionally with thoughts of home.
- In their mission to seek new territory, early explorers created conflict by persecuting and dominating vulnerable indigenous cultures.
- Movement can cause characters to be uncomfortable and create conflict. For example, in E. L. Konigsburg's novel *From the Mixed Up Files of Mrs. Basil E. Frankweiler,* the eleven-year-old protagonist, Claudia Kincaid, and her brother run away from home to the Metropolitan Museum of Art and encounter discomfort and conflict on their mission to solve a mystery.
- People might experience discomfort and internal conflict when moving to a new grade, a new school, or a new city and have anxiety that is associated with such a move.

Besides making connections by bridging what they learn to new situations and content, the goal is for students to demonstrate knowledge for the entire unit by responding to all essential unit guiding questions. In order to do this, *lesson guiding questions* are necessary to introduce factual knowledge that builds the foundation for understanding the more complex essential unit guiding questions. In language arts, students might read a novel, short story, or picture book. You would surely want students to know the characters' names and their personalities, identify the setting, retell the plot, explain the theme or central message, and so forth. Therefore, you would fashion lesson guiding questions to focus students' attention on these aspects of the reading.

By addressing these factually based questions about elements of literature, you are building the bricks for students to eventually grasp the greater unit guiding questions, such as the following: *How does the setting influence characters? How does the character's point of view shape the plot? How do literary works share common themes?* It is with the knowledge of the factual information that students can grapple with the essence of the content represented by the unit questions, which is why they are called the *essential* unit guiding questions. See the following two figures—Figure 2.11, Opinion Piece, and Figure 2.12, Leadership Unit—for a fluid visual representation of sample standards, essential understandings, and essential unit and lesson guiding questions working together to form a comprehensive orchestration of the outcomes. For the leadership

# Opinion Piece

|  | Common Core Standards | Essential Understandings | Essential Unit Guiding Questions | Lesson Questions |
|---|---|---|---|---|
| K | Use a combination of drawing, dictating, and writing to compose opinion pieces in which they tell a reader the topic or the name of the book they are writing about and state an opinion or preference about the topic or book (e.g., My favorite book is . . . ) (NGA, 2010, W.K.1). | People can draw, dictate, and write to communicate their opinions and share recommendations about a book or topic to others. | How can I use drawing and writing to tell others what I think? | • What is my favorite animal, color, book, etc.?<br>• Why is it my favorite?<br>• What can I draw and write about to tell others what I think? |
| Grade 1 | Write opinion pieces in which they introduce the topic or name the book they are writing about, state an opinion, supply a reason for the opinion, and provide some sense of closure (W.1.1). | People can write to express their preferences and share recommendations about a book or topic by supporting their opinions with sound reasons to tell others what they think. | How can I write about my opinions so others understand what I think? | • What is my favorite or most interesting animal, color, book, etc.?<br>• Why is it my favorite?<br>• How can I write sentences to tell others what I think? |
| Grade 2 | Write opinion pieces in which they introduce the topic or book they are writing about, state an opinion, supply reasons that support the opinion, use linking words (e.g., because, and, also) to connect opinion and reasons, and provide a concluding statement or section (W.2.1). |  |  | • What is my favorite or most interesting animal, color, book, etc.?<br>• Why is it my favorite or most interesting?<br>• How can I write at least three sentences to tell others what I think?<br>• What linking words can I use so my sentences flow together?<br>• What ending sentence can sum up my feelings? |

**FIGURE 2.11**

# Leadership Unit

| Mid-Continent Research for Education and Learning (McREL) Standards | Essential Understandings | Essential Unit Guiding Questions | Lesson Questions |
|---|---|---|---|
| **Life Skills Standard 5**<br><br>Demonstrates leadership skills<br><br>2. Knows the qualities of good leaders and followers (Marzano & Kendall, 2000) | Strong, positive leaders share unique characteristics that set them apart from others. | 1. Do positive leaders share common characteristics? | **Lesson 1.1**<br><br>What characteristics do strong leaders share? Who are people that are leaders? What is the definition of a leader? |
| **Behavioral Studies Standard 1**<br><br>Understands that group and cultural influences contribute to human development, identity, and behavior<br><br>5. Understands that various factors (e.g., interests, capabilities, values) contribute to the shaping of a person's identity | Motivating factors, such as an event, circumstance, or mentor, contribute to people becoming strong, effective leaders. | 2. How do people become strong leaders? | **Lesson 2.1**<br><br>Who are different leaders that we have read about in class? Who or what motivated each person? How did this motivating force contribute to each person becoming a strong leader? |
| | There sometimes exists a correlation between overcoming obstacles and leadership; however, one does not guarantee the other. | 3. How can overcoming obstacles contribute to people becoming leaders? | **Lesson 3.1**<br><br>What obstacles did leaders we learn about face? How did they overcome these obstacles?<br><br>**Lesson 3.2**<br><br>Does overcoming obstacles contribute to leadership? Do all people who overcome obstacles become leaders? |
| **Grades K–4 History Standard 4**<br><br>Understands how democratic values came to be, and how they have been exemplified by people, events, and symbols<br><br>6. Understands the ways in which people in a variety of fields have advanced the cause of human rights, equality, and the common good | Leaders can make an impact on others and society by the contributions they make. | 4. How do leaders' contributions make an impact? | **Lesson 4.1**<br><br>What contributions did the leaders we studied make? How does each contribution make an impact on society or you personally? |

**FIGURE 2.12**

unit, I worked with a group of fifth-grade teachers at Ephrata Intermediate School in Pennsylvania. These teachers introduced students to various autobiographical and biographical accounts of leaders who have made a difference. Note that these teachers used the texts about leaders to address reading strategy standards; however, I have entered pertinent standards for leadership only in Figure 2.12 from Mid-Continent Research for Education and Learning's (McREL's) *Content Knowledge: A Compendium of Standards and Benchmarks for K–12 Education* by Robert Marzano and John Kendall (2000). McREL's compendium is a synthesis of standards documents from professional subject-area organizations and selected state standards for fourteen content areas. Therefore, they should resonate with all educators and are easily transferable.

## EXAMPLES OF ESSENTIAL UNDERSTANDINGS LINKED WITH GUIDING QUESTIONS FOR THE LITERATURE READING STRAND

By now, you probably can ascertain the difference between essential unit guiding questions and lesson guiding questions. To drive the point home and provide materials you can use for mapping a unit and teaching the literature strand, I've created several examples in Figures 2.13 to 2.19. What I include is not a complete list, as there are endless possibilities for essential understandings and associated guiding questions. Some cells you will use as is; others will provide ideas to personalize the entries for your targeted unit. Figures 2.13 through 2.19 are available on the companion website, although a portion of Figure 2.13 is included here so you can see how the others are formatted and what to expect.

Whereas Figure 2.13 includes essential understandings and associated guiding questions specific to the Common Core Standards for reading literature, Figures 2.14 to 2.19 (see the companion website) were written to include what is not shown in the Common Core Reading

## Essential Understandings and Guiding Questions Aligned to the Common Core Reading Standards for Literature K–5

| 6. Craft and Structure | | | |
|---|---|---|---|
| **Common Core Standards** | **Essential Understandings** | **Unit Guiding Questions** | **Lesson Questions** |
| **Kindergarten**<br><br>• With prompting and support, name the author and illustrator of a story and define the role of each in telling the story (NGA, 2010, RL.K.6). | Through a collaborative effort, authors and illustrators tell a story; however, each has a specific role to perform. | How do authors and illustrators work together to tell a story? | • What does an author do? Who is the author of this story?<br>• What is an illustrator? Who is the illustrator of this story?<br>• How do authors and illustrators work together to tell a story?<br>• What could you write and draw to tell a story about a topic? |

**FIGURE 2.13** *(Continued)*

| | | | |
|---|---|---|---|
| **Grade 1**<br><br>• Identify who is telling the story at various points in a text (RL.1.6). | Readers benefit from identifying the narrator of a story so they can fully appreciate the perspective from which a story is told. | Why do readers need to know who is telling the story? | • What does the narrator of a story do?<br>• Who is the narrator of this story?<br>• Does the narrator change throughout the story? At what point? |
| **Grade 2**<br><br>• Acknowledge differences in the points of view of characters, including by speaking in a different voice for each character when reading dialogue aloud (RL.2.6). | Effective readers recognize dialogue and acknowledge characters' points of view and how their perspectives contribute to the meaning of a story. | How are characters' points of view different? | • Who are the characters in the story? What do these characters think, say, and do?<br>• Where is dialogue in the story? How do you know this part of the story is dialogue?<br>• When you read aloud, do you change your voice for different characters? Why?<br>• What does point of view mean?<br>• Do characters in the story have different points of view? What are they?<br>• Why do readers need to know about a character's point of view? How does it help to understand a story better? |
| **Grade 3**<br><br>• Distinguish their own point of view from that of the narrator or those of the characters (RL.3.6). | Thoughtful readers consider alternate perspectives from a story's narrator or characters to identify and consider all sides of an issue. | Why is it important to consider all points of view? | • What is the narrator's point of view?<br>• What are different characters' points of view?<br>• Is there another point of view? How are your views different from the narrator or characters?<br>• Why is it important to look at all viewpoints? Which point of view makes the most sense? |
| **Grades 4 & 5**<br><br>• Compare and contrast the point of view from which different stories are narrated, including the difference between first- and third-person narrations (RL.4.6).<br>• Describe how a narrator's or speaker's point of view influences how events are described (RL.5.6). | The narrator's or speaker's point of view can influence how events are described. | How can the narrator's point of view influence the plot? | • What are first- and third-person pronouns?<br>• Who is the narrator of this story? Is it written in first- or third-person point of view? How do the pronouns help you to know?<br>• If the narrator's point of view were different, how might elements of the plot change (e.g., central conflict, rising action, climax, resolution)? How would other elements of the story change (e.g., character, setting)?<br>• What does the narrator of this story want you to think after reading this story? |

**FIGURE 2.13**

Standards for Literature but that I feel are relevant to teach alongside them. As such, I have categorized them differently than the Common Core subheadings—Key Ideas and Details, Craft and Structure, and so forth. Instead, mine are titled Introduction to Literature, Elements of Literature (i.e., setting, character, plot, point of view, theme), Reading Strategies, Literary Connections, and so on. For some of you, these might be more familiar terminology. I embed line items of Figure 2.13 within these new figures to show how the essential understandings and guiding questions I include can augment the Common Core's Reading Standards for Literature if you choose to add them. Rows that are shaded throughout Figures 2.14 to 2.19 indicate my extensions to the Common Core; essential understandings that have a code in parentheses designate actual Common Core Standards. Note that fractions in the code mean more than one grade: for example, *RL.1/2.7* refers to reading for literature, first and second grades, Standard 7.

Figures 2.14 through 2.19, discussed below, are available on the companion website.

*Figure 2.13* Essential Understandings and Guiding Questions Aligned to the Common Core Reading Standards for Literature K–5. In this figure, I created my version of essential understandings and guiding questions aligned to the Common Core Reading Standards for Literature K–5 (NGA, 2010). These standards are grouped into these subheadings: Key Ideas and Details, Craft and Structure, and Integration of Knowledge and Ideas. I included all standards in this category except for Standard 10, Range of Reading and Level of Text Complexity.

*Figure 2.14* Introduction to Literature. When launching a literature unit, it is important to ground students in this genre and help activate their schema. These essential understandings and guiding questions focus on the interrelationship between words and visuals, and introduce the elements of literature that are common across fiction: *setting, character, theme, point of view,* and *plot.*

*Figure 2.15* Elements of Literature. This figure focuses squarely on all the elements of literature. I create essential understandings and guiding questions associated with each element individually (e.g., for plot, *How do authors develop an interesting plot?*) and an integration of elements (e.g., for point of view/plot, *How can a narrator's point of view influence the plot?*). Read through all the figures, because some elements appear in other places like, for example, Figure 2.19, Literary Connections.

*Figure 2.16* Reading Strategies. This figure includes *questioning, retelling, inference, summarizing, prediction,* and *compare/contrast.*

*Figure 2.17* Word Choice/Figurative Language. This figure includes words and phrases of all kinds, such as unknown words, words and phrases that produce rhythm, and literal versus figurative language.

*Figure 2.18* Literary Devices. This figure includes selected literary (or narrative) devices, specifically *allusion, dialect, dialogue, suspense,* and *tone.* Although this figure includes and augments the Common Core's Reading Standards for Literature, I added one language and writing standard because this is where *dialect* and *dialogue* reside in the Common Core.

*Figure 2.19* Literary Connections. Students from an early age learn to make personal connections. This figure includes text-to-self, text-to-text, and text-to-world connections across the grades.

I encourage you to use my examples of guiding questions featured in Figures 2.13 to 2.19 for literature, because that is certainly why I created them. Heed these points, though, when using them:

- Any of my entries can be edited. This probably goes without saying, but I welcome you to alter essential understandings or guiding questions as you see fit to achieve your desired outcomes. Ideas for editing:

○ You might replace *story* with *drama* to have an essential understanding or guiding question work for what you are teaching.

○ You might personalize the statements or questions by using the pronouns *you* or *I* or keep it generic with *readers/writers.*

○ Should you use *authors* or *writers?* This choice is purely yours. Some feel that the word *authors* refers more to published authors in the world. *Writers,* however, is a word that can apply to students themselves as writers, as well as published authors. Use whichever word makes sense to you.

○ You will find the word *text,* which is generic. You might want to replace it with *reading materials,* which is also generic, or specific kinds of text, such as *story, novel, short story, poem, folktale,* and so forth. For the lesson guiding questions, you might use the actual title of the story, poem, or fairy tale that you are using, such as *The True Story of the Three Little Pigs* or "The Marble Champ." Note: Longer works such as titles of novels, movies, CDs, books, magazines, and artwork are all italicized if the title is typed on a computer or underlined if it is handwritten. Shorter works such as a chapter, short story, song, article, or poem are punctuated with quotation marks. The tricky situation is when a story that is featured in its own picture book, like *Chrysanthemum* by Kevin Henkes or *The Little Red Hen* by Paul Galdone, appears in an anthology. I would italicize these book titles.

- Each literature selection is distinctive even though all literature shares common elements. Identify your literary selection first. Then, refer to my choices of essential understandings and guiding questions to choose the ones that best fit the text you are using. Since each reading selection is unique in its themes, character treatment, and plotline, not all questions will apply to each selection. For example, *How do authors develop descriptive settings?* may not apply to a particular story you are focusing on because the author does not use strong word choice or imagery for the setting. However, *How and why do characters change over time?* might work perfectly for that story. That is't to say that you will not touch on descriptive settings with another selection in a different unit.

- Some line items in an entire row might be perfect as stated in the figure. Others, though, may not be quite right for a particular text students will read. As such, it is not necessary to move your eye horizontally across the page and use an entire row in a particular figure verbatim. For example, you might want to pick and choose from different cells or use an essential understanding from the figure and create your own guiding questions to accompany it or vice versa. Furthermore, some lesson questions might be repeated in separate boxes or worded slightly differently for a particular grade level. So, feel free to pull some lesson questions from different line items and fashion your own associations between essential understandings and questions for your targeted unit.

- If a figure has two unit questions in a particular cell, choose the one you like best as you probably don't need both. For some questions, a verb may appear in parentheses. The same principle applies: Decide which verb you like best because you don't need two. Consider your students and choose a verb that they understand. You might have new words in a guiding question that will serve as the focus for the lesson, and you will teach this new term (e.g., *summarize, central conflict*), but the verbs should be ones they already know.

- Maybe you like an essential understanding, but the associated unit question seems too sophisticated or simplistic based on the grade level of your students. Remember that because the unit questions are posted and written in language geared to your students, you can surely alter the unit question accordingly to match verbiage suited to your class. In the same vein, if you teach or support upper elementary and a primary essential understanding catches your eye but isn't quite right, edit it accordingly.

- If you are working with colleagues, consider the progression and complexity of learning from grade to grade. Students are exposed to literature throughout many grade levels. As such, it is important to consider what you want them to glean each year, so carefully consider your interpretation of the standards and the rigor of the literature. Discuss the unit maps you are each creating, and identify essential understandings and questions suitable for students of the grades you are targeting among colleagues.

## EXAMPLES OF ESSENTIAL UNIT AND LESSON GUIDING QUESTIONS FOR GRAMMAR AND CONVENTIONS

This section provides more examples by way of grammar and conventions (i.e., spelling, punctuation, capitalization) that complement and extend the language strand of the Common Core Standards. There is widespread evidence to support teaching these skills in context. Isolated grammar and conventions lessons will not yield student achievement and typically end in disappointment for both the student and teacher. However, if you provide a context for teaching these writing skills by featuring published and student work, and teaching compelling, engaging lessons around a text that students enjoy, then you will be more successful. Such was the mind-set when I worked with the fourth-grade team of teachers in Menlo Park, California, at Oak Knoll School. We had been working diligently on incorporating the research around guiding questions within their literature and nonfiction curriculum, and we wanted to expand the work to grammar and conventions. Even though this content is largely skill based, we were determined to devise essential unit guiding questions that were overarching and could span the year. The following list is what we crafted. These unit questions are posted on the wall all year so students repeatedly understand the purpose for their work in this area.

- How does proper use of grammar and conventions help writers communicate ideas clearly?
- How does dialogue impact writing?
- How can sentence fluency and transitions improve written communication?
- How can strong word choice make writing more colorful and powerful?

We then tied specific lesson guiding questions based on standards to these unit questions and chose reading selections replete with examples of a targeted skill so we could teach grammar and conventions in context. To demonstrate understanding of a particular unit focus, students produced a culminating assessment that included targeted grammar and conventions that complemented the unit. For example, in the September–October narrative unit, which is shown in this chapter, the summative assessment is a short story writing piece. Within it, along with demonstrating understanding of the elements of literature, students show evidence of punctuating and capitalizing dialogue, including adjectives for character descriptions, and so forth. The entirety of Figure 2.20, Grammar and Conventions Map, is located in the companion website and shows the fruits of our labor.

# Grammar and Conventions Map

Writing Focus: <u>Narrative</u>          Literature Selection: <u>*Poppy* by Avi</u>          Timing: <u>September/October</u>

| Skills/Standards | Unit Guiding Questions | Lesson Guiding Questions |
|---|---|---|
| **Grammar**<br>• Define, identify, and distinguish between common and proper nouns.<br>• Define and identify types of verbs; focus on action verbs and verb tense.<br>• Define and identify adjectives.<br>• Identify the various types of adverbs; focus on adverbs that show manner. | How does proper use of grammar and conventions help writers communicate ideas clearly? | **Suggested Questions**<br>• What is a noun? (verb, adjective, adverb)<br>• What is the function of this part of speech in a sentence?<br>• What are examples of this part of speech in the reading selection?<br>• What are some different types of this part of speech?<br>• What is verb tense? How do tenses help readers understand when events happen in a story?<br>• What resources can I use to find the right noun (verb, adjective, adverb) for my writing? |
| **Word Choice**<br>• Use specific nouns, action verbs, sophisticated and descriptive adjectives, and adverbs that show manner in writing. | How can strong word choice make writing more colorful and powerful? | **Suggested Questions**<br>• What are strong versus weak nouns?<br>• What descriptive adjectives can writers use to help readers visualize what they write?<br>• How can action verbs contribute to a strong plot?<br>• How can writers use adverbs at the beginning of sentences?<br>• How can verbs and adverbs improve dialogue tags? (Example: She shouted loudly, "I hate peas!")<br>• What resources can I use to find the right words for my story? |

| | | |
|---|---|---|
| **Punctuation**<br>• Use commas to separate adjectives.<br>• Use apostrophes in the possessive case of nouns. | How does proper use of grammar and conventions help writers communicate ideas clearly? | **Commas**<br>• How do writers use commas to separate adjectives?<br><br>**Apostrophes**<br>• What are the different ways to use apostrophes?<br>• How do writers use apostrophes to show ownership? |
| **Sentence Structure**<br>• Identify subject and predicate.<br>• Identify fragments and write in complete sentences.<br>• Identify run-ons and write sentences without them. | How can sentence fluency improve written communication? | **Complete Sentences**<br>• What is a complete sentence? What is a subject and predicate?<br><br>**Fragments**<br>• What is a fragment? How can I turn a fragment into a complete sentence?<br><br>**Run-Ons**<br>• What is a run-on? How do writers avoid run-ons? |
| **Punctuation/Capitalization/Word Choice**<br>• Punctuate and capitalize dialogue correctly for beginning and end tags. | How does dialogue impact writing? | **Dialogue**<br>• How do readers identify dialogue?<br>• How do writers punctuate dialogue?<br>• How do writers create strong dialogue tags?<br>• How does the dialogue in the story we are reading tell us information about the characters or plot?<br>• How can I use dialogue effectively in my story? (High achievers can identify dialogue that is interrupted by tags; write dialogue using middle tags; e.g., "Herbert," she screamed at the top of her lungs, "watch out for that boulder!") |

**FIGURE 2.20**

## EXERCISE 4: HOW DO EDUCATORS CREATE (OR REVISE) ESSENTIAL UNIT AND LESSON GUIDING QUESTIONS?

At this point, the book has guided you through three exercises that mirror the unit template components: (1) What is the best way to group standards? (2) How are standards used to determine what students should know? and (3) How do educators create essential understandings? Now you are ready for Exercise 4: How do educators create essential unit and lesson guiding questions? Because you will create your own questions, let's look at the two types side by side and analyze them. Ask yourself or discuss with colleagues: *What characterizes each kind of question?* You can peruse Figure 2.21 to foster discussion around this prompt. Know that Figure 2.22 answers this question, so cover it up with a sheet of paper now if you earnestly want to respond to my query without peeking.

The following steps will help you create your own questions for your targeted unit of study.

*STEP 1: Assemble materials.* If you have adhered to the exercises in this book so far, then you should have your grouped standards and the knowledge list entered on the unit template. In addition, you have created and entered essential understandings. Keep the textbook, materials, and resources tied to the unit available. And, of course, you'll need the laptop or paper and pencil. Replenish your chocolate, as needed. If you haven't already,

## Essential Unit and Lesson Guiding Question Examples

| Essential Unit Guiding Questions | Lesson Guiding Questions |
| --- | --- |
| How does setting affect characters? | • What are the major settings in *Because of Winn-Dixie?*<br>• How do these settings affect different characters, such as Opal, Winn-Dixie, and the preacher?<br>• Does the setting affect characters' actions, thoughts, or beliefs? How so? |
| How do authors develop characters? | • What is characterization? What are the methods of characterization?<br>• How does Gary Soto use characterization in "The Marble Champ" to develop the character of Lupe?<br>• What method does Soto use most in describing Lupe?<br>• Is Lupe similar to other characters? How so? |
| How and why do readers compare and contrast information? | • What information would readers compare and contrast? Why?<br>• What are different graphic organizers readers can use to record information to compare and contrast?<br>• How can you use a Venn diagram to compare and contrast characters from fairy tales we read in class? How can you use another graphic organizer? Which does the job best?<br>• What do you learn from comparing and contrasting characters? |

**FIGURE 2.21**

# Features of Essential Unit and Lesson Guiding Questions

| Distinguishing Features | |
| --- | --- |
| **Essential Unit Guiding Questions** | **Lesson Guiding Questions** |
| • Are written in general terms with no proper nouns.<br>• Include present tense verbs and no form of the verb *to be*.<br>• Include at least one concept or maybe two that form a relationship.<br>• Begin with *why* or *how*.<br>• Cannot be answered with a list or finite response; these questions are more provocative and engaging than the straightforward, factually based lesson guiding question.<br>• Can foster transference and connections as students relate the questions to other units of study, other text, the world, or personally.<br>• Are featured prominently on poster board or chart paper in the classroom and kept up all unit long. | • Can be written to elicit factual information specific to a unit of study, so references to characters, titles of books, or particular settings are fair game.<br>• Include at least one skill or concept for each question.<br>• Begin with any type of question: *who, what, where, when, why/how, is, does*<br>• Are foundational as they serve to support the unit question; when teachers conduct lessons associated with all the lesson guiding questions, students should be prepared to demonstrate understanding of the overarching, associated essential unit question.<br>• Are posted individually as the lesson objective for the day(s) on the whiteboard, SMART Board, or easel. |

| Common Features |
| --- |

- **Logical order**. Both types of questions are sequential, so write unit questions that are scaffolded; begin with the less complex to the most in-depth. By the same token, write the associated lesson guiding questions for each unit question in an order for teaching. The only caveat is that you might return to unit guiding questions throughout the course of study. For example, a unit question such as *How do characters change throughout time?* would be revisited frequently throughout a novel and more than once throughout a short story or picture book as characters show change as a result of different factors. The same idea applies to unit questions around reading strategies, such as *How can readers employ the questioning strategy to gain more meaning from the text?*
- **Appropriate timing**. You must consider how much time you have to teach a unit and plan the number of questions accordingly.
- **Language**. It is important that students for whom you are writing this unit can read and understand the words in your questions. However, if you include a concept term that you will expose them to and use it as the basis for instruction, then by all means add it.
- **Distinction**. Make sure that there is no overlap among your questions. If there is too much similarity, combine questions or choose the strongest one. Each question—unit or lesson—should stand alone.
- **Visibility**. Whereas the unit questions are posted and remain visible throughout the entire unit, the lesson questions are featured for each lesson to set the stage, so write them on the whiteboard or interactive board. The commonality is that they are both clearly in the students' line of vision.

**FIGURE 2.22**

peruse the unit templates in Chapter 3 to see other examples of unit and lesson guiding questions, in addition to other component entries.

*STEP 2: Use essential understandings to create unit guiding questions.* Review your essential understandings and circle the concepts that you included in every statement. Using these concepts, create a unit guiding question for each essential understanding that begins with *why* or *how.* Focus on at least one concept. If you want to include two concepts, form a relationship between them as you did for your essential understandings. To assist, use Figure 2.9, Verbs That Show Relationships. Stay true to the guidelines of what essential unit questions entail from what you read in this chapter and that are summarized in Figure 2.22, Features of Essential Unit and Lesson Guiding Questions. You will undoubtedly need to brainstorm a list of possible unit questions for each essential understanding and then wordsmith and combine some to avoid repetition. This should be familiar since you did this in Exercise 3 when you created essential understandings. It is acceptable and sometimes necessary to have two essential unit questions tied to one understanding.

Note: Essential unit guiding questions are not a rewording of the essential understanding to accommodate a question word of *how* or *why* preceding it. You do not want essential unit guiding questions that are too wordy and give away the store. As stated earlier in the section titled "The Nature and Critical Importance of Essential (or Enduring) Understandings," "The essential unit guiding questions are pointed, succinct, and provocative; they guide instruction and promote self-discovery. The essential understandings basically reveal the answers to the guiding questions and give away what you want all students to realize." If needed, reread this section and peruse Figure 2.3 that shows the essential understandings paired with essential unit questions.

*STEP 3: Create lesson guiding questions.* You might complete this step in tandem with Step 2 as you discuss with colleagues, have a conversation with yourself, or use the textbook and other materials to determine what lesson questions are needed to support students in understanding the overarching essential unit guiding questions. Your learning style might be to tackle each essential unit question and its corresponding lesson questions together, or you might prefer to go through and create all unit questions and then return for the more specific and detailed lesson questions. Remember that you want all students to be able to demonstrate understanding of all the unit guiding questions at the end of this course of study. As you create these lesson questions, again use Figure 2.22, Features of Essential Unit and Lesson Guiding Questions, and what you have learned so you are mindful that the goal of lesson questions is to get students to answer the bigger conceptual unit questions. Enter these unit and lesson guiding questions on the appropriate pages of your unit template to correspond with the essential understandings.

*STEP 4: Prepare to post unit guiding questions.* Whereas each lesson guiding question is featured on a whiteboard or SMART Board to identify a specific lesson goal for a class segment, all unit questions are posted throughout the entire course of the unit. Format your unit questions on a computer and add graphics to prepare them for posting. You can take the sheet and have it enlarged at a copy shop for a relatively inexpensive amount. My teacher-clients in Portola Valley, California, requested a machine from their parent–teacher organization that creates poster size visuals so they can regularly create large renderings of the essential unit questions for each unit of study instead of trekking to the local print shop. Of course, you can also create your own posters on easel paper. Some teachers mention that they will feature their unit questions on a SMART Board or a similar interactive board. I veto this idea because you want the unit guiding questions to be visible throughout the whole unit for easy reference to them while teaching.

It might appear that these unit questions are always posted at the outset of the unit. This is not so. You could launch the unit by conducting a simulation, showing a video, or featuring a guest speaker, or in another way that solicits input from students about what they think the upcoming unit will be about based on this introductory activity. After a debriefing discussion following such a launch, you can share the questions and post them. Another idea is to ask students to brainstorm questions in groups that they want addressed in the unit. You might say, *We are beginning a unit on weather. Make a list of questions that you have about this topic that you want to explore together.* Invite each group to share and compile a class-generated list void of duplications. If you conduct this exercise, still prepare your unit and lesson guiding questions so you have unit goals in mind. Because you are the professional, you must be grounded in the standards-based essential understandings so you know the unit outcomes and can be sure selected student-generated questions meet these goals. So when students brainstorm guiding questions, take dedicated time to review and edit them and assign pertinent ones as either unit or lesson questions appropriately. This method helps with student buy-in and involvement while still maintaining the intended purpose of the unit.

## CLOSING

Essential understandings are also referred to as enduring understandings and big ideas because they encapsulate what is most critical that you want students to understand as a result of a course of study. In this chapter, you learned how to create these generalizations that are necessary for professionals to craft to ensure they and their charges are clear-minded about unit goals. The essential unit guiding questions are an expression of the understandings that frame a unit of instruction. These are posted conspicuously so students are guided through the unit with clear purpose. As students respond to more factually based lesson guiding questions, they learn the foundational knowledge to respond to these overarching essential unit questions. One significant goal for students on the journey toward deep understanding is to make connections and transfer knowledge. Using essential understandings and unit guiding questions help support students in this endeavor.

As a result of exercises from this chapter and the previous one, your unit template might include a group of standards, a list of knowledge items, essential understandings, and associated unit and lesson guiding questions. The next chapter presents completed unit templates to use as examples followed by Chapter 4 on assessments.

# 3

# Unit Template With Examples

**T**his chapter provides the blank unit template (Figure 3.1) and its components, which are referenced in previous chapters and cited continuously throughout the book. You can copy the template from this book, download it from my website (www.kathyglassconsulting .com) by clicking on the "Unit Template" link, or access it through the companion website at http://www.corwin.com/mappingelaunits. As you are aware, the template serves as the basis for creating a comprehensive curriculum unit map. This chapter also includes discussion of three comprehensive, completed unit maps as examples of finished products that might result from completing exercises within this book: (1) informative unit for Native Americans and Thanksgiving (Figure 3.2), (2) narrative unit for short story reading and writing (Figure 3.5 beginning on page 78), and (3) argument unit for persuasive techniques and opinion piece writing (Figure 3.10). Although these maps include grade-specific Common Core Standards for grouping purposes, you can easily adapt the informative map for any primary grade and the narrative and opinion units for third to fifth (or even higher) grades. All unit maps and their accompanying assessment pieces—rubrics and checklists— are included in the companion website to this book. As a model, within this chapter is the printed version of the narrative unit map, along with the checklist and rubric.

I frequently collaborate with teachers to write comprehensive units of study. We house each unit in a three-ring binder with the table of contents at the front followed by the unit template, which serves to orient readers to the overall unit contents. Each section of the binder is divided and organized by the unit guiding questions and consists of specific lessons and accompanying student handouts. Examples of such detailed lessons are in Chapter 7. The last section of the binder is the culminating assessment and the rubric that is used to score it. Educators, however, plan for the culminating assessment during unit design prior to teaching a unit and present it to students near the start of the unit.

As you have experienced already, each component on the template provides an explanation and several examples so you can customize your own curriculum unit map. The previous two chapters concentrated on standards, knowledge, essential understandings,

# Unit Template

Unit: _____

Grade: _____ Timing: _____

| Standards |
|---|
| |
| **Knowledge** |
| |
| **Culminating Assessment (Summative)** |
| |

---

**Essential Understanding #_____:**

**Essential Unit Guiding Question #_____:**

| Lesson Guiding Questions | Skills | Activities | Resources | Formative Assessment Evidence |
|---|---|---|---|---|
| Lesson__.__ | | | | |
| Lesson__.__ | | | | |

**FIGURE 3.1**

and guiding questions along with pertinent exercises to apply this work to create your own map. Subsequent chapters continue to focus on other template components.

Following are annotations for some figures in this chapter, and those located on the companion website, that provide cursory, pertinent explanations for the three unit maps. I strongly encourage you to read the narrative unit's figures in this chapter and the other ones on the companion website for specific examples of all template components. You will note that the activity column is very detailed in each map, but this doesn't mean that you have to be so extensive in your own explanations. This is addressed in Chapter 6 when you craft your activities. Essentially, you must determine how comprehensive you want to be in your descriptions of the exercises. That has a lot to do with your own style, who will be using and viewing this document besides you, what lessons you already have that satisfy a certain activity, and how accomplished you are at typing! If an activity is already written, you might be brief in the activity column and reference it in the resources. You will also notice that the activities all begin with a verb and are written as if this sentence frame precedes each bullet: *Students will...*. Each bullet is directed for students because it should be self-explanatory what the teacher needs to prepare, say, or do to conduct the activity. However, if you feel this treatment is incomplete, by all means, insert what the students and teacher will do. In some instances, you'll find an additional, parenthetical remark for the teacher.

In terms of the rubrics, there is a 5-point scale for the opinion paper and a 4-point scale for the other two to illustrate the slight difference. It is a personal and district preference for determining these scales, as there seem to be strong arguments for both versions. As a professional, it is important for you to use a rubric to assess students against a clear criterion. Whether you choose a 3-, 4-, 5-, or 6-point scale is not the issue. The overriding consideration is providing clear, detailed feedback to guide students in self-assessing and improvement.

## INFORMATIVE UNIT MAP (PRIMARY)

*Figure 3.2 Informative Unit Map* (available on the companion website). Although the Common Core Standards for this unit are for kindergarten, this unit on Thanksgiving, located on the companion website, can work for most primary classrooms that address similar standards. As evident from the grouped standards, it involves English language arts (ELA) strands as well as social studies content. The essential understandings and questions that drive the unit are identified in Figure 3.3.

| Essential Understandings | Essential Unit Guiding Questions |
|---|---|
| Different groups share similarities and differences in various aspects of their daily lives then and now. | How are groups of people different and the same then and now? |
| Holidays mark the occasion of a significant event and provide a venue for appreciation and celebration. | Why and how do people celebrate holidays? |
| Individuals can make significant contributions that improve people's lives and make a mark on communities. | How can people make a difference? |

**FIGURE 3.3**  Informative Unit Map (Primary): Essential Understandings and Guiding Questions

*(Text continued on page 89)*

# Narrative Unit Map

## Common Core Standards

### Reading Standards for Literature (RL)

1. Ask and answer questions to demonstrate understanding of a text, referring explicitly to the text as the basis for the answers.

2. Recount stories, including fables, folktales, and myths from diverse cultures; determine the central message, lesson, or moral and explain how it is conveyed through key details in the text.

3. Describe characters in a story (e.g., their traits, motivations, or feelings) and explain how their actions contribute to the sequence of events.

4. Determine the meaning of words and phrases as they are used in the text, distinguishing literal from nonliteral language.

6. Distinguish their own point of view from that of the narrator or those of the characters.

7. Explain how specific aspects of a text's illustrations contribute to what is conveyed by the words in a story (e.g., create mood, emphasize aspects of a character or setting).

### Language Standards (L)

1. Demonstrate command of the conventions of standard English grammar and usage when writing or speaking. (a.) Explain the function of nouns, pronouns, verbs, adjectives, and adverbs in general and their function in particular sentences. (h.) Use coordinating and subordinating conjunctions. (i.) Produce simple, compound, and complex sentences.

### Language Standards (L)

2. Demonstrate command of the conventions of standard English capitalization, punctuation, and spelling when writing. (c.) Use commas and quotation marks in dialogue. (e.) Use conventional spelling for high-frequency and other studied words (e.g., *sitting, smiled, cries, happiness*). (g.) Consult reference materials, including beginning dictionaries, as needed, to check and correct spelling.

3. Use knowledge of language and its conventions when writing, speaking, reading, or listening. (a.) Choose words and phrases for effect.

6. Acquire and use accurately grade-appropriate conversational, general academic, and domain specific words and phrases, including those that signal spatial and temporal relationships (e.g., *After dinner that night we went looking for them.*).

### Writing Standards (W)

3. Write narratives to develop real or imagined experiences or events using effective technique, descriptive details, and clear event sequences. (a.) Establish a situation and introduce a narrator and/or characters; organize an event sequence that unfolds naturally. (b.) Use dialogue and descriptions of actions, thoughts, and feelings to develop experiences and events or show the response of characters to situations. (c.) Use temporal words and phrases to signal event order. (d.) Provide a sense of closure.

4. With guidance and support from adults, produce writing in which the development and organization are appropriate to task and purpose.

5. With guidance and support from peers and adults, develop and strengthen writing as needed by planning, revising, and editing.

## Know

| | |
|---|---|
| • Terms—narrative, dialogue (speaker) tags, coordinating and subordinating conjunctions<br>• Elements of literature—setting, character, theme, point of view, plot<br>• The plot forms the organizational structure of a story.<br>• Dialogue—narrative device and dialogue punctuation<br>• Writing process—prewriting, drafting, editing, revising, publishing | • Conventions/grammar—dialogue punctuation, conjunctions (subordinating, coordinating), parts of speech (pronouns, verbs, adjectives, adverbs)<br>• Sentence variety—simple, compound, complex<br>• Coordinating conjunctions are used in compound sentences to link two simple sentences.<br>• A subordinating conjunction begins a dependent clause that is in a complex sentence. |

### Culminating Assessment (Summative)

Short story narrative scored against a rubric (see "Short Story Rubric").

### Essential Understanding 1: Authors use imagery to create vivid settings that allow readers to connect viscerally with places.

### Essential Unit Guiding Question 1: How do authors develop descriptive settings?

| Lesson Guiding Questions | Skills | Activities | Resources | Formative Assessment Evidence |
|---|---|---|---|---|
| Lesson 1.1<br><br>What is the definition for setting? What are the major settings in the story we are reading? | • Report on a text using relevant, descriptive details (NGA, 2010, SL.3.4).<br>• Demonstrate understanding of figurative language, specifically imagery (sensory detail) (L.3.5).<br>• Choose words and phrases for effect (L.3.3a).<br>• Write using sensory details. | • In groups, make a list in response to this question: *What are different places and times that are in a story?* Place can be anything someone can sit or stand in, like a house, an airplane, or a playground. *Time* can be time of day, month, year, or even season; be prepared to share the list with the class.<br>• Review the class-generated list of places to assist with arriving at a definition for setting (with the teacher's help); write down the definition; revise the class list, as needed, based on definition. *The setting of a story includes the time and place that events in the story happen. It answers the questions where and when.*<br>• Answer: *What are other settings in books we've read in class or you have read?*; add these settings to the class list. | • Literature—novel, short story, or picture book that includes descriptive setting<br>• Student journals | • Participation in group and whole class activities<br>• Definition of setting in student journals |

**FIGURE 3.5** *(Continued)*

**79**

| Lesson | Skills | Activities | Materials/Resources | Assessment |
|---|---|---|---|---|
| **Lesson 1.2** <br><br> What are sensory details? What sensory words and phrases does the author use to make these settings seem so real? | See list of skills on page 79. | • Listen to a descriptive paragraph about a setting; sketch what you hear. <br>• After listening, respond to this question: *What words did the author use that helped you to see the setting in your mind's eye?*; see the published paragraph in written form and circle any descriptive words that helped with visualization; as an **option**, volunteers can show how their detailed pictures match written description. <br>• Write down a definition of sensory detail in student journal; note that the root word for sensory is sense. <br>• Listen to other setting paragraphs and identify words and phrases that appeal to each sense; record words and phrases on a sensory detail graphic organizer. (For **differentiation** by **readiness**, assign students different paragraphs with varying degrees of challenge matched to readiness levels; for struggling students, prepare the graphic organizer by filling in some words or giving these students word labels to place in appropriate spots on the organizer; support with one-on-one or small group coaching, as needed.) | • Literature with strong imagery for setting <br>• Student journals <br>• Descriptive setting paragraphs (for **differentiation** by **readiness**) <br>• Graphic organizer for sensory details (For **differentiation** by **readiness**, partially complete organizer in advance and/or make labels for struggling students.) | • Sketch based on hearing descriptive paragraph <br>• Participation in discussion <br>• Paragraph with descriptive words circled <br>• Sensory definition in student journals <br>• Graphic organizer (for **differentiation** by **readiness**) |
| **Lesson 1.3** <br><br> How can you write a descriptive setting with sensory details? | | • In pairs, read different setting paragraphs with sensory details; highlight sensory words and phrases; compare and discuss what you highlighted with another pair or small group. (**Teacher**: Do **not** include the topic sentences for these paragraphs.) <br>• Answer this question: *What is a topic sentence?* Listen to paragraphs and identify the topic sentence; add topic sentences to the paragraphs with sensory details that were missing them. <br>• Choose any setting; complete a clean copy of a sensory detail graphic organizer; use words and phrases you create, ones from your organizer in Lesson 1.2, or ones from other stories. | • Setting paragraphs with sensory details and **no** topic sentence <br>• Other paragraphs with topic sentence and details <br>• Sensory detail graphic organizer <br>• "Descriptive Setting Student Checklist" | • Highlighted words and phrases in paragraph <br>• Participation during activity and discussion <br>• Topic sentences <br>• Graphic organizer <br>• Setting paragraph (**differentiation** by **interest** and **learning style**) |

- Using student checklist, create setting paragraph with a topic sentence and sensory details in pairs or individually; get input from others and revise paragraphs. (For **differentiation** by **interest** and **learning style**, choose any setting; choose to work individually or with partners)

**Essential Understanding 2:** Characters' traits, motivations, or feelings drive their actions and contribute to plot development.

**Essential Unit Guiding Question 2:** How do characters move the plot forward?

| Lesson Guiding Questions | Skills | Activities | Resources | Formative Assessment Evidence |
|---|---|---|---|---|
| Lesson 2.1 What are personality traits? | Explain the function of adjectives in general and their functions in sentences (L.3.1a). | • Generate a list of words to insert in the blank: *the very _____ man*; verify that each word makes sense grammatically; answer: *What is a name for this group of words that can fit in the blank?* (Answer is *adjectives*).<br>• From the list, identify those adjectives that refer to a personality trait and *not* physical appearance (e.g., lazy, generous, courageous, evil); add other traits to the list.<br>• Create and share sentences that show what a person does or feels to support specific traits; underline the traits (adjectives) (e.g., *The man is lazy because he never gets off the couch.*)<br>• Share and discuss sentences and the quality of support for traits. | • Chart paper for brainstorming | • Participation during activity<br>• Class-generated adjective list<br>• Sentences |

**FIGURE 3.5** (*Continued*)

| | | | | |
|---|---|---|---|---|
| Lesson 2.2

What traits describe characters in the story? What actions or feelings support these traits? What sensory words describe characters? | Describe characters in a story (RL.3.3). | • Write the definition of *character* in student journal: A *character is a person in a story. Characters have personality traits. These traits are revealed by what characters look like, say, do, think, and feel.*<br>• Focus on this question: *What traits refer to any of the characters in the story we are reading? How do you know?*<br>• **Teacher:** Prepare several cards with one trait written on each card that reflect traits characters in the story you are reading in class exhibit. (For **differentiation by readiness**, make sets of cards at varying degrees of difficulty; distribute appropriately challenging set to each homogeneous group.)<br>• In groups, take turns pulling a personality trait card and discussing what one selected character says or does to support this trait; repeat with another character; be prepared to share your group discussion with the class.<br>• Respond: *We talked before about setting and sensory details. What sensory details does the author use to describe a character's physical appearance? Is the character's appearance related to his or her personality trait? How?* (For **differentiation by readiness** or **learning style**, allow students to respond on paper or orally one-on-one or through a digital or taped response.) | • Student journals<br>• Teacher-prepared cards of personality traits linked to characters in the story (**differentiation** by **readiness**) | • Participation during activity and discussion<br>• Definition of character in student journals<br>• Oral discussion or written response |
| Lesson 2.3

What is plot? How do characters' | Explain how characters' actions contribute to the sequence of events (RL.3.3). | • Write down the definition of *plot* in student journal: *Plot is another element of literature. It is a pattern of related events that resolve a problem.*<br>• **Teacher:** Prepare sentence strips of different events in the plot of a story you read aloud to students. | • Student journals<br>• Sentence strips of plot<br>• Cubing prompts and cubes (Figure 5.3) | • Definition of plot in student journals<br>• Participation during sequencing activities and discussions |

| Lesson Guiding Questions | Skills | Activities | Resources | Formative Assessment Evidence |
|---|---|---|---|---|
| traits, actions, or feelings move the plot forward? | | • Listen to story; in pairs, sequence sentence strips according to the events in the story; confirm order of events with classmates.<br>• Determine and discuss what moved the events in the plot along by answering: *How do character's traits, actions or feelings move the plot forward?*<br>• Using another story, discuss with others who read this same story the order of events and what moved the plot forward. (For **differentiation by readiness** and **interest,** students use independent reading book or literature circle book that is appropriately challenging and personally interesting.)<br>• **Option**—Play cubing game in small groups that focus on character, setting, and plot. (See Figure 5.3 for prompts.) | • Literature for modeling<br>• Literature for independent or group activity (**differentiation** by **readiness** and **interest**) | • Optional: participation during cubing activity; written and oral responses |
| **Essential Understanding 3:** Writers use dialogue to develop experiences and events or show the responses of characters to situations. | | | | |
| **Essential Unit Guiding Question 3:** How does dialogue help to develop a story? | | | | |
| **Lesson Guiding Questions** | **Skills** | **Activities** | **Resources** | **Formative Assessment Evidence** |
| Lesson 3.1<br><br>Where is dialogue in the story? How do readers identify dialogue? | Use dialogue to show the response of characters to situations (W.3.3b). | • Read short text aloud (choral reading) using expression for characters; respond to this question: *What helps you to figure out when to change your voice for different characters?* (**Teacher:** Choose a story with distinct characters that will require students to change their voices during reading, such as with a lion or mouse. This helps to observe whether or not they can detect dialogue.)<br>• Listen to another story; knowing that dialogue is offset by punctuation and includes dialogue or speaker tags, locate dialogue in the story by placing sticky notes in these spots. (**Teacher:** Walk around the room to see and discuss where individual students put sticky notes. For **differentiation by readiness,** reteach those who have inaccurately placed sticky notes, so they are aware that dialogue punctuation indicates the words of a speaker in a story.) | • Short piece of reading that includes distinct dialogue, such as a fable<br>• sticky notes<br>• Brief story with dialogue (making sure each student has a copy so they can place sticky notes)<br>• Various stories that include dialogue (**differentiation by readiness**) | • Participation during activity and discussion<br>• sticky note locations |

**FIGURE 3.5** (Continued)

| Lesson | Objective | Learning Activities | Assessment | Materials |
|---|---|---|---|---|
| **Lesson 3.2**<br>What is the purpose of this dialogue? How does dialogue help readers learn about characters? | | • Using yet another story, individually place sticky notes on the dialogue; compare where you put these notes with group members who have read the same story and agree that these spots indicate dialogue. (For **differentiation** by **readiness**, arrange students in groups based on readability levels and assign a story with the appropriate level of challenge; provide teacher or adult assistance to those groups needing support in identifying dialogue.)<br>• As a group, read just the dialogue and answer this question: *How does this dialogue help readers to learn about the characters? What would the story be like if the dialogue were not included?* | • Observation during activity and discussion<br>• sticky note locations | |
| **Lesson 3.3**<br>How do writers punctuate dialogue? | Use commas and quotation marks in dialogue (L.3.2c). | • Look at dialogue examples and articulate and point to what is common among the punctuation and capitalization. (**Teacher**: Show several examples of dialogue with beginning tags to compare; e.g., *Susan cried, "I am hungry for dinner." Then do the same with end tags; e.g., "I am hungry for dinner," Susan cried.*)<br>• Punctuate sentence strips by using manipulatives of elbow macaroni to show quotation marks and commas, and small beads for periods; refer to "Dialogue Punctuation Rules" to help with this exercise; on paper, write out these sentences using proper dialogue punctuation. (For **differentiation** by **readiness**, arrange students in pairs or trios; prepare and distribute appropriately challenging sentence strips to students; for high achievers, include dialogue with an interrupted tag, such as *"Please," her mom begged, "take out the garbage."*) | • Observation during activity<br>• Written sentences with properly punctuated and capitalized dialogue (**differentiation** by **readiness**) | • Examples of dialogue with beginning and end tags<br>• "Dialogue Punctuation Rules" handout<br>• Elbow macaroni pasta for quotation marks and commas; small beads for periods<br>• Dialogue sentence strips (**differentiation** by **readiness**) |

**Essential Understanding 4:** Students move through the writing process with a clear sense of criteria prior to writing and synthesize all they have learned into their final work.

**Essential Unit Guiding Question 4:** How do writers create a short story?

| Lesson Guiding Questions | Skills | Activities | Resources | Formative Assessment Evidence |
|---|---|---|---|---|
| Lesson 4.1<br><br>How do writers create a short story? | • Establish a situation and introduce a character (W.3.3a).<br>• Organize an event sequence that unfolds naturally (W.3.3a).<br>• Use descriptions of actions, thoughts, and feelings to develop events (W.3.3b).<br>• Provide a sense of closure (W.3.3d). | • In groups, brainstorm a list in answer to this question: *What makes a strong short story?*; share list with class; cross-reference list with teacher-prepared checklist. (**Teacher:** This activity is detailed in Lesson 5 in Chapter 7 to introduce checklist to students.)<br>• Brainstorm for story on a graphic organizer; show it to your teacher before drafting your story. (For **differentiation by readiness** or **learning style**, assign students an organizer based on readiness level so students who are more advanced can include more events in the plot and might even attempt more suspense; provide choices of graphic organizers within each challenge level so students can select one based on learning style.)<br>• Using your checklist as a guide, draft your short story. (For **differentiation by readiness**, create and provide tiered checklists.) | • Lesson 5 in Chapter 7 "Short Story Student Checklist" (**differentiation by readiness**)<br>• Short story graphic organizers (see Figure 5.11 for graphic organizer websites) (**differentiation by readiness** and **learning style**) | • Graphic organizer (**differentiation** by **readiness** and **learning style**)<br>• Student story draft |
| Lesson 4.2<br><br>How does the writing process work? | Develop and strengthen writing as needed by planning, revising, and editing (W.3.5). | • Answer these questions: *What is the writing process? How have you used it before?*<br>• Understand the steps in the writing process; review poster of steps in the process. | • "Writing Process" poster | • Participation in discussion |

**FIGURE 3.5** (*Continued*)

| Lesson 4.3<br><br>What are temporal words? How do I include them in my story? | • Use temporal words and phrases to signal event order (W.3.3c).<br>• Develop and strengthen writing as needed by planning, revising, and editing (W.3.5). | • Read two story excerpts and determine which flows better and why. (**Teacher:** Show a text excerpt that includes transitions and one that is choppy and does not; allow students to arrive at the conclusion that one is missing these transitional words which accounts for the lack of fluidity.)<br>• Focusing on the excerpt that includes transitions, circle them all; answer this question: *In stories, what is the purpose of these transitional words and phrases?* (Possible answers: They allow reader to understand sequence, such as the series of events better; e.g., *When the boy caught the fly ball…* or *After he finished his homework…* Or they allow readers to understand time order; e.g., *In the morning…* or *On the next day…*)<br>• In pairs, go on a scavenger hunt through a story and find other transitions; compare transitions with the class and create a class-generated chart of transitional words and phrases. (For **differentiation** **by readiness**, assign students appropriately challenging text that includes various levels of transitions.)<br>• Review your first draft of your story and insert transitional words and phrases where there are none or replace existing ones to make them stronger. | • Two text excerpts—one with and one without transitional words and phrases<br>• Various literature (**differentiation by readiness**)<br>• Short story rough drafts | • Participation in discussion<br>• Circled words<br>• Participation in scavenger hunt and generating class list<br>• Short story revision |

| | | |
|---|---|---|
| Lesson 4.4<br><br>What are different types of sentences? How can I use a variety of sentences to make my writing flow? | • Use coordinating conjunctions (L.3.1h).<br>• Produce simple and compound sentences (L.3.1i).<br>• Develop and strengthen writing as needed by planning, revising, and editing (W.3.5). | • With partners, pair sentence strips together that contain the same topic; create one sentence from these two sentences and answer this question: *What word can you use to pair two sentences together?* (**Teacher:** Create many pairs of sentence strips, such as these: (1) *The boy slept peacefully. He was awakened by the thunder.* (2) *Mrs. Smith enjoys eating peas. She likes broccoli, too.* (3) *Dr. Green gave me aspirin. I would get better.*) (For **differentiation by readiness,** create and distribute appropriately challenging pairs of sentences to partners of like readiness levels; provide labels of these coordinating conjunctions for struggling students to use: *and, but, so.*)<br><br>• Name the words that are used to make a sentence using two sentences (coordinating conjunctions); write the definition of compound sentence in student journals: *A sentence formed by using two independent clauses or simple sentences that are merged together with a coordinating conjunction. Coordinating conjunctions are these words: and, but, so.*<br><br>• Sort various sentences into piles: simple and compound sentences. (**Teacher:** Prepare these sentences for students to sort; make header cards.) (For **differentiation** by **readiness,** arrange students in homogeneous groups; prepare and distribute appropriately challenging sentences; include complex sentences as a third sorting option for some students, as well as include sentences with other coordinating conjunctions. Note that by the end of the year, though, third graders are expected to know complex sentences, too.) | • Sentence strips of simple sentences (**differentiation** by **readiness**)<br>• Labels of coordinating conjunctions (**differentiation** by **readiness**)<br>• Student journals<br>• Sentence strips for sorting activity: simple, compound, complex (**differentiation** by **readiness**)<br>• Short story rough drafts | • Participation during activities and discussion<br>• Definition of compound sentence in student journals<br>• Short story revision |

**FIGURE 3.5** (*Continued*)

| | | | |
|---|---|---|---|
| | | After sorting, verify for accuracy; note the punctuation for compound sentences: A comma is always after the first simple sentence and before the coordinating conjunction: *He wanted to eat cake, but he had to settle for cookies.* (For **differentiation by readiness**, convene high achievers together and teach how to use a semicolon for compound sentences as an alternative to using a comma.)<br>• Review your short story and then revise for sentence variety. | • Student published short story (**differentiation by readiness**) |
| Lesson 4.5<br><br>How do writers revise and edit their work so it does not have errors? | • Develop and strengthen writing as needed by planning, revising, and editing (W.3.5).<br>• Demonstrate command of the conventions of standard English grammar and usage when writing (L.3.1) and capitalization, punctuation, and spelling when writing (L.3.2). | • Have peers and teacher review drafts and make comments using student checklist as a guide for conversations; use input to revise paper.<br>• Use resources to correct spelling and replace weak words with stronger ones; rely on classmates and teacher to check for grammar and conventions errors; make necessary editing corrections. (For **differentiation by learning style**, create and include pictures with story. For **readiness**, make available resources at varying levels of challenge.)<br>• Submit published story. | • "Short Story Student Checklist" (**differentiation by readiness**)<br>• Peers and teacher<br>• Various resources—dictionary, thesaurus, online resources (**differentiation by readiness**)<br>• Student short story |

**FIGURE 3.5**

***Figure 3.4*** (available on the companion website). *Primary Rubric: Informative/Explanatory Writing.* Throughout many lessons in the unit, students use a combination of drawing and dictation or writing to produce various pages. Therefore, the culminating assessment is a compilation of these writing pages for a class (or individual) book. Teachers score their work against this rubric.

# NARRATIVE UNIT MAP (ELEMENTARY)

***Figure 3.5*** *Narrative Unit Map* (see pages 78–88). This map, featuring "The Art of Entertainment," focuses on narrative reading and writing for third grade but can definitely be adapted for second through fifth grades. Figure 3.6 identifies the understandings and guiding questions for this unit.

| Essential Understandings | Essential Unit Guiding Questions |
|---|---|
| Authors use imagery to create vivid settings, which allow readers to connect viscerally with places. | How do authors develop descriptive settings? |
| Characters' traits, motivations, or feelings drive their actions and contribute to plot development. | How do characters move the plot forward? |
| Writers use dialogue to develop experiences and events or show the responses of characters to situations. | How does dialogue help to develop a story? |
| Students move through the writing process with a clear sense of criteria prior to writing and synthesize all they have learned into their final work. | How do writers create a short story? |

**FIGURE 3.6**   Narrative Unit Map (Elementary): Essential Understandings and Guiding Questions

***Figure 3.8*** *Short Story Student Checklist.* Students produce a short story as the unit culmination. This checklist, which guides students as they write, is fairly generic and can be used for different grades and different readiness levels of students across grades.

***Figure 3.9*** *Narrative: Short Story Rubric.* In Chapter 4, there is a section dedicated to rubrics that includes more detail about scoring guides. For the grammar and conventions areas, there are two choices of criteria in this narrative rubric (see pages 93–94 of Figure 3.9) and also for the opinion writing rubric featured on the companion website. One is quantitative; the other is more subjective. Figure 3.7 provides an example of these criteria, so decide with your colleagues which scoring approach you all prefer so there is consistency among your group.

| | Quantitative | Subjective |
|---|---|---|
| **Capitalization**<br><br>Use correct capitalization (NGA, 2010, L.4.2a). | 4—One error<br>3—Two to three errors<br>2—Four to six errors<br>1— Seven or more errors | 4—Minor errors<br>3—Some errors<br>2—Many errors<br>1—Serious errors; hinders reading |

**FIGURE 3.7**   Quantitative Versus Subjective Scoring Decision

*(Text continued on page 94)*

# Short Story Student Checklist

Remember what you know about elements of literature. Use this checklist to guide you in writing a story.

## Ideas/Content and Organization

☐ I write a story that has one clear <u>main idea</u> and stays on-topic.

☐ I include an original <u>title.</u>

☐ I correctly <u>indent </u>for each new paragraph.

☐ I include <u>descriptive details</u> about
   ☐ setting
   ☐ characters
   ☐ events

☐ I include a <u>plot</u> with a beginning, middle, and end.

### ➡ Beginning

☐ I write an exciting and attention-getting story beginning to <u>interest</u> my reader.

☐ I <u>describe</u> my main <u>character</u> and <u>setting.</u>

☐ I include a <u>central conflict</u> (or problem) to my story.

### ➡ Middle

☐ I thoroughly explain the events of my story in a <u>logical order</u> so my story makes sense.

☐ I include <u>transitional words and phrases</u> to connect paragraphs and show sequence (e.g., *After an uncomfortable dinner, Sally walked out the door.*)

### ➡ Ending

☐ My ending <u>resolves the central conflict.</u> It answers questions a reader might have about what happened.

☐ My ending is <u>not abrupt.</u>

## Voice

☐ I know why I am writing (<u>purpose</u>) and to whom I am writing (<u>audience</u>).

## Sentence Fluency

☐ I write <u>complete sentences</u> so there are no <u>fragments.</u>

☐ I have no <u>run-on sentences.</u>

☐ My sentences <u>begin in different ways.</u>

## Word Choice

☐ I use strong nouns, adjectives, and adverbs and <u>sensory details</u> to <u>describe</u> my <u>setting, characters,</u> and <u>events.</u>

☐ My <u>dialogue tags</u> include strong verbs.

## Conventions

☐ I try my best to <u>spell</u> all words correctly. I use the dictionary for words I don't know how to spell.

☐ I end my sentences with correct <u>punctuation</u> and use commas where I should.

☐ I punctuate <u>dialogue</u> correctly.

☐ I <u>capitalize</u> appropriate letters.

☐ My sentences make sense and do not have <u>grammar</u> errors.

☐ My <u>writing is legible and my paper is neat.</u> I pay attention to the <u>right and left margins.</u>

**FIGURE 3.8**

# Narrative: Short Story Rubric (Grade 4)

| Components | Points |
|---|---|
| **Title**<br><br>Include original title. | **5**—Extremely original; sophisticated<br>**4**—Original title<br>**3**—Title provided<br>**2**—Weak title; doesn't match story<br>**1**—Missing a title |

| Ideas/Content and Organization and Word Choice | **Beginning**<br><br>Orient the reader by establishing a situation and introducing a narrator and/or characters (NGA, 2010, W.4.3a); create an interesting and attention-getting beginning; introduce setting; state central conflict. | **5**—Very clearly interesting and attention-getting beginning; setting and main character clearly introduced without too much detail; very clear central conflict; sophisticated<br><br>**4**—Clearly interesting and attention-getting beginning; setting and main character clearly introduced; central conflict clearly stated<br><br>**3**—Adequately interesting and attention-getting beginning; setting and main character adequately introduced; central conflict stated<br><br>**2**—Minimally interesting and attention-getting beginning; setting and main character hardly introduced; weak or unclear central conflict<br><br>**1**—Not interesting or attention getting beginning; setting and main character not introduced; no central conflict |
|---|---|---|
| | **Middle/Logical Sequence/Suspenseful**<br><br>Organize an event sequence that unfolds naturally (W.4.3a); develop plot (attempt suspense). | **5**—Thoroughly developed, logical sequence of significant events; clearly identified suspense<br><br>**4**—Mostly developed, logical sequence of significant events; somewhat suspenseful<br><br>**3**—Adequately developed sequence of events; logically sequenced (attempts suspense)<br><br>**2**—Weakly developed sequence of events; haphazard sequence<br><br>**1**—No development of events; hard-to-follow sequence |
| | **Conclusion**<br><br>Provide a conclusion that follows from the narrated experiences or events (W.4.3e); answer questions a reader might have about what happened; not abrupt. | **5**—Narrated events resolved completely; sophisticated<br><br>**4**—Resolved without reader having any unanswered questions<br><br>**3**—Narrated events mostly resolved<br><br>**2**—Weak ending or abrupt<br><br>**1**—No ending |
| | **Descriptive Details**<br><br>Use description to develop experiences and events or show the responses of characters to situations (W.4.3b); use concrete words and phrases and sensory details to convey experiences and events precisely (W.4.3d) and for setting. | **10**—Consistent, sophisticated use of descriptive words and sensory details to write about experiences/events, setting, and character<br><br>**8**—Clear use of descriptive words and sensory details to write about experieinces/events, setting, and character<br><br>**6**—Some use of descriptive words and sensory details to write about experiences/events, setting, and character<br><br>**4**—Limited use of descriptive words and sensory details to write about experiences/events, setting, and/or character<br><br>**2**—Rare or no use of descriptive words and sensory details |

**FIGURE 3.9** (Continued)

| | | |
|---|---|---|
| **Ideas/Content and Organization and Word Choice** | **Dialogue**<br><br>Use dialogue to develop experiences and events or show the responses of characters to situations (W.4.3b). | 5—Entirely meaningful dialogue moves plot forward by helping to develop events and/or show characters' responses to situations<br><br>4—Meaningful dialogue moves plot forward<br><br>3—Dialogue somewhat meaningful and adequately moves plot forward<br><br>2—Unnecessary dialogue, too much dialogue, or not very meaningful; hardly moves the plot forward<br><br>1—No dialogue or little dialogue that fails to move the plot forward |
| | **Paragraphing**<br><br>Know when to begin a new paragraph and how to indent paragraphs. | 5—Paragraphing and indenting completely intact<br><br>4—Most paragraphing and indenting intact<br><br>3—Some minor paragraphing and indenting errors<br><br>2—Unclear paragraphing and indenting<br><br>1—No paragraphing/indenting |
| | **Transitions Between Sentences and Paragraphs**<br><br>Use a variety of transitional words and phrases to manage the sequence of events (W.4.3c). | 5—Thoughtful use of transitional words and phrases from sentence to sentence and from paragraph to paragraph to help the story sequence; sophisticated<br><br>4—Usually uses appropriate and enough transitions to sequence events<br><br>3—Adequate use of transitions to sequence events; story still flows even if some transitions are missing or somewhat inadequate<br><br>2—Weak use of transitions or many are missing; very choppy<br><br>1—No transitions |
| **Voice** | **Point of View**<br><br>Use consistent point of view throughout paper (first or third person). | 5—Maintains consistent first- or third-person point of view throughout paper; no second-person point of view<br><br>4—Might get off track once<br><br>3—Might get off track twice but seems to mostly understand point of view<br><br>2—Inconsistent point of view<br><br>1—Clearly unaware of point of view |
| | **Audience/Purpose**<br><br>Be aware of task, purpose, and audience (NGA, 2010, W.4.4) | 5—Clearly aware of task, purpose, and audience<br><br>4—Generally aware<br><br>3—Somewhat aware<br><br>2—Little awareness<br><br>1—Seems altogether unaware |

| | | |
|---|---|---|
| **Sentence Fluency** | **Sentence Beginnings**<br><br>Include a variety of sentence beginnings — subjects, prepositional phrases (L.4.1e), adverbs. | 5—Thoughtful use of sentence beginning variety using subjects, prepositional phrases, and adverbs; sophisticated<br>4—Consistently uses sentence beginning variety<br>3—Sometimes uses sentence beginning variety<br>2—Most sentences beginning in the same way<br>1—All sentences beginning in the same way by either the same word or the same type (e.g., all subjects, same words) |
| | **Sentence Variety**<br><br>Include a variety of sentence structures—simple, compound, complex. | 5—Thoughtful use of sentence variety; includes compound-complex sentences<br>4—Consistently uses sentence variety<br>3—Sometimes uses sentence variety<br>2—Most sentences similar in structure<br>1—All sentences similar in structure |
| | **Run-Ons and Complete Sentences**<br><br>Produce complete sentences, recognizing and correcting inappropriate fragments and run-ons (L.4.1f). | 5—No run-ons; all complete sentences<br>4—One run-on or one fragment<br>3—Two run-ons or fragments<br>2—More than two run-ons or fragments<br>1—Unclear about sentence structure altogether |

| | | | |
|---|---|---|---|
| **Presentation/Conventions** | **Presentation**<br><br>If handwritten, use legible penmanship, proper margins and heading; if typed, adhere to proper formatting; all papers neat. | 5—Very neat paper; complete adherence to proper formatting and even uses sophisticated formatting<br>4—Neat paper and adherence to proper formatting<br>3—Somewhat neat and adherence to proper formatting<br>2—Messy; haphazard formatting<br>1—Unacceptably messy; proper formatting ignored | |
| | **Grammar**<br><br>Demonstrate command of the conventions of standard English grammar and usage (L.4.1). | 5—No errors<br>4—One error<br>3—Two to three errors<br>2—Four to six errors<br>1—Seven or more errors | **OR** 5—No errors<br>4—Minor errors<br>3—Some errors<br>2—Many errors<br>1—Serious errors; hinders reading |
| | **Capitalization**<br><br>Use correct capitalization (L.4.2a). | 5—No errors<br>4—One error<br>3—Two to three errors<br>2—Four to six errors<br>1—Seven or more errors | **OR** 5—No errors<br>4—Minor errors<br>3—Some errors<br>2—Many errors<br>1—Serious errors; hinders reading |

**FIGURE 3.9** *(Continued)*

| Presentation/Conventions | Punctuation<br><br>Use commas and quotation marks to mark direct speech; use comma before a coordinating conjunction in a compound sentence (L.4.b, c); punctuate sentences correctly. | 5—No errors<br>4—One error<br>3—Two to three errors<br>2—Four to six errors<br>1—Seven or more errors | **OR** | 5—No errors<br>4—Minor errors<br>3—Some errors<br>2—Many errors<br>1—Serious errors; hinders reading |
|---|---|---|---|---|
| | Spelling<br><br>Spell grade-appropriate words correctly, consulting references as needed (L.4.2d). | 5—No errors<br>4—One error<br>3—Two to three errors<br>2—Four to six errors<br>1—Seven or more errors | **OR** | 5—No errors<br>4—Minor errors<br>3—Some errors<br>2—Many errors<br>1—Serious errors; hinders reading |

Student: _____     Highest Possible Points: _____

Total Points Attained: _____

Comments:

**FIGURE 3.9**

This narrative rubric aligns with fourth-grade standards, but this unit is easily adaptable to third, fourth, and even fifth grades because these grades have similar expectations.

## OPINION UNIT MAP (UPPER ELEMENTARY)

*Figure 3.10 Opinion Unit Map.* This map, available on the companion website, focuses on opinion pieces and persuading people to change their beliefs and take action. To give you a snapshot of this unit, Figure 3.11 features the understandings and guiding questions.

*Figure 3.12 Opinion Writing Student Checklists.* Three checklists are included in the companion website for opinion writing to illustrate three versions based on differentiation by readiness. It is important to note that this assignment is differentiated by readiness not only for the writing expectations as shown on the checklists, but also in terms of the varying degrees of readability levels of the resources students use to gather information for their writing. The checklist with a heart symbol is for struggling students, the second version with a clover symbol is for at-grade-level students, and the third version with the spade symbol is for more advanced students. You can use this technique of a heart, clover, and spade for other checklists and assignments as well. I devised this symbol system for tiered

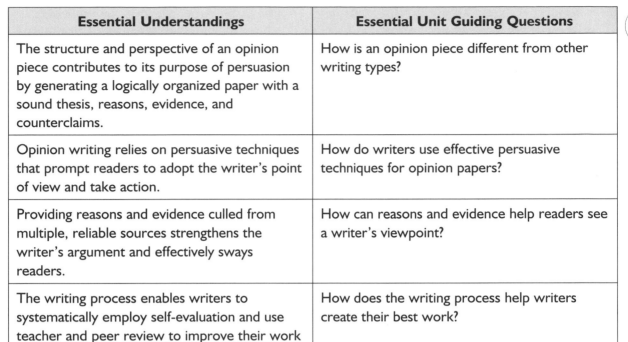

| Essential Understandings | Essential Unit Guiding Questions |
|---|---|
| The structure and perspective of an opinion piece contributes to its purpose of persuasion by generating a logically organized paper with a sound thesis, reasons, evidence, and counterclaims. | How is an opinion piece different from other writing types? |
| Opinion writing relies on persuasive techniques that prompt readers to adopt the writer's point of view and take action. | How do writers use effective persuasive techniques for opinion papers? |
| Providing reasons and evidence culled from multiple, reliable sources strengthens the writer's argument and effectively sways readers. | How can reasons and evidence help readers see a writer's viewpoint? |
| The writing process enables writers to systematically employ self-evaluation and use teacher and peer review to improve their work to produce optimal results. | How does the writing process help writers create their best work? |

**FIGURE 3.11** Opinion Writing Unit Map (Elementary): Essential Understandings and Guiding Questions

assignments so they are easy to find on the computer and do not have an inherent association like *1, 2, 3* or *A, B, C* might. All versions meet grade-level standards, though. For the opinion piece, most students write a multiple-paragraph paper with an introduction, body, and conclusion. However, if individual students need more modification, expect a single paragraph that includes a topic sentence (reason), supporting evidence, and closure. This opinion paper is also differentiated by interest in that students choose their own topic as the basis for their writing. Be mindful, though, that students choose appropriately challenging topics of interest. If struggling students choose a topic where the resources are scarce and those that are available are well above their reading level, it can prove frustrating.

*Figure 3.13 Opinion Writing Rubric.* Although there are three versions of the checklist, this one rubric found on the companion website can be used to score any of the papers. The "Components" column indicates what is omitted from a heart version so you are careful when you score not to include these expectations.

*Figure 3.14 The 4-6-8-10 Rule.* This figure explains a formula teachers can use to convert the rubric grades to a letter grade. It was devised by Vicki Spandel (2001) and featured in her book *Creating Writers: Through 6-Trait Writing Assessment and Instruction.* You would first score students using the rubric and arrive at a percentage. Then, use the mathematical formula explained on the 4-6-8-10 rule to arrive at a grade. What typically happens with scoring using the numbers is that when teachers translate them to a grade, it is lower than a holistic grade a teacher would issue. This formula, in essence, allows for the mismatch between number and letter grades. In using this conversion consistently with teachers who assign letter grades, it is pretty miraculous how the conversion nets out to a letter grade that coincides with what a teacher would have initially granted. In her forthcoming edition of *Creating Writers,* Spandel (2013) raises an excellent point about using several samples of a

student's writing as the basis for formulating a grade. She does not advocate scoring one individual piece, arguing that reviewing strengths and weaknesses across a compilation of work offers the most meaningful picture of the student as a writer.

# The 4-6-8-10 Rule

Vicki Spandel (2001), in her book *Creating Writers: Through 6-Trait Writing Assessment and Instruction*, created a mathematical conversion for arriving at letter grades from number scores. She states about this conversion: "…you are *not* giving the student extra points by adding in these percentages; you are not *giving* the student *anything*. You are simply making up for the fact that measurement on a continuum is by nature slightly imprecise, so we have to adjust it to make it fit our grading system" (p. 379). Her system could be adapted for use with the rubrics in this book. Here is how it works:

First, figure out the basic percentage for a student's paper. For example, if the paper is worth 80 points and a student scores a 68, the basic percentage is 85%. Now, add the conversion as shown below. For the 85% paper, the conversion would be 91%.

**Conversion**

- For scores over 90%, add 4 points to the total. Example—92 original percent + 4 = 96% conversion
- For scores over 80%, add 6 points to the total. Example—85 original percent + 6 = 91% conversion
- For scores over 70%, add 8 points to the total. Example—73 original percent + 8 = 81% conversion
- For scores over 60%, add 10 points to the total. Example—69 original percent +10 = 79% conversion

*Note:* For scores right on the edge (60, 70, 80, 90), add one additional point. For example, if the percentage is 80%, then add 80 + 6 + 1 to arrive at 87%.

**FIGURE 3.14**

# CLOSING

These maps may at first appear daunting in their extensive treatment of a unit of study. But as you embark upon the project of getting at the real essence of a unit, and its supporting foundational knowledge, you will feel empowered by how you can teach with more depth, with more insight, and with more focus. As a result, your students will benefit from this approach to teaching as they glean more from your wise guidance. As you continue reading and building your map, you will see the beauty in this process and all it entails. Onward we go.

# 4

# Assessments

> How will we know if students have achieved the desired results and met the standards? What will we accept as evidence of student understanding and proficiency? The backward design approach encourages us to think about a unit or course in terms of the collected assessment evidence needed to document and validate that the desired learning has been achieved, so that the course is not just content to be covered or a series of learning activities.
>
> This backward approach encourages teachers and curriculum planners to first think like an assessor before designing specific units and lessons, and thus to consider up front how they will determine whether students have attained the desired understandings.
>
> —Grant Wiggins and Jay McTighe (1998, p. 12)

There are three types of assessments to provide teachers and students with necessary information for optimal learning and growth: (1) *preassessments* (also called *diagnostic assessments*), (2) *formative* (also called *ongoing*) assessments, and (3) *culminating* (also called *summative*) assessments. The material in this chapter includes a variety of assessment instruments, such as rubrics, checklists, assignment sheets, and preassessments to use as written or adapt for the grade and subject you teach or support. I also include three culminating assessments in Chapter 3 to accompany the unit template examples; in this chapter are other alternatives. Formative assessments are addressed more thoroughly in Chapter 5 as they align with learning activities; however, I do include some here. At the end of this chapter, you will complete Exercise 5 in which you identify the culminating assessment for your targeted unit.

For those of you who have developed professional learning communities, assessments are a major tenet of this model. In his article "What Is a 'Professional Learning Community'?" Richard DuFour (2004) identifies three significant questions that educators must address together in their professional learning communities. The question he poses—"How will we know when each student has learned it?"—is what assessments should uncover.

## CULMINATING ASSESSMENTS

When teachers disseminate new information or content to students, the students will not necessarily learn what is presented. But a multitude of learning opportunities teachers design and conduct will help students to work with these new ideas to process them. Formative assessments—or assessment *for* learning—allow students to practice and learn the material. These ongoing assessments also serve to inform teachers about their instruction so they can enrich, reteach, reinforce, or modify instruction, as appropriate. (See Chapter 5 for more about formative assessments.) After students grapple with and explore this new information for a period of time that represents the length of a unit of study, teachers then ask them to demonstrate that they have indeed mastered the content presented. This is referred to as the culminating product or summative assessment, which essentially is evidence *of* learning after a considerable unit of study. These culminating assessments need to call upon students to prove they have mastered the intended content goals presented throughout the unit. Therefore, they must be designed to incorporate the "big three": what students have come to *know, understand,* and be able to *do* (KUD). Teachers need to accompany these assessments with rubrics so there are clear and appropriate criteria for success. Creating these assessments and rubrics alongside identifying the KUDs in a curriculum unit map enables educators to have a clear direction for the overarching unit goals. This practice of identifying assessment evidence at the genesis of planning a course of study is a hallmark of the backward design approach.

Products come in many forms, so teachers need to selectively find and create meaningful and effective assessments to do the job of allowing students to show what they learned. Whereas a traditional final objective exam can reveal factual information that students have come to know, it will not do the trick to altogether allow students to demonstrate deep understanding. Therefore, if you prefer objective tests, consider issuing them along with another type of product for a comprehensive assessment of how well students have mastered all the unit goals. For example, in a language arts classroom, products can include a performance, poster project, interview, or formal writing assignment (e.g., opinion paper, research project, summary). In a science class, a summative assessment could be writing a lab report or building a scale model of the Earth, sun, and moon. In math, students can respond to various math prompts and even create and solve their own based on criteria. Differentiating products is a powerful and valuable means of allowing students to exhibit what they have learned. (See Chapter 6, "Differentiated Instruction," for other ideas.) Teachers should present the summative assessment to students at or near the beginning of the unit so all students are well aware of expectations and have specific goals in mind as they work to accomplish each task that leads to the final product.

Since you will identify a summative assessment for your unit during this chapter, I include some culminating opportunities for students to demonstrate understanding. See these brief explanations of figures that include student assignment sheets or materials. Later in this chapter I include examples of rubrics and checklists. Although each figure is geared to a grade level or cluster, some can be adapted to accommodate the grade level and subject matter you teach or support.

*Opinion Writing.* Figure 4.1 provides the student assignment sheet for writing an opinion paper, which is geared for upper elementary. Students can use the brainstorming sheet in Figure 4.2 as they plan for this piece. For this assignment, you can lead students through the steps of collecting research and taking notes so they accumulate evidence, such as facts, data, anecdotes, and so forth. The opinion writing checklist and rubric from Chapter 3 can serve as suggestions for accompanying assessment instruments.

*American Revolution Newspaper.* Causes of the American Revolution Newspaper, Figure 4.3, is an assignment sheet I created with Nancy Rhodes, a fifth-grade teacher. She had the keen idea of having groups of students produce a colonial newspaper. This might seem like a typical assignment, but her twist is to have groups choose to write from a Patriot or Loyalist point of view so their newspapers would each be told from a different perspective. In addition, each student in a group has the choice to write a feature article, news story, or editorial. All writing responds to guiding questions and focuses on a topic. Besides the individual accountability of writing an article, students work together to produce other aspects of the newspaper (e.g., illustrations, advertisements, etc.), discuss viewpoints, and ensure that all contributions respond to guiding questions. The assignment sheet provides more detail of the task. In addition, students each use a checklist and accompanying graphic organizer for the type of article they will write. Figures 4.4 and 4.5 are examples of a checklist and graphic organizer, respectively, for students who choose to write a news article.

*Character Study.* The four choices featured in Figure 4.6, Character Highlights, allow students a choice in demonstrating their understanding of a character in a way that resonates with them. You can adapt this project to a historical figure or hero and modify it for younger students.

*Multiple Intelligence Options.* Using Figure 4.7, Project Choices, students each have an opportunity to select the project that fits their learning style. While it is generic and can work with any unit, it refers to guiding questions so there is an assumption that you have written and incorporate these in your unit. To guide students as they work on their projects, introduce the Project Checklist in Figure 4.8. For younger students, narrow down the list to a few choices and modify what is entailed for each project.

*Games.* Typically games are considered a formative assessment, and Figure 4.9, Nonfiction Game, can serve as such. However, after students play the game based on a particular text, have them create their own game board as a culminating assessment. To play this game, provide beans, pennies, paper clips, or other sorts of tokens that are moved around the board. Place these tokens in the "start" box. Instead of dice, although you can surely use them, students can flip over a card from a stack that reads 1, 2, or 3 to signify the number of spaces they will move up if they get the answer correct, or back if the answer is wrong. The questions on the game board in Figure 4.9 should be based on a nonfiction text that you can read to the whole class and then divide students into groups to play. Or you can differentiate by having students read different books in small, homogeneous groups and play the game. Some groups might need adult supervision to play; others may not.

*(Text continued on page 110)*

# Writing an Opinion Paper

## Find a Topic

Choose one of the topics below as the focus for an opinion paper or consider your own topic from the ideas listed.

| Topics | |
|---|---|
| classroom seating | household chores |
| homework policy | limits on watching television |
| curfews for kids under age 18 | noise pollution |
| access to websites | air pollution |
| school uniforms | **Ideas** |
| laws about noise | issues about animals |
| litter on school campus | any city or state law |
| afterschool sports | any school policy or rule |
| | television programming |

## Brainstorming

Review and then complete the "Opinion Writing Brainstorming" using the research you collect to gather information for your evidence. When you finish, show it to your teacher.

## Writing Process

Once your teacher has approved your brainstorming, begin the rough draft of your opinion paper. Use the "Opinion Writing Checklist" to guide you while writing so you can make sure you have satisfied all the criteria. When you finish your rough draft, follow the steps your teacher has assigned to get to the final copy.

## Due Dates

Brainstorming/Research _____

Rough Draft _____

Self-Review _____

Revising/Editing _____

Peer/Teacher Review _____

Revising/Editing _____

Final Copy _____

**FIGURE 4.1**

# Opinion Writing Brainstorming

⇨ **Introduction (First Paragraph)**

| |
|---|
| **Attractive Opening**—Introduction attracts and draws in the reader. |
| **Thesis**—Writer clearly states a position on one issue. |

⇨ **Body Paragraphs**

Here are my <u>reasons</u> and my <u>evidence</u> to support each reason:

| | <u>Reasons</u>—topic sentence | <u>Evidence</u>—relevant and accurate evidence including facts, quotes, data, examples that are not common knowledge |
|---|---|---|
| **Paragraph 2** | | |
| **Paragraph 3** | | |
| **Paragraph 4** | | |
| **Counterargument** | Others might feel… | But this is weak because… |

⇨ **Conclusion (Last paragraph)**

| |
|---|
| Restate thesis and sum up main points: |
| Include a call to action: |

**FIGURE 4.2**

# Causes of the American Revolution Newspaper

**Final Project.** You will work in a group to create a Loyalist *or* Patriot newspaper focusing on the causes of the American Revolution. Each group member will write his or her own newspaper article from the perspective of a Loyalist or Patriot. Together as a group, you will lay out the articles to look like an authentic newspaper of the colonial time period.

## What type of newspaper article do I write?

You will choose to write a feature article, a news article, or an editorial. However, you must have a group discussion about who is writing which kind of article so that there is a balance among the three types of newspaper articles. In addition, you will make one other contribution to the paper (see "What else do I contribute to the newspaper?"). Use the checklist and graphic organizer for each article type to guide you while writing.

## What else do I contribute to the newspaper?

- **Advertisement**—The ad must reflect the time period. Consider what kinds of ads would be appropriate before creating one, such as persuading someone to fight for a side or to buy a certain colonial product.
- **"Flag"**—Create a flag for the newspaper that includes a name, date, and location.
- **Maps with captions**—Include one or more historically accurate maps with captions to accompany articles.
- **Illustrations**—Include one or more illustrations with captions.

## What do I write about?

Each of you will select a **topic** for your article. Within your article, you must address at least **two guiding questions** and write from the **perspective** of either a Loyalist or Patriot. As a group, discuss which questions you will each address in your article so that your group newspaper addresses all guiding questions.

| Guiding Questions | Topics | |
|---|---|---|
| 1. How can differences in political and economic beliefs and interests create conflict? | A. French and Indian War | M. Paul Revere |
| | B. Stamp Act (and Sugar Act) | N. Samuel Adams |
| 2. How can people who share interests work together to change for the better? | C. Townshend Acts | O. George Washington |
| | D. Boston Massacre | P. Thomas Paine/ *Common Sense* |
| | E. Boston Tea Party | |
| 3. How might political independence create risks and rewards? | F. Coercive or Intolerable Acts | Q. Thomas Jefferson |
| | G. Iroquois Confederacy | R. Patrick Henry |
| 4. How do government documents reflect key political ideals and a system of government? | H. Committees of Correspondence | S. Ben Franklin |
| | I. First Continental Congress | T. King George III |
| | J. Second Continental Congress | U. John Adams |
| 5. How can individuals make a difference in creating political change? | K. Declaration of Independence | V. Loyalists |
| | L. "Taxation without representation" | W. Patriots |

## How do I get information for my article?

Use multiple sources to get the content you need for your article, such as facts, details, examples, quotes, and definitions. Your textbook can be one source, but use others, such as reliable websites, books, and other resources. Use the school and classroom library, as well as the public library, for resources.

**FIGURE 4.3**

# News Story Checklist

## Ideas/Content and Organization

☐ I write a <u>news story</u> with a lead and supporting paragraphs.

☐ I focus my news story on a <u>particular topic</u> and also respond to the <u>guiding questions.</u>

☐ I write an attention-grabbing and appropriate <u>headline.</u>

☐ I include a <u>byline</u> and <u>dateline.</u>

☐ I <u>indent</u> each paragraph appropriately.

☐ My news story follows the <u>inverted pyramid</u> format so my most important information is at the beginning in the lead, and the least important is at the end.

### ➡ Beginning (Lead)

☐ My <u>lead paragraph</u> answers the questions <u>who, what, where,</u> and <u>when.</u> The lead includes the most important facts about my topic.

### ➡ Middle

☐ My <u>body paragraphs are clearly structured,</u> with topic sentence, support, and ending sentence.

☐ I <u>support each topic sentence</u> by using <u>evidence,</u> such as facts, quotes, data, and/or examples from many credible sources. I answer the <u>why</u> and <u>how.</u>

☐ I <u>cite my sources</u> so readers know where I got my information.

### ➡ Ending

☐ My <u>ending</u> includes the least important details of the news event.

## Word Choice

☐ I use specific and accurate <u>vocabulary</u> suited to my topic.

☐ My <u>news story does not include unclear language</u> since I use specific verbs and nouns to explain the news event.

## Conventions

☐ I use correct <u>punctuation and capitalization</u> in my news story and headline, and also for any quotations.

☐ I <u>spell</u> all words correctly.

☐ I use <u>correct formatting.</u> My news story, title, and any illustrations complement the formatting of the other items in this group newspaper and reflect the colonial period.

☐ My sentences make sense and do not have <u>grammar</u> errors.

☐ I write using <u>present tense verbs</u> since my news story reflects a current colonial period event.

## Sentence Fluency

☐ I write <u>complete sentences</u> and do not include fragments or run-ons.

☐ I use <u>a variety of sentence structures:</u> simple, compound, and complex.

☐ My <u>sentence beginnings vary</u> so that each sentence does not start in the same way.

## Voice

☐ I write my news story in <u>third-person point of view.</u> I keep this consistent point of view throughout my article.

☐ I know to whom (<u>audience</u>) I am writing and why (<u>purpose</u>) I am writing.

**FIGURE 4.4**

# News Story Organizer

Perspective: _____ Loyalist _____ Tory

| Event | |
|---|---|
| What newsworthy event happened that you will cover in your article? | What guiding questions will you address that relate to this event? |

| Beginning (Lead) | |
|---|---|
| Who? | What? |
| Where? | When? |

| Middle (Why? How?) | |
|---|---|
| Topic Sentence 1 | Support—What is your evidence? Use facts, quotes, data, and/or examples from many credible sources to answer the *why* and *how*. |
| List sources: | |
| Topic Sentence 2 | Support—What is your evidence? Use facts, quotes, data, and/or examples from many credible sources to answer the *why* and *how*. |
| List sources: | |
| Topic Sentence 3 | Support—What is your evidence? Use facts, quotes, data, and/or examples from many credible sources to answer the *why* and *how*. |
| List sources: | |

| Ending |
|---|
| Identify the least important details: |

**FIGURE 4.5**

# Character Highlights

## Speech

Write a speech that a character might make about one of the following:

☐ a particular event or situation
☐ a conflict
☐ another character

In the speech, respond to the guiding questions. Then, deliver the speech to the class live or pretaped as if you were this character. Submit the typed speech to your teacher after delivering it.

## Illustrations

Draw a series of detailed, creative, and accurate illustrations that reflect a character's feelings or decisions about an event or situation, a conflict, or another character. Beneath each drawing, provide an appropriate caption. Make sure to address the guiding questions in your project. Present these pictures in an order that makes sense.

## Research

Write 8 to 10 questions that you would want to pose to a character if you had the chance to meet. Include the guiding questions in your list along with other questions you want answered. Then, answer each question. You can do this activity with a partner in which you each pose questions, and then discuss answers to your partner's questions. Submit neatly typed and formatted questions and answers to your teacher.

## Poetry or Prose

Choose a character. Then write prose or poetry using these line starters based on your reaction to this character's achievements, contributions, or decisions. Include the guiding questions in your work. Create an original title.

☐ I wish that …       ☐ I see that …
☐ I realize            ☐ I believe
   that …                 that …
☐ I decide            ☐ I feel that …
   that …              ☐ I hope
☐ I wonder               that …
   about …

**FIGURE 4.6**

# Project Choices

Choose one of these projects to demonstrate your understanding of our unit. Make sure you *address all guiding questions* in whichever project you select. You will present your project to the class. Read the "Project Checklist" to guide you as you work.

### Game

Create a game that includes game cards, directions, a game board, and anything else that others would need to actually play the game. Provide questions as well as answers. Be creative in the visual appeal of the game and the strategy required to play.

### Play

Write a script and perform a play. You may perform your play live or videotape it and show it to the class. Use props and costumes. For the script, include narration and actors'/actresses' lines. Make sure to have a beginning, middle, and end. Submit your script to your teacher.

### Song

Create lyrics to a song. You might create a song from scratch by making up the melody and lyrics, or you might create lyrics to a familiar tune. Record the song on audio- or videotape and share it with the class. If you play an instrument, use it as you sing. Include a chorus and at least three verses. Submit your song lyrics to your teacher.

### Picture Poster

Create a picture poster in which you create five drawings accompanied by captions that are each at least four sentences. First make a poster layout in which you draft the text and sketch drawings before finalizing your project. Remember to provide a title for your poster.

### Technology

Choose a project using technology, such as a PowerPoint, iMovie, or other ideas you have. Get approval before beginning your project to determine expectations.

### Trial

You are a prosecuting attorney putting one of the people you learned about on trial for a crime or misdeed this person has committed. Prepare your case on paper with all your arguments and support each one with facts from the person on trial's life. You may videotape yourself in a mock trial, using friends or family to play roles in a court scene. Submit the written version of the case to your teacher.

### Party

Plan a party for a guest list based on our unit. Complete each of the following to ensure a successful party: (1) design an invitation to the party which would appeal to those coming, (2) describe what each person should wear to the party, (3) explain the menu for the party from appetizers to dessert, and (4) describe the games or entertainment in detail. Display this information however you see fit, such as poster, technology, book, or other way.

### Short Story or Sequel

Write a short story or sequel focusing our unit's guiding questions. Your writing should include a *setting, character, plot,* and *point of view.* Also write descriptive details to make it interesting. Feel free to include pictures for your story.

### Radio or TV Interview

Create a script and then tape an interview of someone related to our unit.

Pretend the person is being interviewed by a magazine or newspaper reporter. Introduce the person at the beginning of the radio or TV program and ask intriguing questions that would interest the listener, including the guiding questions. Have a friend or family member ask the interview questions while you assume the role of the figure. If you are videotaping the program, wear a realistic costume. Creativity is encouraged, such as including introductory music for the program, any necessary sound effects, pertinent commercials, and so forth. Submit your script to your teacher.

**FIGURE 4.7**

# Project Checklist

## PROJECT

☐ I <u>show I am knowledgeable about this topic.</u> It is obvious that I have done my research.

☐ It is clear that I read the "Project Choices" sheet because I <u>satisfy each point for my chosen project.</u>

☐ I respond to all the <u>unit guiding questions</u> accurately and thoroughly.

☐ I include <u>at least five facts</u> in my project.

☐ I <u>use accurate terms and descriptive words.</u> I have checked all of my facts to make sure they are correct.

☐ My writing includes <u>proper grammar and conventions</u> (periods, capitalization, punctuation).

☐ I <u>indent</u> as needed.

☐ If my project requires <u>artwork,</u> it is colorful, accurate, creative, and neat.

☐ My writing is <u>organized</u> in a way that makes sense and all of my main points are clearly written.

☐ It is obvious that I have done my <u>personal best.</u>

## PRESENTATION

☐ I <u>rehearse</u> several times in preparation for my presentation.

☐ I <u>make note cards</u> for my presentation, if appropriate.

☐ I practice my words so that I do not need to look down at my note cards too frequently. I <u>look at the audience</u> while presenting.

☐ When I speak, I make sure I am <u>loud</u> enough for everyone to hear.

☐ I make sure I <u>speak clearly.</u>

☐ My <u>pacing is good</u> – it's not too slow or too fast.

☐ My presentation is <u>organized</u> so it is easy for the listener to understand my main points.

☐ I review all of my notes and am <u>prepared for any questions</u> that the audience will ask me.

**FIGURE 4.8**

## Nonfiction Game

| | END |
|---|---|
| What did you learn that you didn't already know? | What fact from the book is the most interesting to you? Why? |
| What is an index? Find the index in your book and show it to your group. | Explain the meaning of two words that you learned from this book. |
| Explain how this book is organized. | What else do you want to know about this topic that isn't in the book? |
| Why are some words in bold type? | Find a labeled picture, chart, or diagram in your book. |
| If you could talk to the author, what would you tell him or her? | Summarize what you learned. |
| Was anything confusing about the book? Ask questions to your group about what confused you. | What new words can you use this week that you learned from the book? How would you use them? |

| What is the title of the book? Who is the author and illustrator? | What are other topics that are similar to this topic? |
|---|---|
| What is a table of contents? Does your book have one? | |
| What is a caption? Find a caption in your book. | |
| If you don't know what a word means, where do you go in the book to help you? | |
| What are two facts that are in the book? | |
| **START** | |

**FIGURE 4.9**

## RUBRICS

To assess culminating products, teachers use rubrics—comprised of a set of criteria directly linked to standards and learning objectives—to assess student performance on a targeted written essay or project. You have undoubtedly seen various types of rubrics, and have probably noticed that most have these two unvarying elements: performance factors and levels of quality. The performance factors can be general, but they are more effective in giving students feedback and assessing their work if they are written for a specific assignment (e.g., topic sentence, specific details, descriptive word, etc.). Quality levels can be numerical, in word form, or a combination of both. For example, the rubric can be written on a 4-, 5-, or 6-point scale or include words like *developing, emergent, capable, advanced,* and *exemplary.* Figure 4.10 illustrates these rubric features and the gradation of quality levels; have yourself a chuckle reading it.

## Performance Factors

| ↓ | Outstanding | Very Effective | Effective | Marginally Effective | Ineffective |
|---|---|---|---|---|---|
| **Producing Quality Work** | Leaps tall buildings at a single bound | Must take a running start to leap over tall buildings | Can only leap over short buildings or medium buildings (no spires) | Crashes into buildings when attempting to jump over them | Cannot recognize buildings at all, let alone jump them |
| **Using Work Time Effectively** | Is faster than a speeding bullet | Is as fast as a speeding bullet | Not quite as fast as a speeding bullet | Would you believe a slow bullet? | Wounds self with bullets when attempting to shoot gun |
| **Accepting Responsibility** | Is stronger than a locomotive | Is stronger than a tornado | Is stronger than a hurricane | Shoots the breeze | Full of hot air |
| **Job Knowledge** | Walks on water consistently | Walks on water in emergencies | Washes with water | Drinks water | Eyes water |
| **Communicating Effectively** | Talks with God | Talks with employees | Talks to himself/ herself | Argues with himself/ herself | Loses arguments with himself/ herself |

**FIGURE 4.10** Sample Rubric

*Source:* Kadushin, A., & Harkness, D. (2002). *Supervision in social work* (4th ed.). New York: Columbia University Press.

The rubrics included in this chapter, and others throughout the book, align to the Common Core Standards, although I include additional line items in some rubrics. I found that as I was writing these rubrics using the Common Core Standards, there were additional expectations I required of students, such as *title, maintaining consistent point of view,* and *descriptive setting.* So, slight additions appear where I felt it was necessary to include the full spectrum of criteria to satisfy a writing assignment. You might ask: *How can I add criteria?* The designers of the Common Core do welcome teachers to use their professional expertise, and I made sure not to delete Common Core Standards because students will be assessed against them. If you are making significant changes, be mindful to follow proper implementation guidelines, especially if rubric design is a districtwide endeavor. (For more information, see the section "Can States Add to the Standards?" in the Resource, "A Brief Primer on the ELA Common Core Standards," for specifics on the 15% Guideline.)

The rubric format for Figure 4.11, Personal Narrative, is one you might be most familiar with and one that I have regularly used in the past. In recent years, however, I have switched to another format that is featured in all other examples in this book, including Figures 4.12, Opinion Writing Rubric (Grade 2) and 4.13, Fable Rubric (Primary). In using this alternate format, teachers and I have found two key benefits: (1) targeted skills or concepts are highlighted and assessed for a specific assignment (e.g., description, sentence variety, temporal words, dialogue punctuation, plot development, etc.); (2) it gives students concrete feedback for improvement in each of these areas.

A list of rubrics in or referenced in Chapter 3 is as follows:

- Figure 3.4—Primary Rubric: Informative/Explanatory Writing
- Figure 3.9—Narrative: Short Story Rubric
- Figure 3.13—Opinion Writing Rubric (Upper Elementary)

A list of rubrics here in Chapter 4 is as follows:

- Figure 4.11—Personal Narrative Rubric (Elementary)
- Figure 4.12—Opinion Writing Rubric (Grade 2)
- Figure 4.13—Fable Rubric (Primary)

*(Text continued on page 117)*

# Personal Narrative Rubric (Elementary)

| | | 4<br>**Advanced** | 3<br>**Capable** | 2<br>**Developing** | 1<br>**Emergent** |
|---|---|---|---|---|---|
| **Ideas/Content and Organization** | **Title** | Original and captures the central theme of the piece | Appropriate/functional | Unoriginal | Not present or does not match the content |
| | **Main Idea** | Develops one clear, main idea without ever getting off-track; a grade level or more above in sophistication | Develops a clear, main idea that stays on-topic | Generally stays on-topic, but may get off-track | Unfocused, off-track, and may include disconnected thoughts |
| | **Indenting** | First sentence indented using three fingers; if multiple paragraphs used, all indented appropriately | First sentence indented using three fingers | Attempts to indent, but not indented clearly because may only use one finger or letter space | No sense of indenting |
| | **Logical Order** | Details occur in the order in which the event took place; logical and effective sequencing | Logical sequencing present; one minor detail off-sequence | Little logical sequencing | Order of details seems haphazard and rambling; gets in the way of reading |
| | **Beginning** | Includes many details about setting and characters; grabs the reader's attention | Includes some details about setting and characters | Weak or incomplete | No sense of beginning |
| | **Middle** | Explains what happened clearly; a grade level or more above in sophistication | Explains what happened so the reader understands event | Explanation of event weakly stated | No sense of middle; actual event not explained |
| | **Ending** | Leaves the reader with a sense of closure and resolution; originally stated | Present; attempts to provide sufficient closure | Weak; does not tie up loose ends or repeats beginning | No sense of ending |
| | **Transitions** | Entirely appropriate temporal words to signal event order | Mostly appropriate temporal words to signal event order | Missing temporal words or inappropriate ones used | No temporal words to signal event order |

| | | | | | |
|---|---|---|---|---|---|
| **Word Choice** | **Descriptive Words** | Lively verbs and unique, specific adjectives and nouns consistently used; no repetition and unclear language | Sometimes uses lively verbs and specific adjectives and nouns; might use some repetition and unclear language | Few lively verbs or specific adjectives or nouns; repetitive | No lively verbs or specific adjectives or nouns; unclear language |
| **Sentence Fluency** | **Fragments/ Run-Ons** | Writes all complete sentences (no fragments) and does not string two sentences together (no run-ons) | May have one fragment or run-on | Two fragments and/or run-ons | No sense of complete sentence; paper ridden with fragments and run-ons |
| **Conventions** | **Spelling** | Correct, even on more difficult words | Correct on common words, but more difficult words spelled phonetically | Frequent errors, even on common words | Replete with spelling errors; writing too difficult to read and interpret due to spelling errors |
| | **Punctuation** | Entirely accurate; may have quotes used correctly | Usually correct; one minor error | Often incorrect | Missing |
| | **Capitalization** | Appropriate words capitalized correctly | Appropriate words capitalized correctly, although one minor error present | Several capitalization errors | Capitals and lowercase letters used haphazardly |
| | **Grammar** | Grammar and usage always correct | Appropriate grammar and usage used, although one minor error present | Several grammatical errors | Grammar and usage almost always incorrect, which contributes to lack of clarity and style |
| | **Penmanship/ Neatness** | Legible; paper neat and taken care of; margins and spacing appropriately used | Legible, although may have one word difficult to discern; paper neat; margins and spacing used appropriately | Some places difficult to read due to illegible handwriting; somewhat messy; margins and/or spacing haphazard | Whole paper difficult to read due to illegible handwriting; paper messy, smudged, and/or improperly folded; use of margins and/or spacing lacking |
| **Voice** | **First-Person Point of View** | Consistently uses first-person point of view | Mostly uses first-person point of view appropriately | Some errors in using first-person point of view pronouns | Writing in third- or second-person point of view; consistently switches point of view |

**FIGURE 4.11**

# Opinion Writing Rubric (Grade 2)

| | Components | Points | |
|---|---|---|---|
| **Ideas/Content and Organization** | **Title**<br><br>Include title. | **4**—Original, sophisticated title<br>**3**—Accurate title | **2**—Unrelated or weak title<br>**1**—No title |
| | **Topic**<br><br>Introduce the topic or name of the book as the basis for writing (NGA, 2010, W.2.1). | **4**—Clear introduction of topic or name of book as the basis for writing<br>**3**—Adequate introduction of topic or name of book as the basis for writing | **2**—Weakly stated introduction of topic or name of book as basis for writing<br>**1**— No introduction to alert reader to the topic or name of book as the basis for writing |
| | **Opinion**<br><br>State an opinion (W.2.1). | **4**—Clearly stated opinion<br>**3**—Somewhat clearly stated opinion | **2**—Weakly stated opinion<br>**1**—Unclear about opinion or not stated |
| | **Reasons**<br><br>Supply reasons that support the opinion (W.2.1). | **4**—Thoroughly developed reasons that clearly support opinion<br>**3**—Somewhat developed reasons that generally support opinion | **2**—Unclear or limited reasons that weakly support opinion<br>**1**—No reasons stated |
| | **Conclusion**<br><br>Provide concluding statement or section (W.2.1). | **4**—Developed conclusion<br>**3**—Provides a sense of closure | **2**—Weak conclusion<br>**1**—No conclusion |
| **Word Choice** | **Word Choice**<br><br>Use adjectives and adverbs, and choose between them depending on what is to be modified (L.2.1e). | **4**—Entirely strong, descriptive adjectives and adverbs<br>**3**—Adequate use of adjectives and adverbs | **2**—Weak or minimal use of adjectives and/or adverbs<br>**1**— No adjectives or adverbs |
| **Voice** | **Point of View**<br><br>Write in consistent first-person point of view throughout paper. | **4**—Consistent use of first-person point of view<br>**3**—May get off-track once | **2**—Weak sense of point of view<br>**1**—Whole paper in third person or a combination of first, second (you), and third |
| | **Audience/Purpose**<br><br>Show awareness of audience and purpose. | **4**—Clearly aware of both audience and purpose of writing<br>**3**—Aware of audience or purpose | **2**—Unclear about audience and purpose<br>**1**—Unaware of audience and purpose; off-topic |

| | | 4—All complete sentences<br>3—Some run-ons or fragments | 2—Many run-ons and fragments<br>1—Unclear about sentence structure altogether |
|---|---|---|---|
| **Sentence Fluency** | **Complete Sentences**<br>Avoid run-ons and fragments. | 4—All complete sentences<br>3—Some run-ons or fragments | 2—Many run-ons and fragments<br>1—Unclear about sentence structure altogether |
| | **Sentence Variety**<br>Produce, expand, and rearrange complete simple and compound sentences (L.2.1f). | 4—Thoughtful and consistent use of sentence variety; sophisticated<br>3—Sometimes uses sentence variety | 2—Most sentences with the same sentence structure so there is little cadence<br>1—All sentences with the same structure; halted reading |
| | **Linking Words**<br>Use linking words (e.g., *because, and, also*) to connect opinion and reasons (W.2.1). | 4—Thoughtful use of transitions; sophisticated<br>3—Some use of transitions | 2—Weak use of transition; repetition<br>1—No transitions |
| **Conventions** | **Spelling**<br>Generalize learned spelling patterns when writing words; consult reference materials, including beginning dictionaries, as needed to check and correct spelling (L.2.2d, e). | 4—Consistent use of correct spelling<br>3—Mostly spells correctly | 2—Weak command of spelling<br>1—No sense of spelling or phonemic rules |
| | **Grammar**<br>Demonstrate command of the conventions of standard English grammar and usage (L.2.1). | 4—Consistent use of proper grammar<br>3—Mostly uses grammar correctly | 2—Weak grasp of grammar<br>1—No sense of grammar rules |
| | **Capitalization**<br>Capitalizes holidays, product names, and geographic names (L.2.2a) and *I*. | 4—Consistently capitalizes correctly<br>3—Mostly capitalizes correctly | 2—Weak capitalization<br>1—No sense of what to capitalize |
| | **Punctuation**<br>Demonstrate a command of the conventions of standard English punctuation (L.2.2). | 4—Consistently uses punctuation marks correctly<br>3—Mostly uses punctuation marks correctly | 2—Unclear about how to use punctuation marks<br>1—No use of punctuation marks |

**FIGURE 4.12**

# Fable Rubric (Primary)

| | Components | Points |
|---|---|---|
| **Ideas/Content and Organization** | **Title**<br><br>Include original title. | 5—Extremely original; sophisticated<br>3—Title present and matches fable content<br>1—No title or unrelated title |
| | **Description**<br><br>Use frequently occurring adjectives (NGA, 2010, L.1.1f); use words and phrases acquired through conversations, reading and being read to, and responding to texts (L.1.6). | 5—Uses entirely strong description and sensory details for character, setting, and/or plot<br>3—Adequate use of description and sensory details for character, setting, and/or plot<br>1—No description |
| | **Logical Sequence of Events**<br><br>Recount two or more appropriately sequenced events regarding what happened; include some details regarding what happened (W.1.3). | 5—Entirely logical sequence for two or more events; thoroughly developed details<br>3—Somewhat logical sequence; makes sense to reader; adequately developed details<br>1—No events to sequence |
| | **Ending**<br><br>Provide some sense of closure (W.1.3); state moral. | 5—Developed ending; moral clearly stated<br>3—Adequate ending; moral somewhat stated<br>1—No ending or moral |
| **Voice** | **Audience/Purpose**<br><br>Show awareness of audience and purpose. | 5—Clearly aware of both audience and purpose for writing<br>3—Aware of audience or purpose<br>1—Unaware of audience and purpose; off-topic |
| **Sentence Fluency** | **Complete Sentences**<br><br>Produce and expand complete simple and compound declarative and exclamatory sentences in response to prompts (L.1.1j). | 5—All complete sentences; sophisticated sentence variety<br>3—Combination of simple and compound sentences<br>1—Unclear about sentence structure altogether |
| | **Temporal Words**<br><br>Use temporal words to signal event order (W.1.3). | 5—Thoughtful use of transitions; sophisticated transitions<br>3—Uses transitions to signal event order; sometimes can be repetitive<br>1—Weak or no transitions |
| **Presentation/Conventions** | **Presentation**<br><br>Use legible penmanship; submit all papers neatly. | 5—Very neat paper and penmanship<br>3—Adequately neat; mostly legible<br>1—Unacceptably messy; poor penmanship |
| | **Grammar**<br><br>Use singular and plural nouns with matching verbs in basic sentences (e.g., He hops. We hop.) (L.1.1c); use verbs to convey a sense of past, present, and future (e.g., Yesterday I walked home. Today I walk home.) (L.1.1e). | 5—Few, if any, errors<br>3—Some errors that do not interfere with reading<br>1—Several errors that interfere with reading |

| Conventions<br><br>Use end punctuation for sentences (L.1.2b); capitalize the first word in a sentence (L.K.2a); use conventional spelling for words with common spelling patterns and for frequently occurring irregular words (L.1.2d); spell untaught words phonetically, drawing on phonemic awareness and spelling conventions (L.1.2e). | 5—Few, if any, errors<br>3—Some errors that do not interfere with reading<br>1—Several errors that interfere with reading |
|---|---|

*Note:* Teachers can score a 2 or 4 for any line item, as needed.

**FIGURE 4.13**

Rubrics are used to score student work at all grades. However, some teachers present it to students in the upper elementary grades so they are clear about criteria. In this regard, they use the rubric as a teaching tool to score student and published samples and are careful to focus on a few line items at a time. Otherwise, students might feel overwhelmed, and it would negate the purpose of sharing the rubric.

The far left column of each rubric shows any alignment with the Common Core Standards by referencing specific standards in parentheses (e.g., W.1.3 = Writing Strand/Grade 1/Standard 3). As mentioned, I insert other pertinent expectations and list them without a code so they are not misconstrued as part of the Common Core Standards. Figure 4.14 illustrates two line item examples from an upper elementary narrative rubric. For easy reference, the Common Core Standards are in bold and italicized type here and are followed by the letter/number identification. In the completed rubrics, I show the identifications only.

| Beginning<br><br>*Orient the reader by establishing a situation and introducing a narrator and/or characters* (NGA, 2010, W.4.3a); create an interesting and attention-getting beginning; include description of setting; central conflict stated. | 4—<u>Very clearly</u> interesting and attention getting; description of setting and main character thoroughly and clearly stated without too much detail; <u>very clear</u> central conflict; sophisticated<br><br>3—<u>Somewhat</u> interesting and attention getting; description of setting and main character stated; central conflict <u>clearly</u> stated<br><br>2—<u>Minimally</u> interesting and attention getting; description of setting and main character <u>weakly</u> included; central conflict <u>weakly</u> stated<br><br>1—<u>Incomplete</u> and fails to draw in the reader; description of setting and main character <u>minimal or absent</u>; <u>unclear or no</u> central conflict |
|---|---|
| Conclusion<br><br>*Provide a conclusion that follows from the narrated experiences or events* (W.4.3e); answer questions a reader might have about what happened; not abrupt. | 4—Resolved <u>completely</u>; <u>all</u> questions answered; sophisticated<br>3—Resolved with <u>most</u> questions answered<br>2—Weak ending; reader left with <u>many unanswered</u> questions<br>1—<u>No</u> ending |

**FIGURE 4.14**  Sample Rubric Excerpt 1

Rubrics to score student writing rely on some subjectivity by virtue of the wide variance of possibilities, even within a range of student products. Therefore, writing rubrics use adverbs to help differentiate one level from the next. Below are some common adverb groupings that appear on scoring guides. The 3—whether it be on a 4- or 5-point rubric—typically denotes at-grade-level work. Scores of 4 or 5 are challenging to achieve and represent sophistication beyond the grade level.

- 4—thoroughly; 3—adequately; 2—minimally/weak; 1—lacks/none
- 4—entirely; 3—mostly/generally; 2—some; 1—hardly
- 4—clearly; 3—sometimes/some/somewhat; 2—limited; 1—marginally
- 4—minor (errors); 3—some (errors); 2—many (errors); 1—serious (errors)

It is altogether understandable to use *sometimes/some/somewhat* as a 3 (at grade level) for certain line items and *generally/mostly* as a 3 for other line items within the same grade. This would indicate that some line items are a clearer expectation for a certain grade, whereas other benchmarks are still developing. The excerpts in Figure 4.15 from a first-grade narrative writing rubric illustrate this point.

| **Events** Include details to describe what happened (NGA, 2010, W.1.3). | 4—Thoroughly developed details 3—Some details 2—Little details 1—No details |
|---|---|
| **Capitalization** Capitalize dates and names or people (L.1.2a); and the letter *I*. | 4—Consistently capitalizes correctly 3—Mostly capitalizes correctly 2—Weak capitalization 1—No sense of what to capitalize |

**FIGURE 4.15** Sample Rubric Excerpt 2

By the same token, you can differentiate from grade to grade by using *sometimes/some* as the 3 (at grade level) for a lower grade and *generally* as a 3 for a higher grade level, because you have elevated expectations in the upper grade. For example, take the narrative device of *suspense*. In fourth or fifth grade, you might have *some use of suspense* or *attempts suspense* as a 3. However, in middle school, the 3 might indicate *clear use of suspense*. Note that in the Common Core Standards K–8 (NGA, 2010), the narrative device of suspense is not mentioned in writing. Nonetheless, it is a critical narrative device and one I suggest including in your rubrics in the middle school. You might, however, create differentiated rubrics and expect high achievers to challenge themselves to the next level and assign indicators to each rubric number accordingly.

You will notice for the language standards, specifically grammar and conventions skills, that there are two choices of criteria in some rubrics. As mentioned in the preceding chapter with the narrative and opinion writing rubrics that accompany the unit maps, one is quantitative; the other is more subjective. Figure 4.16 provides a specific example; decide with your colleagues which treatment provides the best feedback to your students for improvement.

| | Quantitative | Subjective |
|---|---|---|
| **Capitalization**<br><br>Use correct capitalization (NGA, 2010, L.4.2a). | 4—One error<br>3—Two to three errors<br>2—Four to six errors<br>1—Seven or more errors | 4—No errors<br>3—Minimal errors<br>2—Several errors<br>1—Serious errors; hinders reading |

**FIGURE 4.16**   Quantitative Versus Subjective Scoring

Much like some districts that identify certain standards as *focus* or *power* or *essential,* this can be reflected in the rubrics by weighting certain line items. Or you might merely allot more points for extra emphasis because a particular line item is not only a focus but constitutes a large part of the student's product. See the example in Figure 4.17.

| **Precise Words/Descriptive Details/Sensory Language**<br><br>Use concrete words and phrases and sensory details to convey experiences and events precisely (NGA, 2010, W.4.3d) and for setting; use description to develop experiences and events or show the responses of characters to situations (W.4.3b). | 8—Consistent, sophisticated use of precise words and phrases, relevant descriptive details, and sensory language to capture action and convey experiences/events, setting, and character<br><br>6—Some use of precise words and phrases, relevant descriptive details, and sensory language to capture action and convey experiences/events, setting, and character<br><br>4—Limited use of precise words and phrases, relevant descriptive details, and sensory language to capture action and convey experiences/events, setting, and character<br><br>2—Rare or no use of precise words and phrases, relevant descriptive details, and sensory language to capture action and convey experiences/events, setting, and character |
|---|---|

**FIGURE 4.17**   Sample Weighted Rubric Excerpt

Note that the rubrics like Figure 4.17 and other figures may be construed as generous in issuing a 2 and 1 (Figure 4.16) on the bottom line items instead of a 0. I suggest you have a discussion with your colleagues about how to treat papers that have nonexistent elements. Whatever you decide, surely be consistent so individual teachers aren't operating on their own set of criteria for scoring.

Addressed in the previous chapter and again here, a significant issue raised around the topic of rubrics is how to translate number scores to letter grades. Teachers frequently ask me about this. If you or your teachers issue letter grades, it would behoove you to read the explanation and use the mathematical conversion found in Chapter 3, Figure 3.14, Vicki Spandel's 4-6-8-10 Rule. To reiterate, it is a simplistic way to convert number scores from the rubric to letter scores.

It works like magic for all the clients I serve as it seems to grant students the letter grade a teacher might issue had the paper been scored holistically. To record the scores, some teachers merely use the rubric and highlight line items and put the score at the bottom of the page in a box (see Figure 3.13). On the reverse side of the sheet, teachers can enter additional comments. Since the line items of the rubric are quite specific, comments might include emphasizing a particular strength and one area students might focus on for the next assignment.

## CHECKLISTS

Whereas not all teachers introduce rubrics directly to students because it is not age appropriate, checklists should be front center for all students so they are clear about an assignment's expectations. For primary, you can use a simplified checklist for those who can read it. For those who are not yet reading, continue to reference the checklist and read it often for exposure. Include pictures to help with understanding, as well, like in Figure 4.18 for fables.

Following is a list of checklists in this and the previous chapter. By reading each checklist, you can determine the nature of each assignment. Many can be modified or extended to meet the needs of your student group if the topic is suitable. The criteria on the checklists are categorized according to the six traits, which is a model for instruction and assessment in writing (e.g., ideas/content, word choice, conventions, etc.). You might have noticed that the rubrics are similarly grouped. However, there are other subheadings you can use to cluster line items, such as sentence structure, style, mechanics, development, and so forth.

A list of checklists in Chapter 3 is as follows:

- Figure 3.8—Short Story Student Checklist
- Figure 3.12—Opinion Writing Student Checklist (three differentiated versions)

A list of checklists here in Chapter 4 is as follows:

- *Figure 4.4 News Story Checklist.* Although this checklist supports the Revolutionary War assignment sheet (Figure 4.3), it is purposefully void of references to the war so teachers can use it for other units of study where a newspaper assignment might be appropriate.
- *Figure 4.8 Project Checklist.* As stated earlier in the chapter, this checklist accompanies the multiple intelligence project choices in Figure 4.7. However, it is fairly generic and can work with an assignment a teacher might create.
- *Figures 4.18 and 4.19 Fable Checklist/Primary.* Figure 4.18 is for all students. Figure 4.19 has two choices. The page with a clover symbol (found on the companion website) might be more suitable for at-grade-level students; the page with a spade symbol might work well for your more advanced students.
- *Figure 4.20 All About Animals Checklist.* This checklist can be used for elementary students as they address the informative/explanatory writing standard. It is designed to be a differentiated assignment in which students choose an animal that interests them as the basis for writing an all-about book featuring their selected topic.
- *Figures 4.21 and 4.22 Conventions Student Checklists.* I worked on these conventions checklists with primary teachers in the Hillsborough School District in Hillsborough, California, to use for most any writing assignment for these younger students. Figure 4.22 includes pictures for those students needing this support, and also earlier in the year with the goal of transitioning to Figure 4.21 later in the school year when students become more adept.

# Fable Checklist (Primary)

### Directions

I write a **fable** based on one that I have read and heard in class. I use this checklist as I write to guide me.

### Ideas/Content and Organization

☐ I <u>retell</u> a folktale in writing based on one I have already read or heard.

☐ I include a <u>title.</u>

I <u>begin</u> my folktale with

☐ a descriptive <u>setting</u>

☐ descriptive <u>characters</u>

☐ the problem

☐ In the middle of my folktale, I tell about the <u>events</u> that happen.

☐ I <u>end</u> by telling how the <u>problem is solved</u> and write the <u>moral.</u>

☐ I make sure I <u>stay on topic.</u>

**FIGURE 4.18 Fable Checklist (Primary)—Page 1**

## ♠ Fable Checklist (Primary) ♠

### Voice

☐ I know <u>why I am writing</u> (purpose) and
who will <u>read this paper</u> (audience).

☐ I write in <u>third-person point of view</u> since I write about what
happens to others.

### Sentence Fluency

☐ I write <u>complete sentences.</u>

☐ I have <u>no run-on sentences.</u>

☐ My <u>sentences begin in different ways.</u>

☐ I use <u>order words</u> to connect my sentences.

### Word Choice

☐ I include <u>sensory details</u> so my reader can picture what I am
writing.

☐ I use interesting <u>adjectives and verbs.</u>

☐ I write <u>dialogue.</u>

### Conventions

☐ I use the sounds I know to <u>spell.</u> I use tools to help me.

☐ I use correct <u>end marks</u> at the end of each sentence.

☐ I <u>capitalize</u> appropriate letters.

☐ I read my paper aloud and it <u>makes sense.</u>

☐ My writing is <u>easy to read</u>, and my paper is <u>neat.</u>

☐ I <u>properly space</u> my words and sentences.

**FIGURE 4.19    Fable Checklist (Primary)—Page 2, Differentiated**

# All About Animals Checklist

Write an all-about book for an animal. Use this checklist to guide you while writing.

## Ideas/Content and Organization

☐ I write an <u>all-about book</u> about one animal.
☐ I include a <u>cover page</u> that has the <u>main title</u> and <u>author.</u>
☐ I include a <u>table of contents.</u>
☐ My all-about book has these sections with a title for each section. The first section <u>introduces</u> my topic:

   ☐ <u>Different kinds or types of ...</u>
   ☐ <u>Labeled diagram</u>
   ☐ <u>Facts about ...</u>
   ☐ <u>Funny or strange facts about ...</u>
   ☐ <u>Lists</u>
   ☐ <u>Glossary</u>
   ☐ <u>About the author</u>

   ☐ _____

   ☐ _____

☐ <u>Each section of my book is formatted</u> in a special way.
☐ <u>Each section of my book teaches others</u> about my animal using <u>detail.</u>
☐ I include a <u>title for each new section.</u>
☐ I write paragraphs with a <u>topic sentence and detailed support</u> on appropriate pages.

## Word Choice

☐ I use <u>many new words</u> that I have learned.
☐ I <u>use synonyms</u> so I do not repeat the same words.

## Sentence Fluency

☐ I write <u>complete sentences.</u>
☐ I have <u>no</u> <u>run-on sentences.</u>
☐ My <u>sentences begin in different ways.</u>

## Conventions

☐ I <u>spell</u> all words correctly.
☐ I end my sentences with correct <u>punctuation.</u>
☐ I <u>capitalize</u> names, the pronoun *I*, and the beginning of each sentence.
☐ My <u>sentences make sense</u> and they sound right when I read them to someone else.
☐ I use my <u>best handwriting.</u> It looks like I took good care of my <u>paper</u> because it is <u>neat,</u> too.

**FIGURE 4.20**

# Conventions Student Checklist 1

### Spelling

☐ Do I double-check my spelling?
☐ Do I sound out words I do not know?

### Punctuation

☐ Do I use end marks at the end of each sentence?

### Capitalization

☐ Do I begin each name with a capital letter?
☐ Do I write the word *I* with a capital letter?
☐ Do I begin each sentence with a capital letter?

### Grammar/Usage

☐ Do my sentences make sense?

### Penmanship/Neatness

☐ Do I write as neatly as I can?
☐ Is my paper neat?
☐ Do I space between words and sentences?
☐ Do I use the margins like I should?

**FIGURE 4.21**

Checklists complement the rubrics; both are an expression of the guiding questions. For example, if a guiding question reads: *How do writers use sensory details to describe characters?* then line items on the checklist and rubric must include sensory details, characters, and description. The purpose of a checklist is twofold: (1) to guide students as they work on a project so they are clear about teacher expectations prior to beginning the task, and (2) for teachers to use as a guide for planning and conducting lessons. When students are aware of what a successful project includes through a student checklist or rubric that states expectations, they will have the opportunity to be more successful. Because you expect students to include these skills and concepts in their work, be prepared to teach lessons that are on the checklist and rubric. Furthermore, it is powerful to also show students samples of work and discuss how you would score these papers or projects against the checklist or rubric. It gives more substance to the checklist and rubric—and a higher degree of student success—if there are authentic pieces that highlight strengths and weaknesses of the criteria.

I encourage teachers to appropriately present a checklist to all students rather than merely handing it to them. If distributed without thoroughly engaging students in what is on the page, teachers will be disappointed when students do not use it as a tool. Be proactive, then, and present it formally to allow students to see clear expectations so they complete their task with these criteria top of mind. See Sample Lesson 5 in Chapter 7 for a detailed step-by-step lesson on how to introduce students to a checklist for a short story. You can adapt this lesson to any writing type since the important takeaway is to share what you expect before students write. If students are completing another project besides writing,

## Conventions Student Checklist 2

**Spelling**

☐ sight words

☐ sound out words

**Punctuation**

☐ end marks      . ! ?

**Capitalization**

☐ Sentences begin with a capital letter.

# <u>T</u>he dog ran.

☐ Names begin with a capital letter.

# <u>S</u>am

☐ The word *I* has a capital letter.

# Sam and <u>I</u> went to the park.

**Penmanship/Neatness**

☐ neat handwriting

☐ finger spacing

**FIGURE 4.22**

alter the lesson accordingly. Aren't you better at performing a task when you are clear at the outset about what is expected of you? Students will be too.

## PREASSESSMENTS

It is prudent to conduct a unit preassessment aligned to the unit goals to gauge students' readiness, interest, or learning style. Preassessments are also referred to as diagnostic assessments because it allows teachers to determine students' starting points prior to beginning a unit so they can plan accordingly for student grouping, individual students' strengths and weaknesses, acceleration or reteaching, and attending to other learning characteristics. Preassessments can also alert teachers to misconceptions and incorrect information students might have so they can address them.

It is not within the scope of this book to go into great detail on preassessments; however, I do provide some suggestions in this chapter. Figure 4.23, Elements of Literature Bookmarks, needs to be prepared as bookmarks prior to teachers conducting the preassessment. Copy the page on 100 lb. cardstock, laminate, and cut out these bookmark strips. Give two or more sets to each student. As students read their core novel, independent, or leveled reading books, ask them to insert the appropriate bookmark in the place where an element of literature appears. Walk around the room quietly and approach one student at a time and ask the student to explain why the bookmark is in the spot where it is. These brief conversations with students can provide valuable information about their knowledge of character, setting, and plot. This activity can serve as a preassessment and also be used again as a formative assessment.

# Elements of Literature Bookmarks

**FIGURE 4.23**

Using graphic organizers is one way to assess. Figure 4.24, Preassessment: Beginning, Middle, End, is self-explanatory. I created Figure 4.25 (Make a Web Preassessment) when I taught language arts and issued it before beginning a short story unit to determine what students knew about the elements of literature. The directions are clearly stated in this figure, whereby students take the provided words and phrases and arrange them in a way that makes sense in a graphic organizer they fashion. I also wanted text to support their web, outline, or other organizer, so I asked them to explain their reasoning in a paragraph. A sentence or two is fine, as well.

# Preassessment: Beginning, Middle, End

We will be learning about beginning, middle, and end of a story. Think about your whole day. Circle which part of the day you think this picture shows:

**beginning**       **middle**       **end**

We will read a story. In the chart below, draw a picture or write words or sentences to show beginning, middle, and end of the story.

| Beginning | Middle | End |
|---|---|---|
|  |  |  |
|  |  |  |

**FIGURE 4.24**

*Source:* Strickland and Glass (2009), page 25.

# Make a Web Preassessment

1. On a separate sheet of paper, create a web or other graphic organizer of your choice that uses the following words and phrases in a way that you think makes sense. If you want to add your own words or phrases to your organizer, please do.

| third person | plot | central conflict |
|---|---|---|
| when | character | introduction |
| first person | rising action | time |
| where | theme | place |
| point of view | falling action | elements |
| central message | antagonist | climax |
| setting | resolution | protagonist |

2. Write a paragraph that explains your web.

**FIGURE 4.25**

---

*Source:* Glass (2009), page 92.

The organizer coupled with your students' rationale will give you a clear idea of what they know about the elements—factual knowledge—and also any evidence of higher-order thinking. Some kids may not know the terms and association among the elements, but you can attain a clear sense of what they did or did not know from the combination of the organizer and their writing. Make sure to circulate around the room to observe student behavior during the exercise, which is another means of preassessment. Once they finish their organizers, collect their work and use the exercise as a springboard for discussion. As a class, you can fashion a web of the elements of literature and ask students to volunteer examples of each element based on literature. In lieu of a class-generated web, you can show Figure 4.26, which is a simplistic web you can use with primary age students. Figure 4.27 is for upper elementary, although you can introduce this more sophisticated web by first showing Figure 4.26.

When I reveal these figures, I explain to students that this web forms the basis of our upcoming unit, so it is incumbent upon me as their teacher to teach them these terms. So they won't feel overwhelmed by it, it is important to share with them that at this point many terms might be new to them. This is especially true for Figure 4.27. You can adapt this strategy to almost any content area or unit by using Figure 4.25 as a template for a preassessment prompt and replacing the terms and phrases for your unit of study.

# Elements of Literature Web 1

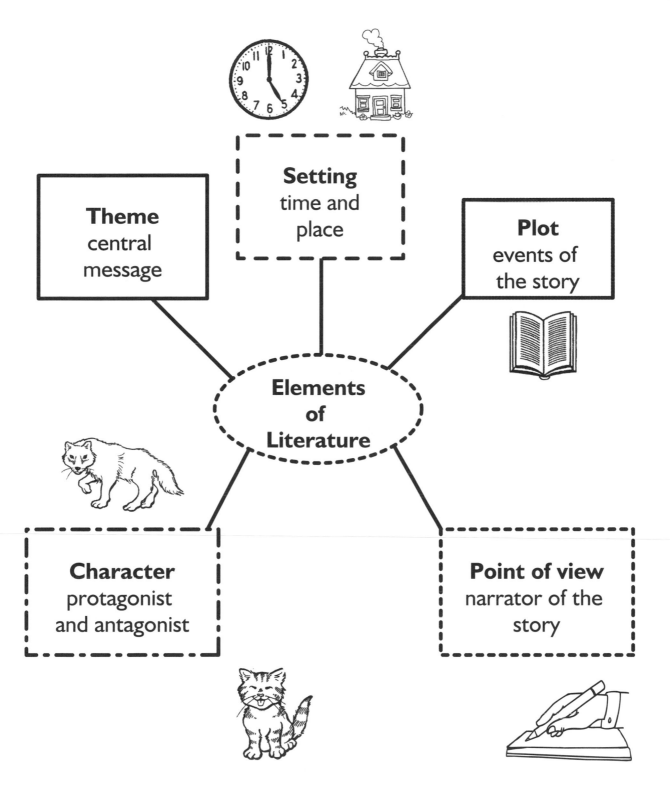

**FIGURE 4.26**

# Elements of Literature Web 2

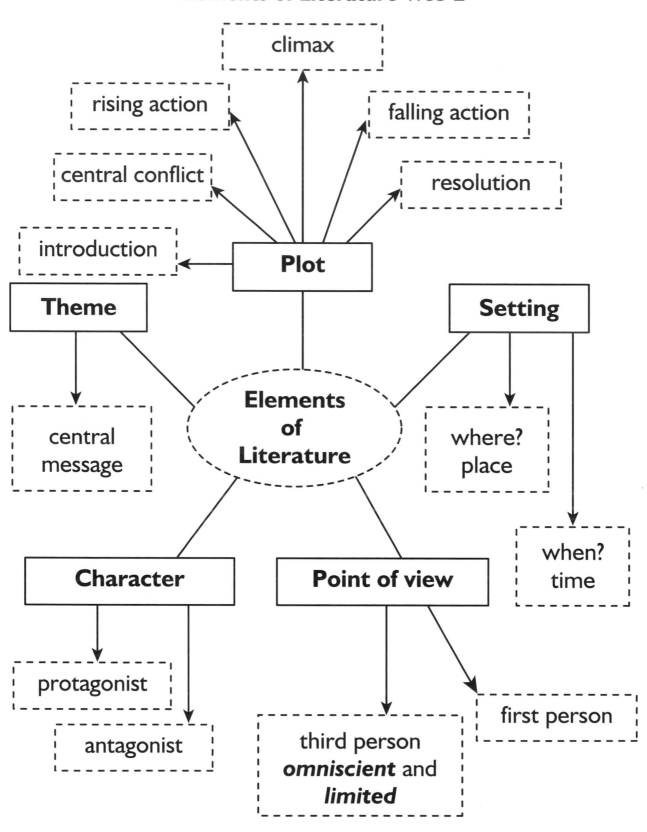

**FIGURE 4.27**

Although you might conduct either formal or informal preassessments for lessons throughout your unit of study, it is worthwhile to issue formal *unit* preassessments to gather as much information as possible on each student. In addition to the web strategy, other formal unit preassessments include asking students to complete a K-W-L chart, respond to a journal prompt, take a pretest, answer questions, annotate a prepared writing sample, create a drawing with accompanying writing related to the unit content, interpret a poem or figurative language, categorize or make a list and provide a rationale, complete a cloze procedure and explain the entries, or create a graphic organizer based on a reading selection. These aforementioned suggestions will allow you to glean readiness levels of learners. You can also issue multiple intelligence and interest surveys to obtain information about students' learning profiles and interests. There are many such questionnaires and surveys on the web, so conduct a search to find them using these key terms: *multiple intelligence survey, multiple intelligence inventory, interest survey, interest inventory.*

Preassessments for individual lessons or groups of lessons might include an informal question and answer session, games, demonstrations (have students show you what they know), observations, predictions, or entrance slips. If you are reading a class book or short story, determine vocabulary words students might know before starting the text. Simply supply the list of words and ask students to provide a definition and a picture or symbol of each word along with a sentence showing meaning. Students who can demonstrate understanding of several words can replace these words with others from the reading on an alternate list that you have prepared. No sense in having students focus on words they already know. Other ideas include *yes/no* cards where students respond to prompts and feature which side of the card they feel represents the correct answer. You can also have students respond on individual whiteboards, handheld electronic gadgets, or the SMART Board.

Be aware that preassessments are not graded but rather a means for collecting useful information so teachers can better plan for their learning. Let students know this, as well. Note, though, that you need to respond to the results of a preassessment if you bother to create and issue one. If you don't, students will wonder why they went to the trouble of responding to the task if you ignore the results. But the time you commit for conducting a preassessment allows you to learn altogether useful information about your students, in order to plan lessons with a clear vision of what instruction the students need.

## EXERCISE 5: HOW DO EDUCATORS DETERMINE AN APPROPRIATE CULMINATING ASSESSMENT?

By now, you have grouped standards, identified what you want students to know, created (or refined) essential understandings, and fashioned essential unit and lesson guiding questions. To determine what culminating assessment you want students to produce to demonstrate their understanding of what you have worked on so far, review all the hard work you have accomplished. What is in front of you on the unit map represents your unit goals. Therefore, find or create a culminating assessment that allows students to show you proof of this essential material. Use the guidance from this chapter and what you have entered thus far on the unit map to identify this culminating assessment. Remember to create or find an accompanying rubric to score their work. Enter the assessment onto your unit map template; the following are some examples of what you might record. Because the culminating assessment is one entry on your map which includes detailed information and a corresponding rubric, feel free to be brief for this particular template component:

- Informative paper using a combination of drawing and dictation or writing based on what it means to be a good citizen: *following rules, sharing, taking turns*
- Opinion piece based on student-selected informational text about an animal
- Short story narrative based on historically accurate characters and setting from social studies unit (historical fiction)
- Personal narrative from the point of view of an organism about its journey through the life cycle
- Demonstration that teaches others how forces make things move
- Live skit or iMovie based on a hero's life

## CLOSING

Although this chapter addresses preassessments, it focuses largely on culminating assessments, along with accompanying discussions on and examples of various rubrics and checklists that provide the criteria for assessing student work. Students will be most successful if they are aware of expectations for a summative assessment prior to working on it. It is imperative that teachers use standards, knowledge, essential understandings, and guiding questions to formulate culminating projects because the goal is for students to demonstrate their understanding of these key aspects of a unit. In a backward design approach, teaching professionals are advised to plan with the end in mind to be clear-sighted about what they really want students to glean in any unit. Once you have a meaningful culminating assessment and rubric, you are ready to keep plugging forward. Next, you will delve into the other template components, including formative assessments, so your unit map will be complete and comprehensive.

# 5

# Skills, Activities, Formative Assessments, and Resources

> *Skills are the actions students should be able to perform or demonstrate as the result of a lesson, a series of lessons, or a unit of study.*
>
> —Carol Ann Tomlinson and Caroline Eidson (2003, p. 239)
>
> *Learning activities are tasks for students designed to develop the knowledge, understanding, and skills specified in the content goals. They should help students perceive, process, rehearse, store, and transfer new information and skill.*
>
> —Carol Ann Tomlinson et al. (2002, p. 56)

At this point, you have accomplished a great deal on your unit map. You are in the home stretch. This chapter addresses the remaining components of the map, except differentiation, which is the focus of Chapter 6. The hard part is over, so if you have made it thus far, the rest might be a breeze.

## SKILLS AND ACTIVITIES

### What Is the Difference Between Skills and Activities?

It is common for educators to confuse skills and activities. Both are written in verbal phrases and seem to indicate what students should do; however, there is a distinction between the two components. In this chapter, I differentiate between skills and activities to show that each has a place in effective curriculum design. I also address teaching and instructional strategies and explain how they are linked, but different from, learning activities.

Teachers select teaching methods and instructional strategies to engage students in targeted learning activities so that students can learn particular skills and also acquire the knowledge and understanding that are defined as the unit outcomes. In other words, learning activities are tasks that serve as the vehicle for students to learn a skill, to acquire knowledge, and to understand key concepts. Figure 5.1 lists skills in one column and activities in the other. Read and study Columns A and B and articulate to colleagues or yourself the differences between them.

## What is the difference between the entries in these columns?

| Column A | Column B |
|---|---|
| • Support reasons with factual evidence.<br>• Summarize current events.<br>• Collect and analyze data.<br>• Create a timeline.<br>• Predict outcomes.<br>• Formulate a hypothesis.<br>• Compare perspectives.<br>• Distinguish between fact and opinion.<br>• Critique a play.<br>• Tally results.<br>• Construct a model.<br>• Work collaboratively.<br>• Arrive at consensus.<br>• Group objects according to shape.<br>• Revise written work.<br>• Find and write examples of imagery.<br>• Identify parts of speech.<br>• Make connections between types of literature.<br>• Distinguish examples of literal and nonliteral language.<br>• Ask and answer questions about key details.<br>• Paraphrase text. | • Interpret graphs of U.S. population growth and analyze data.<br>• Summarize current events about South American immigration.<br>• Create a timeline of the Middle Ages.<br>• Create a timeline of your life including significant events and accompanying illustrations.<br>• List reasons Europeans immigrated to the New World.<br>• Predict outcomes of characters in *Stone Fox*.<br>• Distinguish between fact and opinion in *Beauty and the Beast* or *Cinderella*.<br>• Tally results of your classmates' favorite activities and create a graph that depicts these results.<br>• Ask and answer questions about key details in *Peter Rabbit*.<br>• Construct a model of a double helix.<br>• Compare perspectives of the British and American colonists.<br>• Create a Venn diagram comparing and contrasting two characters in *Esperanza Rising*. |

**FIGURE 5.1**   Skills Versus Activities

You are correct if you noticed that Column B includes items that are more specific and detailed than Column A. Items in Column B include content-specific knowledge indicators aligned to a particular lesson or unit, such as *U.S. population growth, South American immigration, Middle Ages, Cinderella, Peter Rabbit,* and so forth. These personalized words and phrases specific to a unit qualify them as activities rather than skills. Skills, on the other hand, allow for transference of knowledge to different situations. For example, *identify examples of imagery* is a skill that can be applied to many novels, poems, and speeches; *compare and contrast points of view* could conceivably apply to historical figures, characters in stories, politicians, and so forth. However, *compare and contrast the points of view in Little Red Riding Hood and Rapunzel* is an activity expressly tied to those two fairy tales.

As educators, we want to explicitly teach pertinent skills and design opportunities for students to demonstrate understanding of these skills through assessments. But not all statements that are written in verbal phrases and general language and indicate transference are necessarily grade-level appropriate skills. For example, *brainstorm a list* would qualify as a skill for primary-grade students who need to master it. However, if a teacher in sixth grade asks students to brainstorm a list, she would hopefully not feel the need to expressly teach and assess this skill in middle school. The teacher might ask students to brainstorm a list as a springboard activity for a target skill or concept lesson, but it is not an appropriate grade-level skill. So, be conscientious to choose skills that are suited for the grade level of students you teach.

After reading about the difference between skills and activities, take a look at the following Common Core Standards (NGA, 2010). Are they skills or activities?

- Identify the front cover, back cover, and title page of a book (RI.K.5).
- Identify the main topic and retell key details of a text (RI.1.2).
- Ask and answer questions to demonstrate understanding of a text, referring explicitly to the text as the basis for the answers (RI.3.1).
- Use text features and search tools (e.g., key words, sidebars, hyperlinks) to locate information relevant to a given topic efficiently (RI.3.5).
- Explain how an author uses reasons and evidence to support particular points in a text (RI.4.8).
- Integrate information from several texts on the same topic in order to write or speak about the subject knowledgeably (RI.5.9).

I expect that you answered skills, which they are indeed. All of the standards are expressed as skills, so it is incumbent upon educators to identify the key concepts within them and fashion essential understandings and guiding questions so there is a context for these important grade-level expectations.

## What About Teaching Strategies and Instructional Activities?

In designing lesson plans using the unit map as a guide, take into account all of the components on the unit map template. In addition, it is imperative to consider teaching strategies as well as learning or instructional activities because the two go hand in hand. Teaching strategies are what teachers design to orchestrate what students do in a learning activity. Consider teaching strategies, then, as the role of the teacher and learning activities as the role of the student:

**Teaching strategies** refer to the structure, system, methods, techniques, procedures, and processes that a teacher uses during instruction. These are the strategies the teacher employs to assist student learning. **Learning activities** refer to the teacher-guided instructional tasks or assignment for students. These are student activities. (Wandberg & Rohwer, 2010, p. 164)

Both teaching strategies and learning activities are selected based on the learning goals. They should complement and address students' needs for differentiation purposes, be varied instead of repetitive, and allow for student engagement.

There are many confusing and overlapping curriculum design terms, such as *learning or instructional strategies, teaching strategies and methods,* and *learning or instructional activities.* Learning or instructional strategies can be embedded within both teaching strategies and learning activities, and there can be overlap. For example, teachers can feature a graphic organizer during a lesson thereby using it as a teaching strategy. Plus, they might use demonstration or modeling to show students how to complete one, which are also teaching methods. Then, students may be asked to create their own graphic organizers as an instructional activity to learn a targeted skill or concept.

Another overlapping example is the roundtable strategy. Teachers might ask students to employ this process to check for understanding during instruction, but they can also assign it as an instructional activity that students execute. Do not get tripped up on terminology, though. *What is important to discern and account for in lesson planning is what teachers design, orchestrate, and lead and the learning and instructional activities that students perform.* In Figure 5.2, Samples of Teaching Strategies and Learning Activities Aligned to Skills, you will find some overlap of teaching and instructional strategies and activities within both columns of this chart.

Figure 5.2 does not represent the full range of possible strategies and activities, so additional options are listed as follows, as there are a multitude of them. And still, there are other ways to impart learning; however, you will have a wide professional inventory of choices with this list and Figure 5.2.

*Case Studies.* Case studies have been used in business, law, and medical schools for actively engaging students in problem solving and can apply to K–12 schools, as well. In this teaching method, groups of students are presented with a problem to solve that is directly or indirectly based on a real-life scenario. Students work to solve the problem by engaging in discussion and inquiry. Some instructors provide the result of the actual case beforehand as the basis for discussion. Others present the problem and allow students to decide how to solve it, and then present the result of the case as the basis of comparison.

*Debate.* Students focus on different sides of an issue, identify and address counterarguments, and determine the strongest points in order to arrive at a decision. Teachers can collect various differentiated resources for students to use for researching evidence for their arguments and counterclaims.

*Jigsaw* (Aronson, Blaney, Stephan, Silkes, & Snapp, 1978). Groups of students read different but conceptually and topically related material based on readiness or their interests. They prepare notes or graphic organizers together that highlight the major points. Students then redivide into a second group configuration whereby one member from the original group is grouped with others. Students take turns teaching their new group members the reading material from the initial group and together create an assignment that compiles the key points from the collective reading material.

*Lecture.* Lectures are an age-old, familiar strategy in which an instructor delivers an oral presentation that sometimes contains visuals. Even PowerPoint presentations can be classified as a type of lecture because the instructor disseminates information orally to a small or large group. Some lecturers provide opportunities for interaction with the audience; some do not.

*(Text continued on page 142)*

# Samples of Teaching Strategies and Learning Activities Aligned to Skills

| Common Core Standards | Skills | Teaching Strategies | Learning or Instructional Activities (*Students will...*) |
|---|---|---|---|
| • Use linking words and phrases (e.g., because, therefore, since, for example) to connect opinion and reasons (NGA, 2010, W.3.1c).<br>• Link opinion and reasons using words and phrases (e.g., for instance, in order to, in addition) (W.4.1c).<br>• Link opinion and reasons using words, phrases, and clauses (e.g., consequently, specifically) (W.5.1c). | • Identify and use transitional words and phrases to link opinions and reasons. | **Modeling**<br><br>When teachers model for students what they are expected to do, they demonstrate expectations. They might perform a lab experiment, write a paragraph on the overhead or document camera, complete steps to solve a math problem, or act in a certain way to demonstrate sharing or taking turns. Demonstrations can be passive, but teachers can model in a more active way to offer additional support. For example, teachers can model what they demonstrate by using the think-aloud strategy, whereby they talk through their thinking as they complete a task. They can also ask students questions to actively engage them while performing the demonstration. | • Listen to a paragraph from an opinion piece that doesn't have transitional words and phrases. Discuss what makes the writing choppy. (**Teacher:** Do not mention what is missing; let them discover it.)<br>• Read a list of transitional words and phrases aloud with classmates (choral reading).<br>• Listen to a more fluid piece of writing and identify the transitions that make it easier to follow.<br>• Watch the teacher model how to revise a paragraph by inserting appropriate transitions from the list.<br>• Listen to the teacher share his thinking as he completes this task. Answer the teacher's questions as he works, such as the following: *How do I know where to put a transition? What transition will work best in this spot? How do transitions improve writing?*<br>• Use the list of transitions to revise another piece of writing. (For **differentiation by readiness**, give individual students appropriately challenging paragraphs or multiparagraphs to revise to include transitions. In addition, differentiate the list of transitional words and phrases and distribute based on readiness levels.) |
| • Engage effectively in a range of collaborative discussion with diverse partners on grade (4, 5) topics and texts, building on others' ideas and expressing their own clearly (SL.4.1, SL.5.1). | • Build on others' ideas.<br>• Express ideas clearly.<br>• Identify and respond to speakers' points. | **Demonstration Through Video**<br><br>In this example, teachers can show a video of a debate team in action to demonstrate what students will ultimately do. To ensure that the demonstration is not passive, teachers can stop the recording at intervals and engage in discussion with students and answer their questions. | • In groups, debate on different topics of interest using prearranged resources from the teacher. (For **differentiation by readiness** and **learning style**, provide a host of resources at varying readability levels and modalities for accessing information: informational texts, audio centers, videos, software, etc.)<br>• Serve as an audience member to summarize and critique arguments of both sides to arrive at a decision when your team is not debating. |

**FIGURE 5.2** *(Continued)*

| Common Core Standards | Skills | Teaching Strategies | Learning or Instructional Activities (*Students will…*) |
|---|---|---|---|
| • Identify the reasons and evidence a speaker provides to support particular points (SL.4.3). <br>• Summarize the points a speaker makes and explain how each claim is supported by reasons and evidence (SL.5.2). | • Summarize speakers' points and provide a counterargument. | **Demonstration Through Video** (*continued*) | • Complete the following steps in your debating team: <br>  ○ Select a topic. (To **differentiate**, students choose a topic of **interest** to debate.) <br>  ○ Research information about your topic; complete a graphic organizer with key points. (To **differentiate**, students choose graphic organizer for note taking that appeals to their **learning style**.) <br>  ○ State an opinion and support this point of view with reasons and information. <br>  ○ Listen to opposing viewpoints. <br>  ○ Address and acknowledge the opposing viewpoints. |
| • Write narratives to develop real or imagined experiences or events using effective technique, descriptive details, and clear event sequences (W.3.3, W.4.3, W.5.3). | • Identify criteria for narrative writing. | **Roundtable** <br><br> This strategy is used for students to preview or review material, and also for teachers to check for understanding. Teachers pose a prompt or topic. In groups, one piece of paper is rotated around a circle as students input responses to the prompt in list form. The exercise is over when students have exhausted the list of entries. Each group reports out its list to the whole class avoiding duplications. | • Review features of narrative writing after reading several stories and studying about the elements of literature. <br>• Participate in the roundtable activity by entering one word or phrase on a group sheet when it is passed to you in answer to the prompt: "What does a strong short story include?" <br>• Remember to include not only elements of literature, but also what all good writing includes. <br>• Keep passing the paper around the group until everyone has finished contributing. (Examples of contributions are setting, *descriptive words, central conflict/problem, sentence variety, correct spelling, sensory details, etc.*) <br>• In groups, report out to compile a comprehensive class list. <br>• Read the teacher-generated short story checklist of expectations for a writing assignment. (To **differentiate**, create tiered checklists to appeal to **readiness** levels. For this exercise that introduces writing expectations, use the at-grade-level version.) <br>• Compare each line item on the checklist with the comprehensive posted class list. Discuss commonalities and differences; make justified changes to the prepared checklist if there is consensus. |

| Common Core Standards | Skills | Teaching Strategies | Learning or Instructional Activities (Students will...) |
|---|---|---|---|
| • Identify the main topic and retell key details of a text (RI.1.2).<br>• Know and use various text features (e.g., headings, table of contents, glossaries, electronic menus, icons) to locate key facts or information in a text (RI.1.5).<br>• Use the illustrations and details in a text to describe its key ideas (RI.1.7).<br>• Identify basic similarities in and differences between two texts on the same topic (e.g., in illustrations, descriptions, or procedures) (RI.1.9).<br>• Describe people, places, things, and events with relevant details, expressing ideas and feelings clearly (SL.1.4). | • Identify the main topic and retell key details.<br>• Use various text features to locate key facts or information in the text.<br>• Use illustrations and details in the text to describe its key ideas.<br>• Compare information on the same topic using different texts.<br>• Describe animals using details. | **Direct Instruction**<br>This is a methodology that involves explicitly and carefully organized lessons taught directly by the teacher in a prescribed way through explanation, teacher-student interaction, and practice.<br><br>**Cooperative Learning**<br>In this teacher-led strategy, students work together in a small group arrangement to solve a problem or complete a project. Teammates are responsible for their own learning as well as assisting other group members to learn and improve understanding of a topic so there is collective achievement. (Note: With more teacher support and guidance, as is necessary for primary and some tasks in upper elementary, cooperative learning can be a *teaching strategy*. With more student group autonomy, it can serve as an *instructional strategy*.) | • Sit in groups based on a particular animal that interests you for a group project. (To **differentiate**, students work in **interest** groups.)<br>• Listen to an informational text about an animal, such as *Starfish* by Edith Thacher Hurd. Raise your hand or stand up when you hear something that you find interesting and discuss this detail with others in the class.<br>• Assist teacher in making a class list of interesting details. Find pictures that match the text of these details. Review list and discuss with classmates which details are the most interesting.<br>• Use the details to identify the main topic.<br>• Identify the features of informational text and help your teacher make a list of these features. Answer these questions: *Which text features are used to find interesting facts? Which text features help readers to find the main idea?*<br>• In groups, go on a scavenger hunt using a different informational text than *Starfish* to find text features: *Find and point to the index page. Find and point to the glossary. Read one word from the glossary. Find a word in bold print. What does it mean?* and so forth.<br>• In groups, read and listen to books on a targeted animal. Use text features to find details and the main idea. (For **differentiation**, arrange students in groups based on reading **readiness** and **interest** in a particular animal.)<br>• As a group, teach and share with classmates about your animal orally, in writing, or through pictures. (For **differentiation** by **readiness**, students use writing, dictation, or oral means to share.) |

**FIGURE 5.2** *(Continued)*

| Common Core Standards | Skills | Teaching Strategies | Learning or Instructional Activities (Students will…) |
|---|---|---|---|
| • With prompting and support, ask and answer questions about key details in the text (RL.K.1). • With prompting and support, identify characters, settings, and major events in the story (RL.K.2). • With prompting and support, compare and contrast the adventures and experiences of characters in familiar stories (RL.K.9). | • Ask and answer questions about key details. • Identify characters, settings, and major events. • Compare and contrast the characters, settings, and major events of two stories. | **Graphic Organizers** Organizers allow students to use visual diagrams to brainstorm and structure writing projects; help problem solve and make decisions; summarize key ideas in reading, audio, or video; assist with studying; plan research; and more. (Note: In this example, completing a graphic organizer is a teacher-led activity so it is a *teaching strategy*. If students create the organizers on their own, it would qualify as an *instructional strategy*.) | • As your teacher does a book walk of *The Mitten* by Alvin Tresselt, find and point to pictures of characters and setting. Using the pictures, talk about any key details you notice. Ask questions that you might have before reading. (For **differentiation**, ask differentiated questions to appeal to the various **readiness** levels of students.) • Listen to the story and talk about the details you noticed from the book walk. Ask and answer any questions that you or your classmates have about this story. • Using the book walk, help the teacher review another book also called *The Mitten* written by a different author named Jan Brett. Listen as she reads this story. Begin to notice what is the same or different about the characters, setting, and what happens in this story with the same title. • After reading, help the teacher record what is the same and different about these two versions of *The Mitten* onto a chart (graphic organizer). Tell what you liked best about each story. |
| • Ask and answer questions to demonstrate understanding of a text, referring explicitly to the text as the basis for the answers (RI.3.1). • Determine the main idea of a text, recount the key details, and explain how they support the main idea (RI.3.2). | • Ask and answer questions to demonstrate understanding of a text. • Refer explicitly to the text as the basis for the answers. • Determine the main idea of a text. | **Reciprocal Teaching** This reading strategy is designed to allow students to interact with the text and collaboratively work with peers to assist each other in understanding a text. It relies on activating four different comprehension strategies: (1) *predicting*, (2) *questioning*, (3) *clarifying*, and (4) *summarizing*. | • Look at the pictures from *Owls* by Gail Gibbons. Respond: *What do you want to know about owls?* Predict: *Based on these pictures, what do you think you will learn about owls?* • Listen as your teacher reads one section of *Owls* at a time. As you hear each section, respond to any of these prompts: *What do you learn about owls? What other questions do you have about owls?* (**Teacher:** Make a list of student-generated questions.) *Are our predictions correct, or do we need to change them? What part that you heard do you need clarified? How can we summarize this section?* |

| Common Core Standards | Skills | Teaching Strategies | Learning or Instructional Activities (Students will…) |
|---|---|---|---|
| | • Recount the key details and explain how they support the main idea. | **Reciprocal Teaching (continued)** | • Listen to the story again and see if you can answer the questions we have listed. Put a sticky note on pages where answers are found. Respond: *What words on this page give us the answers to our questions?* (For an **extension**, with those questions not answered by the text, invite volunteers to use other resources to answer the questions.)<br>• Explain what the main idea of this book is; find details that tell us so. Respond: *How do our section summaries help us to identify the main idea?* |
| • Explain the meaning of simple similes and metaphors (e.g., as pretty as a picture) in context (L.4.5a).<br>• Use concrete words and phrases and sensory details to convey experiences and events precisely (W.4.3c). | • Interpret figurative language.<br>• Use figurative language in writing. | **Concept Attainment** (Bruner, Goodnow, & Austin, 1956)<br><br>Students compare and contrast teacher-prepared examples and nonexamples of a concept (e.g., proper nouns, similes, shapes, etc.). After sorting these examples and nonexamples, students identify the common attributes of items that qualify as examples and arrive at a definition. They can then add their own examples. Teachers can guide students through discussion and inquiry to compare and contrast the two sets. | • In groups, sort several paragraphs mounted on individual index cards into two piles according to their content. You will have to read all the paragraphs to determine how you might group paragraphs that all share common traits and those that do not. (**Teacher**: Provide paragraphs with sensory detail, simile, and metaphor and paragraphs that lack figurative language.) (For **differentiation**, students are grouped homogeneously. Give different paragraphs to sort based on **readiness** levels so the material is appropriately challenging for students in each group.)<br>• Identify the group of paragraphs that shares attributes. Focusing on this set, discuss and list characteristics that are common among these paragraphs.<br>• Define figurative language (i.e., imagery, simile, metaphor); find examples of figurative language in the assigned paragraphs.<br>• Select and rewrite a paragraph from the set of nondescript paragraphs to include figurative language. (For **differentiation** by **readiness** and **interest**, students select the paragraph that is of interest to them to rewrite; paragraph selections are appropriately challenging for each group.) |

**FIGURE 5.2** Samples of Teaching Strategies and Learning Activities Aligned to Skills

*Literature Circles* (Daniels, 1994). Teachers present a collection of books covering a range of reading levels and topics of interest to students. In groups, students read the same book and are each assigned a specific role that rotates among students, such as *discussion director, illuminator, illustrator, summarizer,* and so forth. The roles are intended to elucidate the reading by providing a structured way to delve into the complexities of a work of literature or nonfiction. Once students are well versed in the roles, the structured aspect of each job is suspended at some point so spontaneity will emerge.

*Museum or Gallery Walk.* Students create various projects based on defined criteria and display them throughout the classroom on walls and tables, for example, posters, PowerPoint presentations, timelines, project cubes, and so forth. Teachers devise several guiding questions or prompts and students respond to them using the museum pieces as the vehicle for gathering this information. Students can view the "museum" (or "gallery") individually, in pairs, or in small groups as the teacher dictates. Upon completion of viewing the projects and responding to the questions and prompts, the class reconvenes and holds a discussion based on findings and impressions.

*Project-Based Learning (PBL).* Students work in groups to explore real-world problems and challenges. This instructional method involves an interdisciplinary approach and is designed to empower students to make decisions, think critically, and collaborate with peers while in pursuit of designing and completing a project.

*Role Playing.* Role playing can be used to explore issues or to better understand a literary text or historical event or figure. Students act out the historical, literary, or real-world situation assuming the roles of historical figures, authentic people, or literary characters who are involved. Some students might observe the role playing; all students offer insights, impressions, and reactions.

*Simulation.* Students mirror a real-world, complex situation by assuming the roles of those involved to gain better insight and understanding. In simulations, participants make decisions and see the results of their actions so they can apply what they learned to life. For example, teachers can ask students to conduct the following: *simulate a trial, assume the role of delegates in the electoral college, create a business plan and simulate running a business to learn about entrepreneurship, operate a store by selling "goods" and exchanging "money," or play games like SimCity to simulate building cities and solving problems associated with city planning.*

*Visualization.* Students listen while a teacher reads a poem or passage aloud or while music or an audio is playing. While listening, students can draw a picture, produce an abstract representation, or create or complete a graphic organizer to record an observation or demonstrate comprehension. Or students can merely listen with eyes open or shut to a situation or a passage. To debrief in a visualization exercise, teachers can pose these questions for students to answer orally, in writing, or a combination of both: *How do images help you to draw conclusions? to make connections? to create interpretations? to recall significant details? to better comprehend?*

Another point to note in Figure 5.2 is the use of separate columns for Common Core Standards and for skills. While the Common Core Standards are indeed expressed as skills, the additional column reflects a targeted portion of a particular Standard that relates to the featured teaching strategy and learning activity. When you compare the two columns, this will be apparent.

# INSTRUCTIONAL STRATEGY: ROLLING DICE OR CUBES

Cubing was originally designed as an instructional strategy for students to use thinking skills to explore a topic or concept. It has since morphed into all kinds of opportunities for students in a variety of ways. In this strategy, students roll a die, a 1-inch wooden cube, or a larger paper cube and respond to a prompt featured on the side that is facing up. Students can respond informally or formally. Informally can entail oral responses; formally can be writing or completing a project. Or they might respond using a combination: first respond orally, gathering input and suggestions to the prompt from peers, and then work independently to respond more comprehensively. Read on for a thorough explanation of two different activity options associated with this strategy and many examples. Option 1 refers to prompts in Figure 5.3 that you can use; Option 2 aligns with Figure 5.4, Question Designer.

## Option 1: What Prompts Can Teachers Feature on a Die or Cube?

Several prompts for die or cube "faces" appear in Figure 5.3 and align mostly to the reading strand for literature and informational text. The prompts use the generic terms *text*, *story*, or *reading* so that they can apply to a picture book, poem, novel, play, or nonfiction. (Later in this section you can read "How Can Teachers Prepare for a Die or Cube Learning Activity?" for logistical information.) Here is a brief explanation of how the provided prompts in Figure 5.3 are categorized:

- *Character 1.* These prompts focus on methods of characterization based on a literary text that teachers share as a read-aloud, or students read independently as a core book or mentor text, or one that students read in literature circles.
- *Character 2.* These prompts are a compilation of questions to better comprehend and analyze characters of any literary text.
- *Setting.* These prompts include probing questions about setting pertaining to any literary text.
- *Theme.* These prompts feature questions relating to this element of literature.
- *General literature.* These simplistic prompts can be used for any selection of literature.
- *Figurative language.* These prompts ask students to find, create, and analyze figurative language in a selected text.
- *Reading 1 and 2.* Both sets of these prompts focus on students engaging with the text more to foster deeper comprehension. Many include various reading strategies calling upon students to predict, compare/contrast, connect, summarize, and so forth.
- *Reading 3.* These prompts are more suitable to primary-age students as they are asked to identify the author and illustrator, and find examples of print concepts.
- *Poetry.* These prompts are specific to a poem students read and then address various aspects of poetic devices and other poetry elements.
- *Sensory Details 1.* These prompts help younger students explore the five senses to describe featured objects, pictures, or a reading selection.
- *Sensory Details 2.* As students roll and see an icon of a sense, these prompts ask students to explain to others words, pictures, or objects associated with the sense.
- *Thinking skills (literature).* The original intent for cubing focused on the thinking skills shown in this row of prompts. These prompts, though, are specific to literature based on the thinking skills.
- *Thinking skills (issue, topic, or concept).* These prompts can be used to further explore an issue, topic, or concept and are more suited to nonfiction and informational text than the previous set of prompts.
- *Nonfiction.* These prompts ask students to identify the different text features associated with nonfiction and informational text.

- *Interest.* When studying different interest-based topics, students can use these prompts to explore their targeted topics more deeply. To foster inquiry and interest, students might toss this cube as a precursor to researching. And students can respond to these prompts based on another student's finished research project to gain more insight into a classmate's topic.
- *Character education.* With adult assistance, primary students can use these prompts to focus on character education.
- *Vocabulary and spelling.* These prompts are used in combination with students' word lists to help them learn new academic terms, vocabulary, and spelling words.
- *Word work.* Students improve word knowledge, such as prefix, affix, synonym, and so forth, with these prompts.

While the prompts are categorized (e.g., *character, theme, thinking skills, character education, interest,* etc.), teachers may customize a die or cube by mixing and matching different cells. You can have a die or cube that includes a compilation of elements of literature, such as one character prompt, one setting prompt, one theme prompt, and so forth. Also, some cells might not even apply to your targeted text, so you might have to adapt some suggested prompts for the activity to be pertinent.

You can fashion your own prompts to accommodate the other strands. For example, here are prompts you can make for targeting the language strand in various grade levels. Students would need a book in hand as the basis for responding to some of these die or cube prompts. For other prompts, they can write their responses on paper or an individual whiteboard or even orally respond:

- Put your finger on a capital letter that **begins** a sentence.
- Find a **name** that is capitalized in a sentence.
- Find two **names** that are capitalized in the story.
- Put your finger on **end punctuation**.
- Act out two **action** verbs that the author uses.
- **Fix this sentence:** the bears ate all of mrs. hunter's food.
- **Fix this sentence:** i love to go shopping with peter.
- **Fix this sentence:** my mom and i like to play scrabble.
- Write one **complex sentence** from the story.
- Write or say the formula for a **complex sentence.**
- Find a **dependent clause** in the story.
- Point to three sentences that begin with an **adverb.**
- Point to two sentences that **begin in different ways.**

## Option 1: How Might Students Respond to Die or Cube Prompts?

This activity is intended as a formative assessment; therefore, students are practicing what you have taught them during some point in the unit. As a precursor and preparation for this activity, ask students to read or listen to a new or familiar text, complete homework, or engage in classroom assignments. Additionally, for this exercise to be fruitful, students need to have some background knowledge related to the targeted prompts, such as elements of literature, types and purposes of poems, reading strategies, and so forth. There are many ways to use this strategy. Choose what works best for the unit goals and students' needs. Following are some ideas; I am sure you have your own, as well.

# Die or Cube Prompts

| | | | | | | |
|---|---|---|---|---|---|---|
| **Character 1** | What does the character **say** that supports a trait? | What does the character **do** that supports a trait? | What does **another say** about the character? | What is the character **thinking** or **feeling**? | What is a **personality trait** for the character? | What does the character **look like**? |
| **Character 2** | How does the character change throughout time? | Why does the character change throughout time? | How can you connect personally with the character? | How is this character like another character? | How can a change in setting affect a character? | How does the story's setting affect this character? |
| **Setting** | What is the definition for setting? | What are the settings in this text? Which is most important and why? | How does the setting impact characters? | What tone does the author create through the setting? | How is a setting in this text similar to the setting in another text? | Explain why the author creates these particular settings. |
| **Theme** | What are two or more themes of this text? | What is the definition of theme? | Cite evidence to support one theme. | What other texts have a similar theme? Explain. | How does the theme of this text connect to the world? | How can you connect personally with the theme? |
| **General Literature** | Who is your least favorite character? Why? | What part made you angry? Why? | What is your favorite part of the story? Why? | If the story were made into a movie, who would be the actors? | How might you change the ending? | What part confuses you? How did you figure it out, or do you still have questions? |
| **Figurative Language** | Create your own **simile** for a setting or character in the text. | Create a **metaphor** for a setting or character in the text. | Find a **metaphor** in the text and explain its meaning. | Find a **simile** in the text and explain its meaning. | Create **imagery** where there is none. | Find **imagery** in the text. Discuss its impact on the reader. |
| **Reading 1** | Identify all characters. What is the central conflict? | Orally summarize the whole text or part of it. | Interpret a part of the text that might confuse others. | Compare and contrast two characters in the text. | Invent dialogue a character might say. Explain why the character would say this. | Would you recommend this reading to others? Why or why not? |

**FIGURE 5.3** (Continued)

|  | | | | | | |
|---|---|---|---|---|---|---|
| **Reading 2** | Make a prediction and explain your reasoning. | Make and explain a text-to-text connection. | What would you say to the author if you met her or him? Be specific. | | How would the text change if written from a different point of view? | How might you change the ending or outcome? Why? |
| **Reading 3** | Who is the author? How do you know? | Who is the illustrator? How do you know? | Point to words that match a picture. | What are new words for you? How can you figure out what they mean? | Point to the title, front cover, and back cover. | What is this whole book about? |
| **Poetry** | What is this type of poem? Does it work for the topic? | What is the purpose of this poem? Is the author successful? | Find a simile or metaphor. What does it mean? Is it strong? | What is this poem's theme? Show evidence. | Find an example of rhythm or rhyme. Is it effective? | What is the tone of this poem? Show evidence. |
| **Sensory Details 1** | What can you **see**? | What can you **feel**? | What can you **smell**? | What can you **hear**? | What can you **taste**? | What does this picture or object remind you of? |
| **Sensory Details 2** | | | | | | |
| **Thinking Skills (Literature)** | DESCRIBE Describe the setting or a character using sensory detail. | COMPARE Compare two elements of literature: theme, setting, character, etc. | ASSOCIATE What does this story make you think about? Make any connections. | ANALYZE Identify and explain examples of figurative language. | APPLY Interpret a meaningful quote from the story. | ARGUE FOR or AGAINST Agree or disagree with a character's action. |

| Thinking Skills (Issue/Concept/Topic) | DESCRIBE | COMPARE | ASSOCIATE | ANALYZE | APPLY | ARGUE FOR or AGAINST |
|---|---|---|---|---|---|---|
| | Describe the issue, concept, or topic using specific detail. | Explain what is similar or different from this issue, concept, or topic. | What does it make you think about? Make any connections. | Describe parts of this issue, concept, or topic to explain it. | How can this issue, concept, or topic be used or solved? | Agree or disagree with the issue, concept, or topic. |
| Nonfiction | What is an index? Find the index and show it to your group. | What are two facts that you learned from this book? | Find two captions. Do they match the pictures, or how would you rewrite them? | What fact is the most interesting to you? Why? | What else do you want to know about this topic that isn't in the book? | Summarize what you learned. |
| Interest | What do you find interesting about this topic? | What more would you want to learn about this topic? | What questions do you have about this topic? | What is this topic like? What does it remind you of? | Who would benefit from learning about this topic? Why? | What are related topics that you would want to learn more about? |
| Character Education | What words describe feelings? | How do I feel? | How can I show my feelings? | How can I understand the feelings of others? | How might my words hurt others? | How can my respectful words make others feel good? |
| Vocabulary | Create a picture or symbol of the word. | Create an advertisement of the word. | Write a poem or song about the word. | Write a simile or metaphor for the word. | Make a visual collage of the word. | Use technology to teach the word to others. |
| Spelling | Say your word three times. | What is a synonym for this word? | Write your word in an artistic way. | Use your word in a sentence. | Tell someone what your word means. | Find and say other words within your word. |
| Word Work | What prefix or affix helps you figure out what this word means? | What is a synonym for this word? | What is an antonym for this word? | Use the word in a sentence to show meaning. | Draw a symbol or picture of the word. | What are nonexamples of this word? |

**FIGURE 5.3**

## Oral Responses

- In a group setting, one student at a time rolls the die or cube and responds to the prompt. Students pass the die or cube so that each has a chance to respond and discuss one prompt at a time.
- Each student in a group rolls and is then the first to respond to the prompt shown. After ample time is given for each to respond, all group members are free to participate in the discussion, which can take many forms. Students can merely agree with the response given, ask for clarification, provide new insight, or counter the response, in which case more discussion can unfold. It is then the next student's turn to roll and have first dibs at responding to the new prompt before open discussion.

## Written Responses

- In groups, students each get a turn to roll the die or cube and take note of what they rolled. Once they all roll, students individually respond to their targeted prompt in writing. Students might first respond orally before working independently or in pairs on the written response.
- Independently, students can each roll the die or cube a set number of times from the six options and then complete the rolled prompts in journals or on separate paper to submit.
- Since these prompts are relatively brief, the oral or written responses can be a precursor to a major writing assignment.

Students can roll the die or cube more than once so different students in a group can respond to the same prompt in a different way. For example, *Find imagery that the author uses in the text* can be used repeatedly as students find different examples. *How can you connect personally with the character?* will generate various responses from different students, too.

For oral or written responses, I suggest you model how to respond and communicate criteria so students are clear about expectations. For oral responses, consider this College and Career Readiness Anchor Standard 1 for Speaking and Listening that would apply: *Prepare for and participate effectively in a range of conversations and collaborations with diverse partners, building on others' ideas and expressing their own clearly and persuasively.*

## Option 1: How Can Teachers Differentiate Die or Cube Prompts?

Arrange students in interest-based or readiness-based groups and prepare cubes accordingly so that each group has customized, differentiated cubes based on different texts, topics, or materials. Students can also prepare their own cubes to use and play with others who are at the same readiness level or share the same interests. To make their own cubes, differentiate the resources (e.g., different textbook excerpts, articles, Internet resources, novels, picture books, etc.) by readiness or interest that they use as the basis for making them. To differentiate by learning style, be flexible and allow students the choice to work individually or in small groups as their mode of working dictates.

As previously mentioned, you can also differentiate by intentionally cutting out different cells from various rows on the prompts provided in Figure 5.3 to appeal to individual and group needs.  If students are arranged in literature circles based on books chosen by interest and readiness, the exercise is differentiated by virtue of this grouping since students will use the text as the basis for response. This same notion applies to leveled reading books, which is naturally differentiated by readiness. You might choose to color-code the cubes for easy reference to correspond to the way in which you have differentiated.

Another option is for students to respond to the unit guiding questions through a project of their choice according to learning style. Following is a bulleted list of some suggestions; other ideas are in Chapter 4's Figures 4.6, Character Highlights, and 4.7, Project Choices. Once students finish their projects, or while they are working on them, they can create die or cube prompts associated with them. Then, they present their projects to students in small groups and instruct them to respond to their die or cube prompts. This would serve many purposes: reinforce the key ideas in the unit for all students, provide a vehicle for students to present their work in small groups in a novel way, and allow students to reflect upon their own projects critically to ensure they are complete and focus on unit goals as they create a single die or cube or a pair. In fact, some students might realize they have to revise their projects if they are struggling with finding die or cube prompts or answers that accompany them.

- Create a book cover that represents the text. Include pictures, a creative title, the author, and a book summary.
- Write a review to entice others to read the text. Do not give the ending away!
- Write and perform a skit of your favorite part of the text. Submit a script with your performance.
- Make a graphic organizer with all the elements of literature and complete it based on the text. Accompany the organizer with a summary paragraph or a paragraph stating your opinion about the text.
- Create a poster with words and pictures that represent major events or aspects of the text.
- Write and perform a song that includes the elements of literature based on the text. Feel free to use a musical instrument.

## Option 2: How Do Teachers Use the Question Designer?

For this option, use Figure 5.4, Question Designer, as a vehicle for probing more deeply into the content of literature or nonfiction text, or even a particular topic or issue. You will need to prepare a pair of dice or cubes. On one die or cube, write or affix question words on each of the six faces as shown on the far left column of Figure 5.4, specifically *who, what, where, when, how, why.* On another die or cube, write or affix these six words that appear on the top row of the same sheet: *is, did, can, would, will, might.* Make several pairs of dice or cubes so that students can play individually, in pairs, or in trios.

Have students take turns rolling the pair of dice or cubes. There will always be a question word coupled with a helping or auxiliary verb when they roll, such as *What will…? Who is…? How might…? Where can…?* The student who rolls generates a question based on targeted informational or literary text to formulate a question about it. They can also use this strategy in response to a lecture, guest speaker, demonstration, or even detailed visual.

As students generate questions, they write selected ones onto the Question Designer in Figure 5.4. There are far too many spaces, so don't require students to fill in the entire sheet. Expect them to fill in a minimum number of questions that include higher-level questioning. To this point, you will need to model this exercise by reading a text to the whole class and discussing how to frame and respond to questions before students begin this activity. They need to be clear about the quality and types of questioning and what represents factual knowledge versus high-order thinking and making connections. You will probably want a combination of both. Show different examples of questions and what you expect, such as those that are answered by facts right in the text and those that are more inferential in nature or that foster prediction. The level of students you teach and readiness levels will indicate how much adult support the class and individuals or groups might need.

Once you model and students have ample time to roll, generate and record their own questions, and discuss answers, ask them to write down four of the questions that they consider to be the highest level along with their answers. They can submit this work to you as a formative assessment. Invite students to write down the more lofty questions even if the dice did not land on *why* and *how* questions. They can invent their own questions that exhibit higher-order thinking. From the modeling exercise that prepared them to complete the Question Designer in Figure 5.4, they should be able to create or identify these deeper questions. Conduct a whole-class debriefing exercise in which each group shares these questions and their answers, and invite others to volunteer their answers to other groups' questions.

## Question Designer

|       | is | did | can | would | will | might |
|-------|----|-----|-----|-------|------|-------|
| Who   |    |     |     |       |      |       |
| What  |    |     |     |       |      |       |
| Where |    |     |     |       |      |       |
| When  |    |     |     |       |      |       |
| How   |    |     |     |       |      |       |
| Why   |    |     |     |       |      |       |

**FIGURE 5.4**

## Option 2: How Can Teachers Differentiate the Question Designer?

Because students generate questions based on the text, topic, or issue, this is a natural way to differentiate. If pairs or small groups are reading different materials based on readiness levels, then these students will create questions based on the varying levels of text readability. If students are focusing together on interest-based topics and issues, they can continue to work in these interest groups to formulate questions. For struggling students, provide adult assistance to help them create appropriately probing questions that span the breadth of the text, topic, or issue. This is important so that students do not continuously create questions, for example, tied to the same character or setting without exploring other elements of literature with a text.

## How Can Teachers Prepare for a Die or Cube Learning Activity?

To prepare for this activity, teachers need to be mindful of grouping configurations for either option and arrange students purposefully to work independently or in pairs, trios, or foursomes. Groups larger than four become too chaotic, and students may not be as engaged or invested in the activity if distracted by too many peers. To determine the grouping, consider your purpose in assigning this activity and differentiate by interest, readiness, or learning profile. Furthermore, determine and communicate to students how the activity will actually be played. (See the oral and written response suggestions under the previous subheading "Option 1: How Might Students Respond to Die or Cube Prompts?")

In terms of logistics, there are many ways to prepare for this activity:

- Of course, you can make your own cube out of bond paper. If you conduct an Internet search for "cubing" or "make a paper cube" you will find a template.
- You can buy wooden dice from a teacher or art supply store and write the prompts on them. If you use this method, be careful not to use a fat-tipped Sharpie on the wooden die because it will bleed.
- Another option is to download my prompts from the companion website and cut and affix them onto a cube with double-sided tape. As an option, you might then decoupage these prompts onto the cubes so they are securely stuck to each side. I did this using wooden cubes and it worked out rather nicely.
- You can also type prompts onto mailing labels and then cut them out and stick them on paper or wooden cubes.

Even though this section focused on making cubes or dice, you might decide to merely copy the prompts onto 100 lb. paper, which is the thickest that can go through a printer. Then, cut these cells out to use as cards. Students can pull a card from a hat, or place several cards face down for them to choose.

# INSTRUCTIONAL STRATEGY: USING MANIPULATIVES

During math lessons, manipulatives abound. Teachers use pattern blocks, tiles, cubes, spinners, tangrams, and more. In other content areas, as well, teachers can customize and differentiate manipulatives so students can engage with learning in tactile and kinesthetic ways. Cubing is one such way to use manipulatives.

This section provides myriad ways to constructively use other manipulatives to enhance learning and engender more participation from kids physically and intellectually. Unlike rolling a cube or die, though, which is solely tactile, the manipulative ideas presented here can be used tactilely *or* kinesthetically. When designed as a tactile activity, students lay out various pieces individually, in pairs, or in small groups and maneuver them on a table, desk, or floor in accordance with directions the teacher communicates based on learning goals. These pieces are distributed in a set that the teacher has prearranged and placed in an envelope. Tactile activities are more controlled as students manipulate several pieces in one location. As an alternative, kinesthetic manipulative activities involve giving each student, or perhaps pair, a card or strip and they circulate around the room to find another student or partnership that satisfies the directive. Kinesthetic requires more movement, of course, but also students need several manipulatives in repetition to grasp a skill or concept. Both are engaging, add variety, and appeal to different learning styles. The dynamics and class management is different for each, so teachers should set ground rules for students to know, practice, and follow before engaging in these activities.

## What Types of Manipulatives Can Educators Use, and How Can They Be Differentiated?

Always be aware of your desired lesson outcomes and students' needs to determine if this strategy would be effective at some point during instruction. Teachers can conduct manipulative activities both informally and formally and as a pre- and formative assessment. Before or during instruction, have the unit and lesson guiding questions visible and communicate them orally so students are aware of the purpose for the activity. The only exception occurs if you want students to discover on their own the relationships between, or common attributes of, the manipulatives to arrive at an understanding. For example, you might have students sort cards of personification examples and nonexamples to determine if they can ascertain the reason for grouping certain cards together. (See "Concept Attainment" in Figure 5.2.) The directive would be as follows:

> *Students, I will give each group a set of cards with sentences on them. Your job is to study all the cards and talk about what some of them have in common. Place the cards that have something in common together and put the other cards in their own pile. Be ready to explain what you found the grouped cards have in common.*

Once students do this sorting, even with some helpful hints, they discuss and analyze what is common among the sentences they grouped together. During this discussion of similarities, share the guiding questions so they continue their learning with this purpose top-of-mind: *What is personification? How does personification enhance writing?*

What follows is a variety of options for this strategy and suggestions about how to best use manipulatives in your instructional program. Although I write as if educators always find or produce the manipulatives, certainly consider asking students to make them as part of their learning. When you conduct an activity using materials you make, a by-product is that students then have a sample. After a particular activity, give them different resources as the basis for making their own manipulatives. This opportunity can help further their learning as they research, read, and amass information to use for this activity. After teachers check for understanding and correctness, student-generated manipulatives can be issued for pairs and small groups to use.

Although Chapter 6 is dedicated to differentiation and includes a multitude of ideas, what follows are specific differentiation ideas for using manipulatives. I begin, though, with these six pervasive differentiation techniques:

1. *Level of adult assistance.* Some students might need more support than others, so offer additional instruction to struggling learners, as needed. By the same token, check in with all students to ensure they are being effectively challenged and taking appropriate risks to learn and grow.

2. *Power of observation.* Observe students informally as they work in partnerships or small groups. Also review their written work, if you assign it, to determine if you need to gather a small group for reteaching or enrichment.

3. *Learning style.* Determine if you want to conduct a tactile or kinesthetic activity based on your learning goals. The activities detailed in this section are written as tactile; however, any of them can be altered to accommodate a kinesthetic activity.

4. *Readiness.* For tactile work, distribute sets of cards or strips to groups based on readiness so each group receives appropriately challenging material. Also consider the quantity you give each group to provide the right number of manipulatives.

5. *Color-coding.* Color-code manipulatives for the different levels of learners. For example, customize a game of bingo for learning vocabulary by color-coding the bingo cards and clues. Specifically, high achievers could have a blue bingo card, at-grade-level students a yellow card, and struggling students a green card. Write clues on blue, yellow, and green cards to match the bingo cards that reflect readiness levels. Give struggling students a hint before playing bingo to listen carefully to clues read from a green card. You can also create various sets of cards to use for other games—concentration, matching, sequencing, or other activities—and color-code each set to reflect readiness levels.

6. *Grouping.* In some activities, group by readiness or interest. Other times, though, allow students to choose to work independently or with a partner they select. Offering this choice responds to differentiation by learning style.

Specific differentiation ideas for using manipulatives include the following:

• *Matching.* Create pairs of manipulative cards for students to match vocabulary words with definitions, terms or concepts with examples or pictures, characters with their personality traits, animals with their habitats, causes with effects, subjects with predicates, and so forth. As with all of these manipulative ideas, matching can be used as a preassessment or formative assessment, or even used for both. See Figure 5.5 for various simile and metaphor cards that you can use. For example, *Her teeth are as straight as* is one card and the matching card reads *white picket fences.* I am a firm believer in using examples students are exposed to, so create your own manipulatives by pulling similes and metaphors from text students are listening to or reading so they see authentic application. However, you can use Figure 5.5 as a model; then students can create their own sets from their literature.

  o **Differentiation**. See the six general ways to differentiate listed previously. For struggling students, you might color-code the cards so that the word, character, animal, or whatever category is being matched is in a color and the corresponding card is in white. This way, students can lay out the pieces into two separate columns and match them more easily. For advanced students, consider creating all white cards instead of color-coding them. For a simile activity, find various similes that show a range of sophistication so you give the appropriately challenging cards to groups of students to match. In addition, give your advanced students metaphors depending upon your student population. Also, add pictures to accompany the similes to those who need the support of a visual.

## Simile and Metaphor Cards

| | | | |
|---|---|---|---|
| He is as smart as | Albert Einstein. | Her teeth are as straight as | white picket fences. |
| The baby's hair was as soft as | fur. | The shot hurt as badly as | a sharp pencil poke. |
| Her eyes were as blue as | the azure sky. | The grains of sand are as fine as | sugar. |
| The dog's bark is loud like | a siren. | His shirt is blood-red like | a persimmon. |
| His forehead was hot like | fire, so I took him to the doctor. | The plane took off effortlessly like | a bird taking flight. |

| | | | |
|---|---|---|---|
| The cat savagely attacked the mouse like | it was its last meal. | The glistening pool called me like | a soft-spoken mother beckoning its child. |
| The shiny pool looked like | a mirror. | Tulips are | tiny teacups for fairies. |
| A drink of lemonade on a hot summer's day | is a refreshing dunk in the pool. | The baby's persistent cries on the crowded flight | were nails on a chalkboard. |
| Sarah, our soccer team's goalie, | is a wide barricade on a highway. | She lights the room with her presence because she | is sunshine all day long. |
| Anything written on the Web is | a public announce-ment. | My heart is | stone sitting empty and cold. |

**FIGURE 5.5**

• *Sequencing.* Ask students to manipulate sentence strips to identify the sequence of a story. As students advance in the grades or are more sophisticated, have them sequence the strips not just in a linear row to signify logical order, but also in a shape to show structure. For example, the basic plot diagram is an inverted check. Have students place the strips in an inverted check design and discuss which strip represents the central conflict, which one is atop the check to show the climax, and so forth. In addition, ask students to take the strips and create a shape other than the inverted check to represent the plot structure they feel the author crafted. They must defend their shapes by using plot element terms (e.g., *introduction, central conflict, rising action,* etc.). For younger students, instruct them to sequence a collection of random pictures, explain why they chose this order, and then introduce *beginning, middle,* and *end.* Next, have them sequence pictures you prepare from familiar stories as a vehicle to check for understanding and also for them to identify and use the terms *beginning, middle* and *end.*

o **Differentiation**. As with all manipulative activities, consider the six general differentiation ideas previously listed. For sequencing, create strips based on readiness as shown in Figures 5.6 and 5.7 for the story *Not Norman* by Kelly Bennett (2005). Figure 5.6 shows strips without pictures whereas Figure 5.7 provides pictures. If using these strips, make sure to cut off the numbers in Figure 5.6 that indicate the sequence. For students who do not need visual aids, instead of making two versions—one with pictures and one without—create two or three sets of sequencing strips for the same story that vary by sophistication and distribute the appropriate level of challenge to each group. Another way to differentiate is to have students read different stories based on interest and readiness and ask them to write accompanying sequencing strips to use with classmates.

## Sequencing *Not Norman* by Kelly Bennett (2005)

| 1. When the boy gets Norman, he wants to trade him for another pet. |
|---|
| 2. The next day, the boy takes Norman to school for sharing. |
| 3. When the boy is about to share, Emily's snake escapes and only Norman listens to him. |
| 4. That afternoon, the boy takes Norman to his music lesson. |
| 5. During the music lesson, Norman sways and glugs to show he likes the tuba. |
| 6. As soon as music class is over, the boy wants to take Norman back to the pet store. |
| 7. By the time the lesson is over, it's too late. |
| 8. That night, the boy is scared by noises at the window, and Norman comforts him. |
| 9. On Saturday, the boy takes Norman to the pet store. |
| 10. Finally, the boy realizes Norman is the best pet ever. |

**FIGURE 5.6** Sequencing Without Pictures

## Sequencing *Not Norman* by Kelly Bennett (2005)

When the boy gets Norman, he wants to trade him for another pet.

The next day, the boy takes Norman to school for sharing.

When the boy is about to share, Emily's snake escapes and only Norman listens to him.

That afternoon the boy takes Norman to his music lesson.

During the music lesson, Norman sways and glugs to show he likes the tuba.

**FIGURE 5.7** (*Continued*)

After music class, the boy wants to take Norman back to the pet store.

By the time the lesson is over, it's too late.

That night the boy is scared by noises at the window, and Norman comforts him.

On Saturday, the boy takes Norman to the pet store.

Finally, the boy realizes Norman is the best pet ever.

**FIGURE 5.7** Sequencing With Pictures

• *Card sort.* As opposed to matching, have students sort cards to categorize them by examples and nonexamples based on the lesson goal. They can sort nonexamples of imagery (*I like my crazy pet dog.*) and imagery examples (*My rambunctious dog Titan jumps on any surface in sight: the green marble kitchen counter, the smooth felt of the pool table, or the coffee table cluttered with leftover snacks.*). If you are studying adjectives, create cards with adjectives from the literature or informational text you are reading and random other words, and have students sort adjectives and nonadjectives. Another sorting opportunity involves giving students two characters as title cards and having them sort personality traits and physical appearances associated with each character. They can sort cards with examples of renewable and nonrenewable energy. In addition to the previous ideas in which students sort cards into two categories, they can sort by more than two, such as sentence beginnings in which they focus on the first words of a sentence (e.g., *proper noun, common noun, pronoun, adverb, dependent clause, prepositional phrase,* etc.), or excerpts from literature you are reading by the method of characterization (e.g., *what a character says, what a character does, what a character looks like,* etc.), and so forth. Or make category cards with various parts of speech, like *nouns,* and then have several cards with actual words (*Mrs. Sommers, doctor, playground, house, Ellen*) for students to sort.

○ **Differentiation**. Realize there are boundless examples of sorting students can do which can be differentiated by using pictures or not (depending on the level of students), creating more sophisticated words or text to sort, and considering the number of items to sort. If you have students finding groups kinesthetically, like parts of speech, give high achievers the lead cards (e.g., *noun*) so when they walk around the room, they can help to seek out students with the associated cards who might need support.

• *Identification cards.* Use the cards in Figure 5.8 that show the elements of an opinion or argument paper with an arrow. Ask students to place each card with its arrow pointing to the appropriate place on a student or published sample showing where the author employed this element. For papers without a particular element present, the student does not use any cards, which itself becomes a discussion opportunity. Of course, this strategy can be used with any genre by creating element cards specific to that writing type (e.g., *setting, plot, character, point of view, theme* for literature). Or create identification cards of the methods of characterization and have students place each card where evidence of the method exists.

○ **Differentiation**. Distribute different student or published samples to student groups based on interest or readiness to use as the basis for this activity. For an extension, have students use identification cards to point out methods of characterization for their independent or leveled reading books and identification cards to indicate elements in a nonfiction textbook or picture book (e.g., captions, bold text, glossary word, table of contents entry, etc.).

## What Activities Can Educators Implement During a Learning Experience Using Manipulatives?

Prior to conducting a manipulative activity, teachers can prepare students for learning by stating the guiding question, making a connection to a previous activity, or conducting a mini-lesson. For example, before I had students categorize sentence strips based on their beginnings, I led a short lesson where I read an excerpt from Louis

## Opinion/Argument Identification Cards

| topic sentence ← | thesis statement ← |
|---|---|
| fact ← | data ← |
| transition ← | transition ← |
| example ← | address reader concern ← |
| conclusion ← | call to action ← |

**FIGURE 5.8**

Sachar's *Holes* and posed the question *What do you notice about the sentence beginnings in this excerpt?* The excerpt is as follows: "He dug his shovel into the side of the hole. He scooped up some dirt, and was raising it up to the surface when Zigzag's shovel caught him in the side of the head. He collapsed. He wasn't sure if he passed out or not. He looked up to see Zigzag's wild head staring down at him" (Sachar, 1998, p. 78). The discussion that ensued set the stage for the manipulative activity that focused on various types of sentence beginnings. (By the way, I made sure to communicate to students that authors take creative license in their work and that the lack of sentence variety was used for effect. We then have a discussion about what he hoped to achieve by using repetitive sentence beginnings.)

After students perform a manipulative activity, augment it with continued formative assessments such as students engaging in oral discussions, making their own manipulatives, finding evidence of the skill they learned in literature and informational text, and so forth. They have worked with partners or small groups, so give them an opportunity to think and process what they learn and demonstrate this learning independently. For the previous example on sentence beginnings, after the manipulative activity, students were instructed to hunt for specific sentence beginnings in published work and then practiced writing paragraphs using a combination of sentences with varied beginnings. Ultimately, they were expected to demonstrate understanding of this skill in a longer writing piece of their own.

### How Can Teachers Prepare for Using Manipulatives?

When I use this strategy, I copy all of my manipulatives on heavy 100 lb. paper. Not all office supply stores carry this high a weight, so go to the larger chain stores. This thickness will go through your computer printer. After copying, you might laminate the sheet for durability and reuse, and then cut out the pieces. To create sets of manipulatives, you can place them in regular business envelopes or coin envelopes. (I am amazed at the different sizes of coin envelopes office supply stores have at our fingertips!) I store my envelopes in plastic shoe boxes with labels on the front for categories, such as "Narrative Unit," "Parts of Speech," or the title of a literary or informational text.

# FORMATIVE ASSESSMENTS

## What Are Formative Assessments, and How Are They Linked to Instructional Activities?

Teachers conduct *formative* (or *ongoing*) *assessments* consistently throughout a unit to collect information about how to modify, extend, enrich, compact, reteach, redirect, or do whatever is necessary to help students make meaning and capitalize upon unit goals. Since these assessments are a vehicle to check for understanding, formative assessments inform instruction and help determine when interventions are necessary. Simply stated, they are assessments *for* learning. Effective teachers use them often and pay attention to the results they collect to service students optimally. They also serve as a means for students to self-assess and self-monitor how they are faring so they can be advocates in their learning. For those of you who appreciate analogies, here are a couple: Just as doctors take the vital signs of patients to inform them of adjustment to a health regimen or gardeners routinely assess their plants and administer more or less fertilizer or water to assure optimal growth, so, too, do teachers check for understanding regularly to further the growth of their students.

Black and William (1998), two British academicians who are leading authorities invested in assessments, state, "the term 'assessment' refers to all those activities undertaken by teachers, *and by the students in assessing themselves*, which provide information to be used as feedback to modify the teaching and learning activities in which they are engaged. *Such assessment becomes 'formative assessment' when the evidence is actually used to adapt the teaching work to meet the needs."* These assessments can be informal or formal activities and are an integral part of the instructional program. Using cubes and manipulatives during an instructional activity are examples of formative assessments that can be used to check for understanding. If students roll a die or sort sentence strips and discuss responses and reasoning, it becomes a more informal method to gauge their understanding. If, however, students respond to the activity orally and then write in their journals or create a graphic organizer to submit to teachers, their responses can be studied more carefully thereby making it a formal assessment. Quizzes, portfolio reviews, journal responses, homework assignments, brainstorming sheets, RAFT (role-audience-format-topic), graphic organizers, notes, outlines, written summaries, pictures with captions, responses to exit cards, dialectical journals, and literature circle sheets are some of the many examples of formal ongoing assessments.

Informal formative assessments can be a valuable tool if teachers carefully observe students engaged in a task, such as think-pair-share, yes/no response cards, responses on a mini-whiteboard, finger symbol responses (thumbs up or thumbs down), or discussion responses. Some teachers take notes to help inform their instruction on individual students through a recordkeeping sheet or sticky notes. This is an excellent idea. Be aware that even though these informal or formal instructional activities engage learners in a task based on unit goals, the task only translates into formative assessment when teachers use the results to gather and respond to the information on student learning.

## RESOURCES

*Resources* constitute the books, handouts, videos, teacher guides, manipulatives, and so forth that are needed for a particular activity. Figures 5.9 and 5.10 provide ample examples. Cross-reference these lists, as you might find some items on one that you would not on another. Of course, you can add to these lists as new digital resources become available, and other resources abound; however, the figures are comprehensive enough for you to use and to help you generate more ideas. Please note that I did not include basic classroom supplies on the lists, such as paper, pencil, crayons, or scissors. However, if you don't typically use chart paper or graphing paper but it is needed for a particular activity, by all means include it. The list is for you, a substitute, colleagues, or others who will teach the lesson, so include everything that would make sense to teach it.

When you get to the exercise at the end of this chapter, you might choose to input resources on your unit map as you enter skills and activities for each lesson. This method might be fairly natural because as you draft these components, you might automatically think about student and teacher resources and materials necessary to make the activity come to life. However, you can also look at Figures 5.9 and 5.10 to stimulate ideas for resources and materials. This might also mean returning to the activities and revising or adding, as needed. For example, if your initial activity does not include a video or guest speaker, but as you review the resources, it seems a great vehicle to teach a particular lesson, then you can add an activity to incorporate this resource.

When a teacher begins to teach a lesson, all of these materials need to be available, so account for them in the map. "It is like a baker who reads a recipe and looks at the ingredients. The ingredients listed are what the baker needs to be successful during the baking project" (Glass, 2009, p. 154). If you have been in the throes of cooking or baking only to find you are out of sugar or some other essential ingredient, you know what I mean. So be proactive and plan in advance for all that you need in a given unit by entering a list on your unit template. In fact, sometimes gathering resources can be a challenge and might even drive decisions about the timing of teaching particular units. This is critical to note as you create a yearlong curriculum map. When I taught language arts, our school had a limited number of class sets of novels, so I would have to collaborate with my grade-level colleagues and plan accordingly so we weren't teaching the same novel concurrently.

Rich resources and materials can enhance any lesson. I am baffled by a recurring comment I hear all too often from teachers about their colleagues' refusal or hesitance to share. I cannot understand why some teachers would not share valuable resources, materials, and lessons with others so that students benefit from their collaboration and sharing. Hopefully that is not an issue at your school, so take advantage of what your colleagues have and together work to find and share resources that meet unit goals and support differentiation. In fact, educators invested in differentiation definitely need support from grade-level colleagues, media specialists, librarians, practitioners in the field, and others; teachers need a wide variety of resources to appeal to differentiation by readiness, interest, and learning profile.

## Resource Ideas for Any Classroom

| General Resources | |
|---|---|
| • biography | • encyclopedia |
| • autobiography | • dictionary/thesaurus |
| • short story | • website |
| • novel | • computer/software |
| • diary | • LCD projector |
| • student journal | • interactive whiteboard (Promethean or SMART Board) |
| • published journal | |
| • drama | • document camera |
| • reader's theater | • artwork |
| • graphic organizer | • calendar with pictures |
| • literary review and critique | • photograph |
| • speeches (audio and text) | • music (CDs, cassettes) |
| • poem | • primary source document |

**FIGURE 5.9** (*Continued*)

- textbook
- video/audio
- librarian
- media specialist
- PowerPoint presentation
- magazine article
- newspaper article
- poster
- pamphlet
- brochure

- guest speaker
- student handout (e.g., for homework, in-class assignments, journal prompts, etc.)
- quiz and test
- student checklist
- published and student examples
- scoring rubric
- teacher resources (e.g., websites, college textbooks, literature guides, etc.)
- content area standards

### Digital Resources

- LibriVox (free audiobooks from the public domain; several options for listening) http://librivox.org/
- Storynory (free audiobooks of orignal stories, fairy tales, myths and histories, poems) http://storynory.com/
- Poem Hunter (database of poems) www.poemhunter.com/
- Many Books (more than 29,000 free Ebooks) www.manybooks.net/
- Wordle (tool to generate "word clouds" from text that students provide) www.wordle.net/
- WebQuests (web-based software for creating WebQuests in a short time without writing any HTML codes; see other educators' Webquests, as well) www.zunal.com/
- Bubbl.us (a tool that allows students to visually web/map understanding of words and concepts; free alternative to Kidspiration) https://bubbl.us/
- iPod Touches
- flip video camera
- graphic organizers

    o www.eduplace.com/graphicorganizer/
    o www.edhelper.com/teachers/graphic_organizers.htm
    o www.teachervision.fen.com/graphic-organizers/printable/6293.html
    o http://freeology.com/graphicorgs/
    o www.educationoasis.com

### Primary Resources

- letter manipulatives (magnetic letters, rubber stamps, letter trace cards, alphabet tiles, etc.)
- individual mini-whiteboards with markers
- picture cards
- art supplies (crayons, gluesticks, glue dots, scissors, washable markers, feathers, Wikki stix)
- plastic tablecoths or shower curtain, plastic smocks
- stickers, bookmarks
- pocket chart, phoneme frames, sentence strips, sight words, flannel board
- finger puppets, stick figurines
- rhythm instruments (sticks, bells, triangle, tambourine)
- timers
- primary reference books (picture dictionary, beginning thesaurus, rhyming dictionary)

**FIGURE 5.9**

## Core Curriculum Resources

| Language Arts | Science |
|---|---|
| • biography<br>• autobiography<br>• short story<br>• novel<br>• diary<br>• student journal<br>• play<br>• prop/costume<br>• reader's theater<br>• literary analysis<br>• speech (written and recorded)<br>• poem<br>• literature and grammar textbook<br>• literature guide (e.g., Novel-Ties, Scholastic, etc.)<br>• video<br>• grammar textbook<br>• book on tape<br>• music<br>• artwork<br>• genre-specific writing rubric (e.g., response to literature, persuasive, etc.)<br>• field trip (e.g., play, symphony, etc.)<br>• VoiceThread (digital tool for sharing stories or conversations with people around the world via voice, text, audio file, or video) http://voicethread.com/<br>• folklore and mythology text http://www.pitt.edu/~dash/folktexts.html<br>• Storykit (iPod app for creating, editing, and reading stories)<br>• Common Core Standards for ELA, Appendix B: Text Exemplars and Sample Performance Tasks (NGA, 2010)<br>• Common Core Standards for ELA, Appendix C: Samples of Student Writing (NGA, 2010) | • newspaper and magazine article (e.g., *American Science Journal*)<br>• science journal article<br>• photograph<br>• field guide<br>• documentary (e.g., *An Inconvenient Truth, Super Size Me,* etc.)<br>• website (e.g., www.fossweb.com/ and www.topscience.org/ for interactive activities; www.scholastic.com/home/ for teacher and parent resources; http://songsforteaching.com/ for music)<br>• perishable lab materials (e.g., pig's intestine, frog, cow's eye, mealworms, crayfish, etc.)<br>• specimens (e.g., rocks and minerals)<br>• aquarium/terrarium<br>• microscope<br>• thermometer<br>• telescope<br>• magnifying lens<br>• balances and scales<br>• chart (e.g., periodic table, blood cells, mitosis/meiosis) and models (e.g., anatomy, torso, plant and animal cells, etc.)<br>• test tube, beaker, plastic slide, petri dish<br>• pH supplies (e.g., meter, papers, indicators, test set)<br>• safety equipment (e.g., safety goggles, apron, plastic covers, etc.)<br>• dissecting set<br>• video (e.g., Bill Nye the Science Guy: *Atoms/Motion, The Magic School Bus*) and documentary<br>• field trip (e.g., weather station, nature preserve, wetlands, planetarium, greenhouse, etc.)<br>• science and technology school resource supplier (e.g., AIMS Educational Foundation, Fisher Science Education, etc.) |
| **Math** | **Social Studies** |
| • math textbook<br>• math manipulatives (e.g., pattern blocks, spinners, tangrams, counters, etc.)<br>• play money<br>• individual whiteboard, markers, erasers | • documentary (e.g., *The Times of Harvey Milk, Why We Fight, Triumph of the Will,* etc.)<br>• recorded and written speeches (e.g., Martin Luther King's "I Have a Dream"; see www.history.com/speeches) |

**FIGURE 5.10** (*Continued*)

- math journal
- math software programs
- website (e.g., http://songsforteaching.com/)
- protractor
- ruler
- geometric shapes
- calculator
- two- and three-dimensional figures
- bank statement/checkbook
- stock report
- data display
- chart, graph, table, diagram
- guest speaker (e.g., architect, engineer, dietician)
- graphing paper
- scales with weights
- abacus
- math literature (e.g., *Eating Fractions, From One to One Hundred, The Greedy Triangle, The Go-Around Dollar,* etc.)
- books and materials by Marilyn Burns

- video (e.g., excerpt from Roots)
- simulation (e.g., Interact materials at www .interact-simulations.com/)
- primary source document (e.g., Declaration of Independence, historical journal entries)
- guest speaker (e.g., Holocaust survivor, history professor, historian, local politician, etc.)
- field trip (e.g., courthouse, walking field trip around school or neighborhood, history museum, factory, etc.)
- historical fiction (e.g., *Little House in the Big Woods, My Brother Sam Is Dead,* etc.)
- WebQuest
- graphic organizer (e.g., Venn diagram, outlines, T-chart, etc.)
- magazine (e.g., *Time for Kids, Newsweek,* etc.) and newspapers
- map, globe, atlas
- Google Earth www.google.com/earth/index .html

**FIGURE 5.10**

---

## EXERCISE 6: What Targeted Skills With Associated Activities, Resources, and Assessments Can Educators Design (and Find) for a Targeted Unit?

For this exercise, you will complete the remaining components of your unit template that are circled in Figure 5.11.

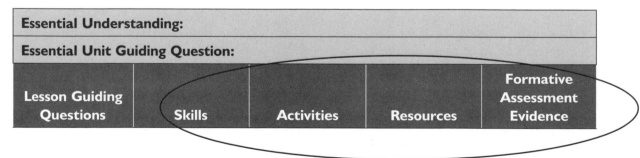

**Essential Understanding:**

**Essential Unit Guiding Question:**

| Lesson Guiding Questions | Skills | Activities | Resources | Formative Assessment Evidence |
|---|---|---|---|---|

**FIGURE 5.11** Unit Template Excerpt 3

You first need to identify targeted skills based on the standards that are associated with each essential understanding and your guiding questions. Remember that these skills must be addressed in context, taught directly, and assessed to demonstrate understanding. Therefore, you will need to sketch appropriate learning activities to teach each skill along with the appropriate resources and corresponding evidence of assessment. If you haven't already, peruse the examples of completed unit maps in Chapter 3 to help you. What follows are some suggestions and reminders for what to record, but surely review this chapter and its figures to support you. The steps for this particular exercise are not numbered because, as mentioned in the previous section on resources, each of you will have your own style in recording entries and it might not be altogether linear from skill through to evidence for each lesson question. Some of you will toggle back and forth between columns as your creative juices flow, you think of resources you already have, or you stop to sketch a graphic organizer to use. So, read the remainder of this chapter and then work on the rest of the template in a fashion that naturally flows. In fact, some of you might want to read ahead to Chapter 6 on differentiation and then begin this chapter's exercise so you can incorporate differentiation as you complete the map. Others may want to finish the map as explained in this chapter and then return to insert differentiation. That's a personal choice for you to make.

*Skills and Activities.* At the beginning of this chapter, the examples of how skills and activities are written in the section "What Is the Difference Between Skills and Activities?" can guide you in recording them on your unit template. They both begin with verbs. However, you will notice that the unit templates are extremely detailed with regard to activities. You need to decide how comprehensive you want to be with this component, as the level of detail might overwhelm some readers. However, consider who is reading your unit map. If others are reading it to develop lessons, then it would be helpful for them if you were to expand upon your activities. If it is for your eyes only or those of a small group of colleagues, you can be brief on the unit template and save the detail for developing the actual lessons. Just be careful to at least record enough in the activities to satisfy teaching the skill.

Figure 5.12, Verbs Based on the Revised Bloom's Taxonomy, can assist with generating activities. As you might know, Benjamin Bloom and his colleagues developed a method of classification on differing levels of intellectual behavior as it relates to learning called Bloom's taxonomy (Bloom & Krathwohl, 1956). It has since been updated by Lorin Anderson, a former student of Bloom's, and David Krathwohl to have more relevancy for twenty-first-century work (Anderson & Krathwohl, 2001). By no means should Figure 5.12 be used as a vehicle for differentiation, as Benjamin Bloom and his colleagues meant for all students to enjoy a rich education by experiencing all levels of intellectual behavior. To relegate struggling learners to the lower levels of remembering and understanding would only do these students a disservice—they should ultimately be evaluating and creating, as well. You surely can differentiate the text or an activity for students, because those who have difficulty with access to a text will not be able to analyze or synthesize it (or even comprehend it!). And all students, even high achievers, will need to comprehend and apply before they can evaluate. So please use Bloom's work or the updated version from Anderson and Krathwohl (2001) as intended and not as a vehicle for differentiation. Tomlinson and McTighe (2006) emphatically make this point in their book *Integrating Differentiated Instruction + Understanding by Design*: "many teachers over the years have used the taxonomy as a framework for a misguided approach to differentiating instruction—that is,

# Verbs Based on the Revised Bloom's Taxonomy

| Remembering | | Understanding | | Applying | |
|---|---|---|---|---|---|
| alphabetize | point to | account for | order | adopt | illustrate |
| check | quote | advance | outline | apply | implement |
| count | recall | alter | paraphrase | calculate | interpret |
| define | recite | annotate | predict | capitalize | make |
| draw | recognize | associate | project | chart | manipulate |
| duplicate | record | calculate | propose | choose | map |
| fill in the blank | repeat | classify | qualify | complete | mobilize |
| find | reproduce | construe | recognize | compute | operate |
| hold | reset | contrive | rephrase | conclude | practice |
| identify | say | convert | report | conduct | put in |
| know | show | describe | restate | consume | put to use |
| label | site | discuss | retell | demonstrate | relate |
| list | sort | estimate | review | determine | schedule |
| locate | spell | expand | reword | dramatize | show |
| match | state | explain | rewrite | draw | sketch |
| memorize | tabulate | expound | select | employ | solve |
| name | tally | express | spell out | exercise | teach |
| offer | tell | identify | submit | exert | use |
| omit | touch | infer | substitute | exploit | utilize |
| pick | transfer | interpret | summarize | generate | wield |
| | underline | locate | transform | handle | write |
| | | moderate | translate | | |
| | | offer | vary | | |

| Analyzing | Evaluating | Creating |
|---|---|---|
| analyze | arbitrate | arrange |
| appraise | appraise | assemble |
| audit | argue | build |
| break down | assess | change |
| categorize | choose | combine |
| check | compare | compile |
| classify | conclude | compose |
| compare | critique | conceive |
| contrast | decide | conceptualize |
| criticize | defend | construct |
| debate | determine | create |
| deduct | editorialize | design |
| detect | evaluate | develop |
| diagnose | give opinion | devise |
| diagram | grade | forecast |
| differentiate | judge | formulate |
| discriminate | justify | generalize |
| dissect | measure | generate |
| distinguish | prioritize | hypothesize |
| divide | rank | imagine |
| examine | rate | integrate |
| experiment | recommend | invent |
| explain | resolve | manage |
| group | score | organize |
| identify | select | originate |
| infer | support | plan |
| inspect | value | predict |
| investigate | verify | prepare |
| order | weigh alternatives | prescribe |
| question | | pretend |
| reason | | produce |
| relate | | propose |
| screen | | rearrange |
| search | | reconstruct |
| separate | | reorder |
| sequence | | reorganize |
| simplify | | role play |
| specify | | structure |
| survey | | suppose |
| test | | synthesize |
| uncover | | visualize |
| | | write |

**FIGURE 5.12**

higher-order thinking for gifted students and basic skills for lower achievers. *Using Bloom's taxonomy as a framework for differentiation is indefensible"* (p. 120). To aptly differentiate, refer to Chapter 6, Figure 6.3, Ideas for Differentiating Instruction, along with other resources you might have to assist you in accommodating the characteristics of the wide variety of students you serve.

Another tool to use to help generate activity ideas is in Appendix B of the Common Core State Standards, where there are sample performance tasks that you might review (NGA, 2010). This appendix is organized by grade clusters (i.e., K–1, 2–3, 4–5) and the performance tasks are tied to their suggested texts that are also included in the same Appendix B.

*Assessment Evidence.* After or concurrent with listing the steps of an activity, record the assessments that you will observe or collect that show tangible evidence of understanding. For example, if students are completing a graphic organizer, the natural piece of evidence that you will look at to check for understanding is the *graphic organizer.* If you have students write a *summary,* then naturally the summary is the piece of evidence. The same applies to a *quiz, poem,* or *journal entry.* If, however, the formative assessment is informal like a game, finger symbols, or mini-whiteboard responses, then what do you record? In these instances, it is important to observe students as they participate in these activities and jot down notes, as needed. On your template, record *observation of participation in group activity,* or something akin to that, based on what students actually do that you observe. Just remember that whatever students do is open game for informing how you instruct and for students to self-assess themselves, so record it all in the unit map to remind you and your students to be keen observers and assessors.

So when recording, input evidence of informal and formal formative assessments, be specific to name the actual handout or assignment, and use nouns or noun phrases to express them, such as *observation during cubing activity, observation during group discussion, "I Am" poem, summary of* Roxaboxen, *Methods of Characterization chart, retelling of* Cinderella, *journal response for immortality,* and so forth.

*Resources.* Record all materials and resources you will need to conduct your activity. Recording generic resources is fine if it makes sense, for example those in this chapter's figures: *various graphic organizers, photographs of national landmarks,* or *picture calendars.* But where you can, be specific in recording your resources for each activity as in the Chapter 3 unit template, such as the exact name of the guest speaker (and even contact information), the title of the movie or song, the name of a handout, and the book or newspaper article titles. Oftentimes the resource and the evidence for assessment are identical entries. For instance, if students create a graphic organizer as an activity, then *graphic organizer* will be in the resource and also the evidence column, because you will touch and assess it. Or, if you have *The Little Red Hen journal prompt* under resources, the companion evidence is naturally *The Little Red Hen journal response.*

## CLOSING

Based on the exercises completed thus far for a targeted unit, you have grouped standards, identified the factual knowledge, created essential understandings and guiding questions, and identified a culminating assessment. To complete the KUD model of know, understand, and do, this chapter focuses on what students will *do*—the skills—and the remaining unit map components. There are myriad engaging ways to design and teach lessons for students to grasp, use, and apply key skills and concepts. To teach within a context of the unit's overarching conceptual understanding, teachers need to design learning activities that include relevant and enriching resources and materials. In addition, they must provide opportunities for students to demonstrate proficiency of the content through assessment. On a unit map, the work of outlining the skills and activities related to the understandings and guiding questions, plus resources and evidence of understanding, prepares educators for designing effective, meaningful curriculum. In the next chapter, you will read about differentiation and return to your unit template armed with ideas to better meet the needs of your students.

# 6

# Differentiated Instruction

> *The key principles of high-quality differentiation include establishing a welcoming and safe classroom, ensuring that what is taught (the curriculum) is of the highest quality, maintaining a commitment to ongoing assessment, offering respectful differentiated tasks, and incorporating flexible grouping practices over time.*
>
> —Cindy Strickland (2009, p. 5)

**A** leading author in the field of differentiation, Carol Ann Tomlinson (2001), provides this often-quoted definition: "In a differentiated classroom, the teacher proactively plans and carries out varied approaches to content, process, and product in anticipation of and response to student differences in readiness, interest, and learning needs" (p. 7). This chapter expands upon this definition and provides some examples. Additional examples of differentiation are woven throughout this book, specifically in the Chapter 3 curriculum unit map examples, Chapter 5 activities aligned with skills, and Chapter 7 complete lessons.

One significant aspect of lesson design is differentiation. This is why the unit map, which serves as the guidepost for creating comprehensive lessons, includes references to it. Differentiation is a necessary part of choosing teaching strategies and instructional activities, as students are individuals who need different paths and opportunities to grapple with and practice learning outcomes. So, too, differentiated resources allow students a variety of ways to gain access to content and understanding. Differentiated assessments provide students the means to demonstrate understanding in a way that resonates with them. Within these components, teachers can indicate appropriate opportunities for differentiation. All students, however, are expected to grasp the standards, essential understandings, essential unit guiding questions, and skills of any given unit, so these are not intended to be differentiated except for individuals with extreme needs. In short, what students should know, understand, and be able to do are non-negotiable when it comes to differentiated instruction. However, to assist students of many different readiness levels, interests, and learning profiles in achieving the goal of proficiency, a teacher needs to differentiate the instructional and teaching strategies, activities, resources, and assessments. Since students—like all people— have individual differences, differentiation should be a priority for educators to include in a unit map as shown in Figure 6.1, a primary-level excerpt from Chapter 3.

---

**Essential Understanding**

Different groups share similarities and differences in various aspects of their daily lives then and now.

**Unit Guiding Question #1**

How are groups of people different and the same then and now?

| Lesson Guiding Questions | Skills | Activities | Resources | Formative Assessment Evidence |
|---|---|---|---|---|
| **Lesson 1.4**<br><br>How is life today different from long ago for Pilgrims and Native Americans? How is it the same for them? | • Draw, dictate, and write to compose opinion pieces. | • Draw, dictate, write about Pilgrims or Native Americans long ago or people now and state an opinion about the topic(s); use books and graphic organizers as aids. (For **differentiation** by **interest**, students choose topic; for **differentiation** by **readiness**, students write or dictate). | • Completed graphic organizer from previous lesson. <br>• Pilgrim and Native American books to use for drawing and dictation or writing (for **differentiation** by **readiness**, provide books at various reading levels). | • Observation during discussion. <br>• Drawing, dictation, writing on chosen topic (**differentiation** by **interest** and **readiness**). |

**FIGURE 6.1** Unit Template Excerpt Including Differentiation

## CONTENT, PROCESS, AND PRODUCT

The *content* refers to what we want students to actually learn as the result of a unit of study. Content is determined by reviewing the state, district, or Common Core Standards and represents what students should understand, know, and be able to do. There are essentially two aspects of differentiating instruction for content: "First, ...we can adapt *what* we teach. Second, we can adapt or modify *how we give students access* to what we want them to learn" (Tomlinson, 2001, p. 72).

If you conduct literature circles in which students read different books, you are adapting *what* you teach. If you have some students working on decimals while others focus on percentages, you are adapting *what* you teach. If you have students working on different vocabulary lists, you are adapting *what* you teach. Let's consider the access piece of content. When you want to learn content about information, where do you turn? For example, when crises erupted in several Arab countries seeking independence or the tsunami decimated Japan, I sought more information by reading the newspaper, listening to news stations, and going online. For students, how do you deliver or make available new information to present content? The typical vehicle is through textbooks, but there are multiple other ways to present or have students *access* content, such as watching a demonstration or video, listening to a guest speaker or viewing a PowerPoint, or reading magazine or newspaper articles in print or online. To also differentiate *how* you allow students access to content, consider the support systems. Some students can grasp content working individually, others might work in partnerships or groups best, and some might need more adult assistance. These various ways of *what* you teach and *how* students gain access to the material provide rich opportunities for differentiation.

Once students are exposed to content, they need to do something with it to make sense of the material and learn. I can read all night about Libya's or Syria's history and the crisis situations, but it probably won't stick unless I actually process the information and do something with it. For me, that might mean making a graphic representation of what I've learned (e.g., outline or bullet points), having a discussion with my husband or peers, and conducting an Internet search to find answers to specific, targeted questions I still might have. This *process* piece in teaching represents most of a unit of study as it involves any activities, assignments, and formative assessments, such as simulations, labs or demonstrations, discussions, games, quizzes, journal writes, and homework.

When teachers ask students to demonstrate knowledge at the end of a comprehensive unit of study, they are expecting their charges to complete a culminating project or summative assessment, which is addressed in Chapter 4. This assessment is also called a *product*. A product—not to be misconstrued as a formative or ongoing assessment— might be presented at the beginning of the unit so students are aware of unit expectations, but it is collected at the end of a long period of study. As mentioned earlier, you might issue a final exam; however, you may provide an additional opportunity for students to demonstrate what they have learned that is more authentic and can effectively show what they have gleaned. Or you can assign one comprehensive and meaningful product in lieu of an exam.

In a differentiated classroom, teachers can differentiate content or process or product. It would not behoove teachers to regularly differentiate all three because the goals of a particular unit may not warrant such an intensive approach. For example, there are times when whole-class instruction is prudent, such as when a guest speaker comes to speak to the class and all students would benefit from the message. Other examples include presenting a video clip to all students, showing them a demonstration, or modeling how to perform a task. So be mindful to differentiate where it is appropriate. Creating a unit curriculum map will help you determine when differentiation makes sense and when whole-class instruction is best employed because it allows you to look at the unit in its entirety.

# READINESS, LEARNING PROFILE, AND INTEREST

In a differentiated classroom, teachers appeal to students' readiness, interest, and/or learning style, as well. Students have varying degrees of *readiness* in approaching specific content. Their capacity or scarcity concerning certain subject matter is contingent upon many variables. Some students lack the background knowledge because they might have moved schools and missed a segment of learning, they might have immigrated from a different country and have a language barrier, they might have been disengaged from school, or they might have a learning issue that precludes them from fully grasping the material at the pace it is delivered to grade-level peers.

Conversely, some students might possess more readiness because they pick up knowledge quickly and retain it, they are voracious readers of a particular subject and independently seek knowledge beyond the classroom expectations, or they have adults in their lives who engage them outside of school in an area of interest. When you take into account students' readiness by using their current level of understanding as a jump-off point and plan accordingly, you will be more apt to get the most learning out of your students. Be aware that when differentiating curriculum by readiness, the goal is to challenge students about 10 percent above what they are able. If students are constantly challenged far above their ability levels, they are acutely frustrated. But if they are repeatedly asked to work way below their ability levels, they are bored and psychologically turned off. As you might have observed, these situations can lead to behavior problems.

*Learning profile* includes the way in which students learn best. When you allow students to demonstrate knowledge or work in a classroom environment that supports individual learning styles, student performance might increase. Howard Gardner (1993) popularized this area with his multiple intelligences: *verbal/linguistic, logical/mathematical, visual/spatial,* and so forth. Robert Sternberg (1996) also is known for his work in the area of intelligence and includes three skill areas: *analytical, creative,* and *practical.* And many of you are familiar with Rita Dunn and Ken Dunn's (1978) work on learning styles: *auditory, visual, tactile, kinesthetic,* and *tactile/kinesthetic.*

However, there are other factors to take into account when appealing to students' learning profile. For example, some students might not be bothered by ambient noise, whereas other students are mildly or severely distracted by it. For those students who are adversely affected by the noise, allow them to sit in the periphery of a classroom configuration. You can even provide noise-cancelling headphones or earplugs during times of particular distraction. There are also students who prefer daylight to fluorescent light. If you have a classroom with windows, invite those who prefer natural light to sit near them. Other factors to consider include the physical temperature of a classroom, optimal energy levels based on certain time of day, and mobility preferences. Learning profile can also take into account working individually or in pairs or small groups. Sometimes there could be opportunities for students to choose their own grouping. If so, allow for this flexibility.

Learning profile and *interest* are closely tied. A student who prefers to demonstrate knowledge through a technology project is also more interested in this type of modality than, say, a short story. But it also has to do with students' areas of interests. For example, content standards might indicate that all students write an opinion piece or research paper, so you need to teach and expect students to produce writing within this genre. To appeal to differentiation by interest, though, you might allow students to choose their own preferred topics as the subject for their papers. Allowing students to select a book for a literature circle is also an example of interest-based differentiation. For math, you might ask students to record various geometric shapes from a visual of their choice that most appeals to them, such as Picasso's modern art, a photograph, Mondrian's artwork, and so on. When assigning a research paper, allow students the opportunity to select a topic of interest to them as the basis for the essay. If biography is what you are teaching, allow students the option of choosing a person as the basis for this paper.

## How Might Teachers Combine Readiness, Learning Profile, and Interest?

Teachers surely can combine two or three of these aspects of differentiation. Look at the following assessment example in Figure 6.2 and consider how it appeals to differentiation by readiness, learning profile, and interest.

| Choose a historical figure from the list below. Then create and present one of the following: interview, poem, song, or art with writing. In your project, address the guiding questions: *Why is this individual a hero? How is his/her heroism linked to freedom? How is this hero like another hero in the past or today?* | |
| --- | --- |
| • Anne Hutchinson<br>• Benjamin Franklin<br>• Thomas Jefferson<br>• Abraham Lincoln | • Frederick Douglass<br>• Harriet Tubman,<br>• Martin Luther King, Jr. |

**FIGURE 6.2** Differentiated Assessment Idea

When I issue the assignment, I briefly give students a snapshot of each individual on the list. Of course, you will make your own list, not to mention the one I provide is incomplete. I typically have as many topics as there are students in my classroom with a couple of extra. Then I ask students to write down their top three choices in rank order and put their name on a slip of paper to submit to me. This appeals to interest in that I allow students to choose their topic; however, that night, I review their preferences and assign one of their three choices based on what I know about each student's readiness. I would not give a student who struggles with content a topic where the resources are scarce and hard to read and decipher. Please note that it is perfectly fine to give more than one student the same topic. In fact, students might glean more as they collaborate on finding and discussing resources and content in preparation for their individual projects. Plus, they can discuss aspects of the topic and assign each other different subtopics as the focus for their projects.

To appeal to learning profile, students choose from the list of project choices, that is, interview, poem, song, or art with writing. It is important to note that all students are held accountable for responding to the essential unit guiding questions since they represent key conceptual understanding. Consider applying this same strategy of intertwining differentiation for readiness, interest, and learning profile for literature circles, poetry selections, character studies, or other learning opportunities.

**EXERCISE 7: HOW CAN EDUCATORS INDICATE DIFFERENTIATION ON THE UNIT MAP?**

In the multiple pages of Figure 6.3, Ideas for Differentiating Instruction, you will find many ways to plan for and employ differentiation for your activities, resources, and assessments. At this point, you might have completed all columns of the unit map and are now learning about ways to differentiate that you will go back and include in your template. The guidelines in the last chapter, however, indicated that some of you might want to read this chapter before completing the skills, activities, resources, and evidence of assessment columns and devise differentiation opportunities as you work on developing those columns. Either approach is fine as long as you include appropriate ways to differentiate for your charges and account for it on your unit template. Since this is a broad category filled with numerous resources, you might choose to build your professional inventory in the area of differentiation.

## CLOSING

The reality in any classroom is that it is comprised of students with all different characteristics. Pervasive diversity is the call to action that teachers must address to meet these students' needs whether it be through responding to their readiness levels, interests, or learning profiles. There are a variety of ways to differentiate content, process, or product to appeal to these student characteristics, so account for this as you create your unit maps. Be mindful that standards, essential understandings, essential unit questions, and skills should not be differentiated as they represent expectations for all students save those with extreme situations. However, educators are encouraged—and even expected—to differentiate activities, instructional and teaching strategies, assessments, and resources, as appropriate, in accordance with learning goals. The last chapter is devoted to lesson design to illustrate the natural subsequent step to developing a unit map.

# Ideas for Differentiating Instruction: Readiness

| | Content | Process | Product |
|---|---|---|---|
| **Readiness** | • Provide **resources and supplemental materials** at varying levels of readability, such as the following:<br>　○ various textbooks<br>　○ newspaper articles<br>　○ magazine articles<br>　○ short stories<br>　○ novels (chapters)<br>　○ diaries or historical diaries<br>　○ videos<br>　○ computer software<br>　○ websites<br>　○ speeches<br>• Consider the **amount** of reading.<br>• Adjust **what** material students are taught. | • Provide **word labels**.<br>• Provide **word lists** at varying levels of challenge for individuals to incorporate in their writing or speaking.<br>• **Modify or extend directions.**<br>• Partially complete a **graphic organizer.**<br>• Assign appropriately challenging **graphic organizers, templates,** and **frames.**<br>• Create an assignment using **cloze procedure.**<br>• Create **tiered assignments** that vary by level of challenge. (As a management tip, use color-coding or symbols.)<br>• Consider the **amount of writing.**<br>• Allow **extra time.**<br>• Provide **reference materials** at varying levels of readiness (e.g., capitalize on different kinds of thesauruses, online resources, and dictionaries).<br>• Create or find **games** and appropriately assign them to individuals, pairs, or groups based on readiness.<br>• Assign particular **computer software.**<br>• Assign **jigsaw** reading to groups based on readiness levels.<br>• Assign students to specific **learning centers.**<br>• **Teach or reteach** a skill, concept, or topic for selected students in need of honing targeted learning.<br>• **Enrich learning** to higher achievers ready for more sophistication or extensions.<br>• Issue multiple levels of **questioning.**<br>• Assign **homework** at varying levels of difficulty.<br>• Assign varied **journal prompts** according to readiness.<br>• Preselect **websites** and assign to students as they investigate a research question (WebQuests).<br>• Issue appropriately challenging sets of **manipulatives** and **cubing prompts.**<br>• Provide tiered **RAFT** assignments (role-audience-format-topic). (Note: Do an online search for RAFT for detailed explanation and examples.) | • Allow **dictation, words, sentences,** or **paragraph writing,** as appropriate.<br>• Create **tiered products** that vary by level of challenge.<br>• Create and issue **RAFT** (role-audience-format-topic) products based on readiness. (Note: Do an online search for RAFT for detailed explanation and examples.)<br>• Create **rubrics** for different levels of learners keeping in mind satisfying standards. |

**FIGURE 6.3** (*Continued*)

# Ideas for Differentiating Instruction: Learning Style

| | Content | Process | Product |
|---|---|---|---|
| **Learning Style** | • Use **gestures, facial expressions, and articulation** when reading or orally presenting new information.<br><br>• Show **visuals** or provide extra visuals to further help students comprehend text or information.<br><br>• Invite students to choose to **read text individually or in partnerships.**<br><br>• Allow students to **access content** in a way that addresses their learning styles, such as the following:<br>  ○ computer software<br>  ○ video<br>  ○ interviews<br>  ○ speeches<br>  ○ demonstrations<br>  ○ text (textbook, articles, poems)<br>  ○ PowerPoint<br>  ○ artwork or photographs<br>  ○ graphic representations | • Have **directions** on tape recorder and written down.<br><br>• Offer **read-aloud or independent reading** as an option, when appropriate.<br><br>• Allow choice of **graphic organizers.**<br><br>• Allow students to **type or handwrite** their work.<br><br>• Provide **choice** in how students **learn new words or facts** (e.g., flashcards, graphic organizers, songs, etc.).<br><br>• Be flexible about **where students work** in the classroom (e.g., in a chair, on the floor, at a table, near the window).<br><br>• Be flexible about **how students work** in the classroom (e.g., working with a partner or alone, using noise-canceling headphones, standing at an upright desk, etc.).<br><br>• Create or find different kinds of **games** and allow students to choose which to play.<br><br>• Use a combination of **tactile and kinesthetic** activities, as well as the more common **auditory** and **visual** ones.<br><br>• Create and issue **RAFT** (role-audience-format-topic) or other assignments during formative assessment with choices that appeal to **multiple intelligences.** | • Allow students **choice** in how they demonstrate knowledge for a summative assessment, such as through writing an article or poem, performing a skit or interview, using multimedia (e.g., PowerPoint or iMovie), drawing, using music, and so on.<br><br>• Create and issue **RAFT** (role-audience-format-topic) products from which students choose. |

# Ideas for Differentiating Instruction: Interest

| | Content | Process | Product |
|---|---|---|---|
| **Interest** | • Provide **resources** with various topic choices (e.g., in an animal unit, provide several books on different animals so students can choose the one that interests them).<br><br>• Provide different **reading genres** to learn about a topic (e.g., biography, autobiography, nonfiction, etc.).<br><br>• Conduct **literature circles.** | • Allow students to choose a **computer program.**<br><br>• Conduct **jigsaw** activity based on topic of interest.<br><br>• Allow students to choose or create **interest centers.**<br><br>• Create or find **games** and appropriately assign them to individuals, pairs, or groups based on interest.<br><br>• Assign varied **journal prompts** according to interest.<br><br>• Preselect **websites** for students to choose from as they investigate a research question.<br><br>• Create and issue sets of **manipulatives** and **cubing** prompts based on interest.<br><br>• Allow students to choose **subtopics** within a greater unit (e.g., for colonial life, choose an individual or topic—clothing, art, religion—as the focus for an activity; in math, sort objects of your choice). | • Work with student(s) to devise an **independent study** that culminates in a product; provide criteria for quality of product and clear work expectations.<br><br>• Assign students to collect a sampling of their best work in a **portfolio.**<br><br>• Allow students to determine a community need and create (or participate in) a **service-learning project.**<br><br>• Provide student choice in a **topic of interest** as the basis for a culminating project.<br><br>• Allow students to select and respond to an **essay question** to demonstrate understanding. |

**Additional Differentiation Support**

- **Adult assistance.** Work (or have another adult work) with individuals or small groups to provide further explanation, reteaching, or enrichment.
- **Extra modeling.** Provide extra modeling before individual, pair, or small group work.
- **Peer support.** Assign peers to help further explain a task or explain it in a different way; be mindful not to overuse peers as tutors as these students need to continue on their own learning paths.
- **Preview.** Preview an assignment at school before it is taught to the whole class, or send an activity home for parents to review it with their child.
- **Language.** Provide instruction in a student's native language or allow students to work with an adult who speaks the same language to discuss content, do a picture walk of the text, or respond to literature.
- **Enrichment.** Provide opportunities for students to extend learning and explore a topic or concept with more depth and complexity.

**FIGURE 6.3** Ideas for Differentiating Instruction

# 7

# Lesson Design

> *Beyond learning about a subject, students will need lessons that enable them to experience directly the inquiries, arguments, applications, and points of view underneath the facts and opinion they learn if they are to understand them. Students have to do the subject, not just learn its results.*
>
> —Grant Wiggins and Jay McTighe (1998, p. 99)

**A**lthough the focus of this book is on creating a comprehensive unit map, it is necessary to address lesson design and where it resides within our work of creating this map. This chapter provides a lesson template along with many examples of lessons that follow the template format. After reading this chapter and using the resources within this book, you can better determine which direction you or those you work with need to go for further individual or group support in a particular area of lesson design.

## LESSON COMPONENTS

### What Are the Components of Lesson Design?

To maximize student achievement, it is not enough to create the map and launch into teaching. The unit map serves as the guidepost for conceptual understanding and factual knowledge, but to have students glean what you intend, there is more. The work you have accomplished in previous chapters provides the framework to engage in lesson design that requires detailed step-by-step directions for each lesson in a unit. Effective lesson design includes its own elements, but it is guided by the tenets of sound unit design that are now familiar to you. Lessons set the stage for students to answer the guiding questions as they learn factual information, hone a skill, apply a concept, and seek understanding. In Wiggins and McTighe's (1998) seminal work on backward design detailed in *Understanding by Design*, the authors call this "Stage 3, the curricular activities and teachings—the design work at the heart of everyday teaching" (1998, p. 98).

To teach students in accordance with goals expressed in the unit map, you need to find or create lessons that are differentiated, employ engaging and thoughtful teaching methods and instructional strategies, contain myriad assessments to inform your instruction, and more. Just like a curriculum unit map has a template with components, so do lessons. The lesson template featured in Figure 7.1 will guide you to incorporate all the aspects of sound lesson design. Some of what you see on the curriculum map will undoubtedly appear on the lesson template. However, lessons include many more details; these are explained in Figure 7.1 and shown in the lesson examples in this chapter. Use this template to support your endeavor to plan for success by designing effective and meaningful lessons—or edit existing lessons you find—that include these components:

- Essential unit and lesson guiding questions
- Lesson overview
- Standard(s)
- Resources/materials (including differentiation)
- Estimated timing
- Step-by-step lesson details (including differentiation)
- Extension (optional)
- Assessments (including differentiation)

# Lesson Design Template

Essential Unit Guiding Question #_____: _____

Lesson Guiding Question #_____: _____

Written by: _____

**Lesson Overview**

Succinctly write an overview of the lesson.

**Standards**

Write the actual standard and associated identification letters/numbers or merely write the identification letters/numbers.

### Resources/Materials

- Include bibliography, as needed.
- Indicate if resource is something that is provided in the lesson or not.
- Indicate *differentiated* resources.
- Not necessary to list basic school supplies, unless for a special project.

### Estimated Timing

- Include how long the lesson will take to conduct (e.g., *two 50-minute class periods*).
- Indicate where in the unit this lesson is taught (e.g., *Teach this lesson after reading Chapter 2* <u>**or**</u> *Parts of this lesson about a change in character are revisited throughout the story as shown in the lesson details*).

### Lesson Details

- Number each detailed step so the lesson is easy to follow.
- Begin each detailed step with a verb phrase (e.g., **Practice** *multiplication*, **Identify** *examples of figurative language*, **Complete** *graphic organizer*). Put each verb phrase in bold type and underline it so teachers' eyes immediately go to it.
- Follow each verb phrase with the detailed directions for conducting the lesson by describing both the teacher's and students' roles. These directions include instructional and teaching strategies to conduct this learning activity.
- Indicate *differentiation*.
- Include grouping.
- Refer to any resources or materials that are listed above in the "Resources/Materials" section. The lesson details need to explain what teachers actually do with these resources and how they are incorporated into the teaching of the lesson.

### Extension

Explain what the extension will involve, such as the following:

- Individual or small groups
- Mandatory or optional
- For some or all students
- Homework or in class
- Necessary materials
- Time estimates for each suggested extension activity

### Assessments

- Express as nouns or noun phrases (e.g., *observation of participation; "What method of characterization?" handout; written journal response*).
- List formal assessments by specific name if it's a handout, quiz, assessment, and so forth (e.g., *Sensory Details graphic organizer, Causes of the American Revolution journal write*).
- List informal assessments (e.g., *observation during class discussion or group activity*).

**FIGURE 7.1**

The lesson template reminds and educates teachers of the necessary components of not only *what* to teach, but *how* to teach it. *What* you are teaching is embedded within the essential understandings, guiding questions, knowledge, and skills as they emanate from standards. These are some of the *how* type of questions that are folded into the design of each lesson: *How will it be differentiated? What will be differentiated? How will students be grouped? How will the teacher deliver the information? What will students be expected to do? How will the teacher collect information informally and formally to inform instruction? What varied resources are needed? How will these resources be presented and used? When is the lesson taught within the unit and how long is it? How do teachers bridge from lesson to lesson so this one makes sense and flows with the other lessons? Are there extensions that make sense? If so, for whom?*

## What Are Examples of Lessons That Include the Components?

In this chapter are several lessons aligned to the Common Core that you can use and teach if they are in accordance with your unit goals. Read the guiding questions to help you determine if a lesson focus reflects material you teach. You might adapt aspects of the lessons for the level of students you teach, or use the strategies within the lessons and revise the content to accommodate what you teach. Each lesson is just that—a lesson. Therefore, be mindful that they each are examples of lessons couched within a greater unit. In other words, there are lessons before the ones featured and lessons afterwards; they work in cooperation with one another to meet entire unit goals. So when you create lessons, do so in the sequential order that you mapped out in the unit template so you can bridge learning from one to the next and also give students a preview to an upcoming lesson within your unit.

*Lesson 1.* The guiding question for this lesson—*What is believable or unbelievable?*—is associated with a fairy-tale unit for primary students. The teacher begins by referring to prior lessons that introduced the unvarying elements that most fairy tales have in common and then zeros in on two specific elements as the basis for this lesson: (1) *There are magical or unreal characters like a fairy or an animal.* (2) *There are magical events (or things) that happen that are not real like a fairy doing magic or an animal talking.* Students focus on individual statements related to fairy tales and identify whether each is believable or unbelievable. They then review familiar fairy tales and study their pictures to discern which illustrations are believable and which are unbelievable. The lesson subsequent to this one focuses on the actual text of a selected fairy tale as children identify the believability and unbelievability of what is written.

*Lesson 2.* The guiding question in this lesson—*What sentences belong together to form a paragraph?*—leads students in an activity putting sentence strips together in a logical order; this shows their knowledge of topic sentence first followed by supporting details. Prior to this lesson, they identified the topic sentence and details from a summary writing sample. This lesson uses a tactile or kinesthetic instructional strategy as students are given sentence strips from various paragraphs. They find other students with sentences that form a paragraph, and then together they arrange their strips logically and explain the rationale for the order. After this lesson, students begin drafting paragraphs for a nonfiction summary writing assignment.

*Lesson 3.* This lesson introduces point of view through narrative writing as a precursor to understanding writer's perspective for an opinion piece. Students identify the perspective of characters in familiar fairy tales, namely the wolf in *The Three Little Pigs,* and juxtapose this narrator's viewpoint with that of the wolf in *The True Story of the Three Little Pigs.* They answer the guiding questions: *What is point of view? What impact does a narrator's viewpoint have on the reader?* Students then complete a graphic organizer comparing and contrasting point of view and other elements of literature from different texts. The lesson ends with an explanation that subsequent activities will be centered on expository writing, namely opinion piece, and how its purpose and organizational structure are different than narrative, but that a writer's perspective is an element of both.

*Lesson 4.* In this lesson guided by these questions—*What are settings? What are different types of settings?*—students define setting, generate examples of various types of settings, and recognize an author's use of settings from published excerpts. This lesson is a precursor to students learning about how authors use figurative language to create descriptive settings, which they will ultimately apply to their own stories.

*Lesson 5.* This lesson accompanies Chapter 4 on assessments by showing how to present students with a checklist, rather than merely handing it out to them. Students need to have ownership for the checklist so they actually use it effectively. Passing it out won't do the trick. Try this lesson to engender buy-in for a given writing assignment. This guiding question—*What are the expectations for my short story?*—is for narrative writing; however, you can adapt the strategy to any writing type. The important factor is that students are fully aware of writing expectations prior to sitting down to craft their first draft. You will conduct this lesson about a week or so into the unit, so it serves a dual purpose of checking for understanding of the elements of a writing type.

## NEXT STEPS

Designing lessons is a natural subsequent step to unit mapping. However, after you create lessons, there are a few more steps in the process. To give you a context for where lesson design fits into the overall curriculum plan and what you might do after you've written or found lessons, see the following sequence:

1. *Create a unit map.* When you arrive at lesson design, your unit map should be complete with these components:

   - Grouped standards
   - Knowledge
   - Essential understandings
   - Essential unit and lesson guiding questions
   - Culminating assessment with criterion
   - Differentiation
   - Activities
   - Skills
   - Resources

2. *Design lessons.* This is the focus for this chapter.

3. *Pilot the unit.*
   - After you complete your lessons, you are ready to pilot the unit. When doing so, take detailed notes. If you and colleagues are teaching it concurrently or within the same school year, take notes separately in preparation for reflection that you can do

together. Determine the best system for taking notes: in a journal, on the computer, e-mailed notes to yourself, notes jotted down in the margins of the lessons, a note-taking or dictation app on an electronic device, or whatever works best for you. Your notes should be specific to each lesson and include answers to these types of questions: *Did the grouping work out? Is there another way I could have differentiated? What worked really well? What did not work so well and should be nixed? Were the instructional activities and teaching strategies varied enough? Were they successful in engaging students? Were there classroom management issues I need to address by editing a lesson? Is there an extension activity I could add? A lesson I should add? Was the timing correct, or did the lesson go on too long or did I not allow enough time? What differentiated resources or materials should I add or delete? Were the unit and lesson guiding questions right on, or should I add, delete, or revise any of them? Should I include additional preassessments for lessons or formative assessments? Are there other options for summative assessments that might work?*

- You can now ask certain students if you can keep original samples of their work or make copies. You can use these student samples as a means for reflection and also the following year for students to critique within a formal lesson. To this end, collect weak, on-target, and strong samples. If you don't have a lesson that includes reviewing and critiquing student samples, I suggest adding one, as it's an invaluable way to help students improve their own work. I do not use student samples from kids in my current class to critique. This is because peers can be too generous and not want to offer the insights needed to revise for fear of hurting feelings, or they can be unnecessarily harsh. Either way, it is safe to take off the names and use samples from a different class or the year prior.

- With this arsenal, you can enter into reflection and then revise the unit accordingly.

4. *Reflect and then revise lessons.* This is the ideal time to convene with colleagues who taught the same unit or, if you solely taught the unit, carve out your own time to engage in reflection. Come to this meeting with your notes and student samples to prepare for discussion. You might have a teacher serve as facilitator for the meeting who keeps your group on task and also has an organized plan for your time together. Specifically, you might use the questions delineated in Step 3 as the basis for discussion. Furthermore, you will undoubtedly find that lessons will need revision, so have a plan for this step, which might entail dividing up duties among colleagues and assigning due dates to review each other's lessons and offer feedback. If you work alone, come up with your own timeline for revising these lessons. Even though you will not teach this unit until next school year, time has a tendency to creep up on us.

5. *Reteach.* The next time you teach this unit, there should not be many changes but there could be some. Take notes and make these changes on the spot, if you can, so the unit is intact and ready for the following year.

6. *Create a unit map for another unit.* And so the cycle goes; it is time to gear up for another unit of study and begin the process again. Eventually, with time, you will have a library of effective and meaningful units of instruction.

7. *Create a grade-level yearlong curriculum map; articulate across grade levels.* The issue of other types of curriculum mapping is addressed in the Introduction. To briefly reiterate, the unit map that is your focus while reading this book constitutes one piece—albeit critical—of a unit you teach within your school year. In addition, it is an altogether worthwhile and useful endeavor to create a yearlong curriculum map

of your entire school year if you haven't yet undertaken such a project. After your grade level has embarked upon creating a yearlong map that delineates all units you will teach and accounts for all standards you are responsible for in a given school year, your school or district can create a map that articulates units of study across grade levels. This extensive exercise will uncover gaps and unnecessary repetition. Your grade level and district might already have such mapping documents or have plans to create or revise them based on the new Common Core Standards. If not, there are a great many books and ample computer software to help with such a project. My book *Curriculum Mapping: A Step-by-Step Guide for Creating Curriculum Year Overviews* (2007) is one resource among many on the market for such work.

## CLOSING

Although comprehensive lesson design is not the primary purpose of this book, I would be remiss if I did not address it and provide comprehensive examples of lessons, which are included in this chapter. After educators create a unit map, it is the lessons that make it come alive. They include step-by-step details focused on guiding questions that articulate the roles of students and teachers, ways to differentiate, grouping configurations, needed resources and materials, suggested timing, and ways to assess. After teachers design or find lessons for the unit, each lesson needs to be piloted so teachers can ascertain the effectiveness of each one. Teachers take notes during the piloting phase, collaborate with colleagues who teach the same unit, and make a plan for revision. Ultimately, teachers repeat the process of creating a unit map, designing lessons, piloting, and revising for each unit taught in a school year. This process is ongoing and may take several years, so teachers should not expect that within one year they will have comprehensive unit maps and accompanying lessons totally complete. However, capitalizing upon the strength of colleagues is strongly recommended. To be efficient with time, teachers might create a curriculum map together and then divvy up lesson design among colleagues, offering feedback and ideas along the way.

## A FINAL NOTE

This is the last chapter, so aside from the following lessons, and the Resource section, I take leave. Therefore, I think it appropriate to close this book with some final words. It is no easy task to plan engaging and conceptually sound curriculum. Educators who embrace this work are doing their charges an enormous service because these students will glean so much more than factual knowledge from a given unit. They will be given the opportunity to go way beyond to transfer information and make myriad connections. The approach to planning with key concepts forever present, using guiding questions to frame learning, and delivering instruction in an engaging way are powerful forces in helping students to grow intellectually and ignite excitement in learning. As you continue your efforts and develop units around the map, remember that you are doing important work. Once you catch the fever, which I of course have, you will find there are so many possibilities and endless opportunities to teach under an umbrella of profound meaning and purpose. So, you should commend yourself for the work you've accomplished as you have plodded through the chapters in this book. Go forth with a renewed spirit and a more elevated way of thinking, and be the awesome mentor you were destined to be.

# LESSONS

## LESSON I WHAT IS BELIEVABLE OR UNBELIEVABLE?

### ESSENTIAL UNIT GUIDING QUESTION

How are fairy tales unbelievable?

### LESSON GUIDING QUESTION

What is believable or unbelievable?

---

**LESSON OVERVIEW**

Teachers define the word *unbelievable* and help students identify whether statements posed are believable or unbelievable. Then, students find examples of unbelievable fairy-tale characters and events in pictures.

---

### STANDARDS

- Recognize common types of texts (e.g., storybooks, poems) (NGA, 2010, RL.K.5).
- With prompting and support, describe the relationship between illustrations and the story in which they appear (RL.K.7).
- With prompting and support, compare and contrast the adventures and experiences of characters in familiar stories (RL.K.9).

### RESOURCES/MATERIALS

- Believable or Unbelievable? (Figure 7.2)
- Various fairy tales with many pictures
- Sticky notes

### TIMING

Approximately one 50-minute lesson, or teachers can break the lesson into smaller chunks for workshop time.

### LESSON DETAILS

1. *Connect to previous learning.*
   - Remind students of what they learned in the previous lessons about the elements of fairy tales, specifically the following:
     - There might be a *beginning* like "Once upon a time..." or a similar phrase.
     - There are *magical or unreal characters* like a fairy or an animal.
     - There are *magical events (or things)* that happen that are not real like a fairy doing magic or an animal talking.
     - There is a *good character.*

- ○ There is a *bad character.*
- ○ There are *certain numbers*, such as three animals or three times somebody says something.
- ○ There might be a *royal character*, like a king or queen.
- ○ There might be an *ending* like "And they lived happily ever after" or a similar phrase.

- Tell them that today the focus in on these two elements:

- ○ There are magical or unreal characters like a fairy or an animal.
- ○ There are magical events (or things) that happen that are not real like a fairy doing magic or an animal talking.

- Explain that when characters, events, or things seem unreal or magical, they are also called *unbelievable.* This is a new word for them, so share the root word and explain that the prefix *un* means "not." Tell students that today they will focus on this question: *What is believable or unbelievable?*

2. *Identify statements as believable or unbelievable.*

- Tell students that you will read aloud many statements one at a time. After you read each one, pause and have them determine if the statement is believable (or true) or if the statement is unbelievable (or false). These statements are in Figure 7.2, Believable or Unbelievable? Feature it on the document camera or make an overhead transparency of it. Reveal one statement at a time.
- Use the think-aloud strategy for the first two statements on Figure 7.2. This means you will be talking aloud what you are thinking in your head to show kids how you process information and work out how to do something. Model how to respond to each statement using finger symbols: show a thumbs-up sign for statements that are believable; use a thumbs-down for those that are unbelievable; and, make a fist for those statements you are unsure about.
- Read additional statements one at a time. After reading each statement, instruct students to turn and talk to a partner to determine if each statement is believable or unbelievable. Have each pair use the finger symbols you modeled to respond to each statement. Verify each answer. Statements 3, 6, and 9 are believable and true.

3. *Explain how learning links to ongoing reading work.*

- Tell students that the question *What is believable or unbelievable?* applies to fairy tales because one main characteristic of fairy tales is that something is unbelievable, as they learned in the last lesson. It could be an unbelievable character, an unbelievable setting, or an unbelievable event. That is the charm of fairy tales. Return to the statements and briefly identify what specifically is unbelievable in each statement: *character, setting,* or *event.*

4. *Identify what is believable or unbelievable in fairy-tale pictures.*

- Recall a familiar fairy tale as the basis for modeling this activity and have the book in hand. Focus on one or two pictures and ask students what part of the text explains these pictures. You might feature these pictures—one at a time—on a document camera or merely hold up the book for all to see. Ask if these pictures represent what is believable or unbelievable. Tell students they will be looking at fairy-tale pictures and doing the same exercise.
- Instruct students to work in pairs and review several pictures from fairy tales. As they review each picture, tell them to discuss with their partners if the picture is believable or unbelievable. You might have them use sticky notes to flag those pictures that are unbelievable by writing a *U* and those that are believable with a *B.*
- Then, have them go further to discuss what about the picture is unbelievable: *characters, setting,* or *event.*

- ○ **Differentiation.** Have several different types of familiar fairy tales replete with pictures available for students to peruse. To differentiate by readiness, provide appropriately challenging fairy tales to pairs of students. For high achievers, they can write character, setting, or event in addition to the initials U and B on sticky notes and affix them to appropriate pictures.

5. ***Know that there are believable and unbelievable characteristics in other books students read.***

- Ask students to report to the whole group some examples of what they saw in their fairy-tale pictures. In discussion, compare and contrast these characters, settings, and events from the various books students read.
- Explain to the class that today and every day, they will encounter stories that have unbelievable and believable characters, setting, and events. Have a couple of volunteers share their experiences with reading believable or unbelievable aspects of a story.
- Tell students that in the next lesson they will listen to a fairy tale and identify parts of the text that are believable and unbelievable.

## EXTENSIONS

- Look for examples of unbelievable characters, places, or objects in magazines. Have students cut out examples that they see and bring them into class.
- Watch a Disney fairy tale (e.g., *Beauty and the Beast, Sleeping Beauty,* etc.) and record what is unbelievable.

## ASSESSMENTS

- Participation in discussions and activity
- Placement of and writing on sticky notes

# Believable or Unbelievable?

1. A fairy godmother waves her magic wand and a pumpkin turns into a carriage.

2. A princess bites into an apple and falls into a deep sleep for years and years.

3. A prince invites people to come to the castle for a party.

4. A hen bakes a cake.

5. A little pig builds a house of straw.

6. A wolf lives in the forest.

7. Bears sleep on beds and eat oatmeal for breakfast.

8. Princesses kiss frogs and they turn into princes.

9. Brick houses are stronger than houses made from straw.

**FIGURE 7.2**

## LESSON 2 WHAT SENTENCES BELONG TOGETHER TO FORM A PARAGRAPH?

### ESSENTIAL UNIT GUIDING QUESTION

How do I determine the main idea and supporting details?

### LESSON GUIDING QUESTION

What sentences belong together to form a paragraph?

---

### LESSON OVERVIEW

Students circulate around the room (or work in table groups) to find a complete paragraph that includes the main idea and supporting details. This lesson is preparation for students to write a summary based on a nonfiction text.

---

### STANDARD

Determine the main idea of a text; recount the key details and explain how they support the main idea (NGA, 2010, RI.3.2/RI.4.2).

### RESOURCES

- Activity Sentence Strips (Figure 7.3)
- Summary Paragraphs (Figure 7.4)
- Various expository paragraphs

### TIMING

This lesson takes one to two 40- to 50-minute class periods.

### LESSON DETAILS

1. ***Set the stage for learning.***  Say to students:

   *Earlier you determined the main idea and supporting details from an article. Now you will do an activity in which you each have a sentence strip and you find others who have sentences that belong together to make a paragraph. When you find others who have sentences for your paragraph, you will stand together in the logical order of how the paragraph should be read. You will also be ready to state the main idea and what details prove it is the main idea.*

2. ***Find sentences to make a paragraph.***

   - Prepare for this activity by copying Figure 7.3, Activity Sentence Strips, onto cardstock (100 lb. paper), laminating them, and cutting out the sentence strips. These strips include sentences for four separate paragraphs.
   - Give each student a sentence strip or a pair of students one strip. Instruct them to walk around the room and find others who have a sentence that belongs with theirs. Together, they formulate a paragraph that includes a topic sentence and supporting details.

- Tell students that once they have found others who have sentences that belong together with theirs, they are to discuss the correct order of the strips to form a paragraph: topic sentence (with main idea) first followed by supporting details.
- Once all students are in their groups and have determined the correct paragraph order, convene together as a whole class in a circle with each group standing together. Instruct everyone to face inward so all students see the strips everyone is holding.

3. *Verify paragraph order, topic sentence, and supporting details; add details.*

   - Ask each group to read its paragraph and explain to the class their rationale for why they placed the sentences in the order that they did. In their explanation, they must make it clear which card shows the topic sentence and how the other sentences support it. Classmates agree or disagree with the group; discuss, as needed, to arrive at agreement.
   - After everyone agrees, have the class verify the correct order against the summary paragraphs in Figure 7.4 that you feature on the SMART Board, document camera, or overhead. If the class impressions are different than the prepared summary, discuss what changes need to be made to which version—the students' or the summary paragraphs.
   - As a class, discuss other supporting details the author could have used to support the topic sentence in each paragraph and create additional sentences orally.

     ○ **Differentiation.** Copy the topic sentences in a different color and give these strips to higher achievers. Tell them their job is to help seek out others. Also, some paragraphs are more challenging than others; therefore, distribute strips for paragraphs according to ability level. It is fine to give the same paragraph to more than one group.

4. *Illustrate disjointed paragraphs (optional).* Invite students to make confusing paragraphs with the sentence strips by using the topic sentence from one paragraph and supporting details from other paragraphs. Mix up the sentences so even the topic sentence doesn't appear first. Have students read their creations and talk about why it is so confusing (and funny!). This can be done with the prepared strips or new ones that students create.

5. *Practice identifying topic sentence and supporting details.* Provide pairs with two or three paragraphs that you can copy from social studies or science textbooks. They are to highlight or underline the topic sentences and number the supporting details. If a paragraph is missing a topic sentence, they are to create one. In addition, they add one more supporting detail.

   ○ **Differentiation.** Find paragraphs with various readability levels. Distribute appropriately challenging paragraphs to students. Encourage high achievers to add more sophisticated details.

6. *Prepare for next lesson.* Tell students that in the following lesson, they will complete a graphic organizer to brainstorm for their summary writing piece.

## EXTENSION

Invite students to go home and discuss the structure of a paragraph with family members or older siblings. Together they are to find a paragraph that includes the topic sentence–supporting details construction and cut out a sample to share with the class. Students should be prepared to discuss the main idea of the paragraph and one important or interesting detail.

## ASSESSMENTS

- Participation in activity
- Highlighted or underlined and numbered paragraphs
- Paragraphs from home (extension)

## Activity Sentence Strips

In Paula Angle Franklin's article "Indians of North America," she states that some Native Americans created mounds that were in the shape of living animals.

(as cited in Blau, Elbow, Killgallon, & Caplan, 1995, p. 347)

These mounds can be found within southern Wisconsin, Illinois, Iowa, and Ohio.

The animals depicted in these mounds vary: bears, deer, panthers, wolves, turtles, and birds.

According to Deborah Kent in her article "America the Beautiful: Louisiana," a distinct type of music is found in Louisiana.

(as cited in Blau et al., 1995, p. 342)

Cajun bands that travel through Louisiana towns play accordion music at all-night dances.

The bands feature instruments such as a fiddle, a guitar, an accordion, and a set of steel triangles.

Many of the lively tunes they play came from France in the early 1700s.

The songs, sung in French, usually concern American subjects, such as the unbelievable fierceness of swamp mosquitoes.

In the article "Why Leaves Change Color in Autumn" from *World Book,* changes take place inside a leaf during the fall that cause it to change colors.

(as cited in Kemper, Nathan, & Sabranek, 1995, p. 217)

The green chlorophyll that covers a leaf begins to fade away.

This allows the colors yellow and orange to be seen.

Also, the tiny tubes inside a leaf close up at the stem and hold in sugar and sap.

**FIGURE 7.3** (*Continued*)

(Continued)

| |
|---|
| The sugar may turn the sap red or purple, which shows through the leaf. |
| Then, once the leaf dries up, it turns brown. |
| "Earthquake Disaster," an article in *Science Weekly,* is about an earthquake that struck India.<br><br>(as cited in Robb, Richek, & Spandel, 2002, pp. 146–147) |
| The quake happened on January 26, 2001. |
| Thousands of people were trapped and more than 18,000 were killed. |
| It registered 7.9 on the Richter scale. |
| To understand why quakes happen, scientists use the theory of *plate tectonics*. |

**FIGURE 7.3**

## Summary Paragraphs

In Paula Angle Franklin's article "Indians of North America," she states that some Native Americans created mounds that were in the shape of living animals. These mounds can be found within southern Wisconsin, Illinois, Iowa, and Ohio. The animals depicted in these mounds vary: bears, deer, panthers, wolves, turtles, and birds.

(as cited in Blau et al., 1995, p. 347)

According to Deborah Kent in her article "America the Beautiful: Louisiana," a distinct type of music is found in Louisiana. Cajun bands that travel through Louisiana towns play accordion music at all-night dances. The bands feature instruments such as a fiddle, a guitar, an accordion, and a set of steel triangles. Many of the lively tunes they play came from France in the early 1700s. The songs, sung in French, usually concern American subjects, such as the unbelievable fierceness of swamp mosquitoes.

(as cited in Blau et al., 1995, p. 342)

In the article "Why Leaves Change Color in Autumn" from *World Book,* changes take place inside a leaf during the fall that cause it to change colors. The green chlorophyll that covers a leaf begins to fade away. This allows the colors yellow and orange to be seen. Also, the tiny tubes inside a leaf close up at the stem and hold in sugar and sap. The sugar may turn the sap red or purple, which shows through the leaf. Then, once the leaf dries up, it turns brown.

(as cited in Kemper et al., 1995, p. 217)

"Earthquake Disaster," an article in *Science Weekly,* is about an earthquake that struck India. The quake happened on January 26, 2001. Thousands of people were trapped and more than 18,000 were killed. It registered 7.9 on the Richter scale. To understand why quakes happen, scientists use the theory of *plate tectonics.*

(as cited in Robb et al., 2002, pp. 146–147)

**FIGURE 7.4**

## LESSON 3 WHAT IS POINT OF VIEW? WHAT IMPACT DOES A NARRATOR'S VIEWPOINT HAVE ON THE READER?

### ESSENTIAL UNIT GUIDING QUESTION

How does an author's viewpoint impact readers?

### LESSON GUIDING QUESTIONS

What is point of view? What impact does a narrator's viewpoint have on the reader?

---

**LESSON OVERVIEW**

In this lesson, students identify point of view of the narrator in stories and the influence this viewpoint has on readers, and then they compare and contrast different points of view and other elements. As an option, they orally state how a fairy tale would change if told from an alternative point of view than the traditional version.

---

### STANDARD

- Compare and contrast the point of view from which different stories are narrated, including the difference between first- and third-person narrations (NGA, 2010, RL.4.6).

### TIMING

This activity encompasses approximately two 50-minute lessons.

### RESOURCES

- *The True Story of the Three Little Pigs* by Jon Scieszka
- Any version of *The Three Little Pigs*
- *The Three Little Pigs* by James Marshall
- *Red Riding Hood* by James Marshall
- Various comparison/contrast graphic organizers (easily attainable through a web search)
- *Dear Mrs. LaRue* by Mark Teague
- *The Short and Incredibly Happy Life of Riley* by Colin Thompson and Amy Lissiat
- *I Am the Dog, I Am the Cat* by Donald Hall

### LESSON DETAILS

1. ***Identify point of view and its impression on readers.***

   - Tell students they will listen to a story called *The True Story of the Three Little Pigs* by Jon Scieszka. Tell them you will read the first two pages and then stop so they can answer these questions: *Who is the narrator of this story? In other words, from whose point of view is this story told?* Read the first two pages and then stop for discussion based on these two previous questions.

- Explain that the narrator of a story writes from a certain point of view. This point of view provides perspective and also leaves the reader with an impression. Read the rest of the story and discuss with students this narrator's perspective using this question as a springboard for discussion: *How does this viewpoint influence readers?* Have them identify parts of the story that support how the narrator's viewpoint influences them as readers.

2. *Defend points of view* (optional).

- Explain to students that they will be defending a position of a character in a fairy tale. Mention a particular fairy tale like *Cinderella*. Ask students to name the characters (e.g., Cinderella, stepmother, stepsister, prince). Briefly discuss how each character has a particular point of view and if the story were told from this viewpoint it would be different. Recall *The True Story of the Three Little Pigs* to illustrate how a story can change based on a different point of view.
- Tell students they will (1) identify a fairy-tale character, (2) state a viewpoint, and (3) provide evidence to support this position. They will share these three elements orally with the class.
  - **Differentiation**. Read *Red Riding Hood* and/or *The Three Little Pigs* by James Marshall for struggling students; help them generate characters and their positions. Allow others to use any fairy tale. They may not need the book in hand for this assignment.

3. *Compare and contrast points of view* (model).

- Tell students you will model how to complete a graphic organizer that compares and contrasts two fairy tales. Afterwards, they will read a story and complete their own graphic organizer as you have demonstrated.
- Read a version of *The Three Little Pigs*. Discuss answers to these same questions: *Who is the narrator of this story? In other words, from whose point of view is this story told? How does this viewpoint influence readers?*
- Compare and contrast points of view, other elements of literature, and literary devices of the traditional fairy tale you just read with *The True Story of the Three Little Pigs*. As a class, complete a comparison/contrast graphic organizer that compares aspects of these two versions.

4. *Compare and contrast points of view* (independent practice).

- Have multiple copies of the following list of three books on hand for students to use as the basis for comparing and contrasting point of view and/or other elements of literature. Students read one book and complete a comparison/contrast graphic organizer individually or in pairs.
  - *Dear Mrs. LaRue* by Mark Teague
  - *The Short and Incredibly Happy Life of Riley* by Colin Thompson and Amy Lissiat
  - *I Am the Dog, I Am the Cat* by Donald Hall
  - **Differentiation.** Provide various comparison/contrast graphic organizers. Allow students to choose one based on learning style; however, some are very simplistic (traditional two-circle Venn diagram), so challenge higher achievers to select a more sophisticated organizer or use the three-circle Venn diagram. Differentiate by readiness not only with a more sophisticated graphic organizer, but also with the elements that serve as the basis for comparing and contrasting. All students are expected to focus on points of view; consider also *theme, setting, character, dialogue, writing style,* and so forth for individual students.
  - **Differentiation.** Assign the appropriately challenging book to individual students or pairs. *I Am the Dog, I Am the Cat* presents a straightforward treatment of comparison/contrast of characters so it is not as challenging as the other two selections. In *Dear Mrs. LaRue*, a dog

named Ike has an opinion about his situation at obedience school. His viewpoint, which is featured in pictures, is juxtaposed with his owner's, Mrs. LaRue, or the school officials. Readers must read and also carefully view the pictures to get these different points of view. This story requires some inferencing skills. In *The Short and Incredibly Happy Life of Riley*, who is a mouse, the authors compare and contrast this mouse's life with humans who are portrayed in this book as entitled. It has a sophisticated and strong theme.

- When finished, invite students to share an oral summary of their story and what they learn about viewpoint based on their organizers. Ask them to briefly offer their own impression for which viewpoint they prefer and why.

5. *Debrief.* End by explaining to students that point of view is a powerful element of writing as they have experienced with stories in this lesson. Explain that narrative writing isn't the only text type that includes the element of point of view. It is also a part of expository writing, particularly opinion pieces, which rely heavily on the writer's point of view. In opinion pieces, the purpose of writing and the organizational structure are different, but the writer purposely intends to leave an impression on the reader and has a distinct viewpoint. Tell them they will be studying opinion pieces and eventually writing their own. In doing so, they will need to establish a point of view and use reasons and evidence to support their positions.

## ASSESSMENT

- Participation in discussion
- Presentation of fairy-tale character's point of view (optional)
- Graphic organizers

## LESSON 4 WHAT IS SETTING?
## WHAT ARE DIFFERENT TYPES OF SETTINGS?

### ESSENTIAL UNIT GUIDING QUESTION

How do authors create descriptive settings?

### LESSON GUIDING QUESTIONS

What is setting? What are different types of settings?

> **LESSON OVERVIEW**
>
> In this lesson, students define setting, generate examples of various types of settings, and recognize an author's use of setting from excerpts.

### STANDARDS

- Compare and contrast two or more characters, settings, or events in a story or drama, drawing on specific details in the text (NGA, 2010, RL.5.2)

### RESOURCES

- Butcher (or chart) paper
- Markers
- Setting Categories (Figure 7.5)

### TIMING

This lesson occurs in approximately a 1-hour class period.

### LESSON DETAILS

1. **Define setting.** Conduct a class discussion about setting by asking *What is setting?* Guide students to define setting as anything that answers *where* and *when*, or includes *time* and *place*. Further explain that setting not only includes time and place but also involves the physical details and circumstances in which an event takes place and characters reside or move, such as the background, atmosphere, or environment. With student support, generate a list of setting categories. Arrive at the categories shown in the Figure 7.5 or add your own. Then, provide only one or two examples, as in the figure, to model an activity students will do in Step 2 of this lesson.

| Climate | Geographical Features |
|---|---|
| 75 degrees Fahrenheit, humid, sleet | mountains, oceans |
| **Buildings/Places** | **Time Periods** |
| Shea Stadium, airplane, playground, Disneyland, Florida, Australia | winter, dawn, 5:00 p.m., lunchtime |

**FIGURE 7.5** Setting Categories

2. *List examples of settings.*

   - Post butcher paper around the room on the walls or on tables along with markers. Label each sheet with a setting category. Use the ones provided in Figure 7.5—*climate, geographical features, buildings/places,* and *time periods*—or your own. You can certainly add a category.

   - Instruct students to circulate around the room and add words on any of the butcher papers to provide examples of categories just like you modeled. Encourage them to write as many as they can. You might even assign one butcher paper to a small group and have them all work on making contributions to this sheet. Then call "time" and rotate the butcher paper so another group adds contributions to their classmates' entries. When they add to the butcher paper, tell them to read what was written to avoid duplications. They can even cross out entries that do not go with a particular category, but they must confer as a group before anyone can cross out anything. Rotate papers until all groups have had a chance to focus on each category.

   - Post all the butcher paper on the wall or on different easels. Discuss if any entries are on the wrong sheet or if any need to be omitted. To prepare for Step 3 below, hang up some clean sheets of butcher paper.

3. *Identify examples of settings.*

   - Copy Figure 7.6, Setting Excerpts, onto 100 lb. cardstock, laminate, and cut out the setting strips. Give each student a strip to read and identify the words or phrases that indicate setting. Instruct students to walk around the room with their strips in hand and discuss the settings with at least two people to confirm or rethink the words or phrases that indicate a particular type of setting.

     ○ **Differentiation.** Include excerpts of various settings from different literary texts that include varying degrees of difficulty. Distribute appropriately challenging strips to students based on readiness levels. Some require students to interpret figurative language to better understand the setting. (Note: Even though I include setting strips for you in Figure 7.6, I suggest you create your own from text students have read in class or will read this year.)

   - When students have conferred with others and know the type of setting, have them enter their words or phrases from the strips onto the butcher paper with the appropriate category. If they have settings that do not fit into a category already posted, then they use the clean butcher paper and devise their own setting category.

   - Hold a discussion about the various types of settings using these questions as a springboard for debriefing: *What new types of settings did you create? What words or phrases associated with setting are most powerful and why? Did you find any strong examples of imagery where you visualize in your mind's eye what the author writes? Did any of you have sentence strips that needed interpretation? How so?*

4. *Find settings in literature.* Instruct students to peruse their independent reading books or a class story to find examples of settings to add to the butcher paper. As they hunt for these settings in literature, have them put sticky notes on the pages. Walk around the room and quietly ask students to show you where they found examples of settings. Have them explain what type of setting each example shows.

   ○ **Differentiation.** Pay attention to where students put sticky notes and what they share with you. In a small group, reteach setting to students who are struggling to understand this element of literature.

5. *Debrief.* Review the many different types of settings. Tell students they will be writing their own stories. In their writing, they can create their own settings. Explain that in the next lesson, they will focus on figurative language so they can create descriptive settings that come alive for readers.

**EXTENSION**

Invite students to find pictures of various types of settings and add captions to create a collage to share with the class or post on a bulletin board.

**ASSESSMENTS**

- Observation of participation during discussion and activity
- Setting collage (extension)

# Setting Excerpts

"The first week of August hangs at the very top of summer, the top of the live-long year, like the highest seat of a Ferris wheel when it pauses in its turning."

*(Tuck Everlasting* by Natalie Babbitt, 2007, p. 3)

"On the left stood the first house, a square and solid cottage with a touch-me-not appearance, surrounded by grass cut painfully to the quick...."

(Babbitt, p. 6)

"So the road went humbly by and made its way, past cottages more and more frequent but less and less forbidding, into the village."

(Babbitt, p. 6)

"But the wood had a sleeping, otherworld appearance that made you want to speak in whispers."

(Babbitt, p. 6)

"The pastures, fields, and scrubby groves they crossed were vigorous with bees, and crickets leapt before them as if each step released a spring and flung them up like pebbles."

(Babbitt, p. 46)

"An ancient green-plush sofa lolled alone in the center, like yet another mossy fallen log, facing a soot-streaked fireplace still deep in last winter's ashes."

(Babbitt, p. 51)

"The sweet earth opened out its wide four corners to her like the petals of a flower, ready to be picked."

(Babbitt, p. 45)

"Poppy turned to the left and saw a red barn. It was considerably larger than the house but had only a few windows. The roof was pitched and covered with sheet metal. At the front end of the barn the roof jutted out to form a door hood."

*(Poppy* by Avi, 2005, p. 122)

"On rocky islands gulls woke. Time to be about their business. Silently they floated in on the town, but when their icy eyes sighted the first dead fish, first bits of garbage about the ships and wharves, they began to scream and quarrel."

*(Johnny Tremain* by Esther Forbes, 2003, p. 1)

"All through October the days were still warm, like summer, but at night the mercury dropped and in the morning the sagebrush was sometimes covered with frost. Twice in one week there were dust storms."

*(When the Emperor Was Divine* by Julie Otsuka, 2002, p. 77)

"The sky turned suddenly gray and then a hot wind came screaming across the desert, churning up everything in its path. From inside the barracks the boy could not see the sun or the moon or even the next row of barracks on the other side of the gravel path. All he could see was dust."

(Otsuka, p. 77)

"There across the road, it looked like any rocky hill—nothing but sand and rocks, some old wooden boxes, cactus and greasewood and thorny ocotillo—but it was a special place."

*(Roxaboxen* by Alice McLerran, 1992, p. 1)

"The street between Roxaboxen and the houses curved like a river, so Marian named it the River Rhode."

(McLerran, p. 2)

"After a while they added other streets. Frances moved to one of them and built herself a new house outlined in desert glass, bits of amber, amethyst, and sea-green: A house of jewels."

(McLerran, p. 7)

"The barn was pleasantly warm in winter when the animals spent most of their time indoors, and it was pleasantly cool in summer when the big doors stood wide open to the breeze."

*(Charlotte's Web* by E. B. White, 1952, p. 13)

"It was the kind of barn that swallows like to build their nests in."

(White, p. 14)

**FIGURE 7.6**

## LESSON 5 WHAT ARE THE EXPECTATIONS FOR MY FINISHED STORY?

### ESSENTIAL UNIT GUIDING QUESTION

How do writers know what a story should include?

### LESSON GUIDING QUESTION

What are the expectations for my finished story?

---

### LESSON OVERVIEW

Students brainstorm what they think a strong story entails based on what they have learned so far in the unit. Teachers show a prepared checklist of student writing expectations. Students compare their brainstormed list with the teacher's checklist. As they compare their list with the teacher-prepared checklist, students reinforce elements of literature and have an opportunity to study the expectations.

---

### STANDARDS

- Communicate knowledge of standard English grammar and usage (NGA, 2010, L.3.1) and capitalization, punctuation, and spelling when writing (L.3.2) this text type.
- Write narratives to develop real or imagined experiences or events using effective technique, descriptive details, and clear event sequences (W.3.3).
  a. Establish a situation and introduce a narrator and/or characters; organize an event sequence that unfolds naturally.
  b. Use dialogue and descriptions of actions, thoughts, and feelings to develop experiences and events or show the response of characters to situations.
  c. Use temporal words and phrases to signal event order.
  d. Provide a sense of closure.

### RESOURCES

- Short Story Student Checklist (Figure 3.8 in Chapter 3)
- Suggestions for Using a Checklist (Figure 7.7)—teacher resource
- Let's Review (Figure 7.8)
- Personal Narrative Revision Sheet 1 (Figure 7.9)—primary
- Personal Narrative Revision Sheet 2 (Figure 7.10)—elementary
- Revision Sheet: Short Story (Figure 7.11)—upper elementary

### TIMING

This activity is to occur after a few days of beginning the narrative unit so students are aware of the elements of literature from the introductory lessons.

## LESSON DETAILS

*Note to teachers:* Presenting a writing checklist to students *prior to teaching* will serve to explain what the finished product will entail and how students will be assessed. The lesson written here is a formal way to orient students to a checklist. When students are aware of expectations for writing or any project in advance of working on it, they have a higher likelihood of producing better results. If you continuously use checklists in your classroom, which is recommended, students may not always need something as formal as this lesson to engender ownership of items on the list. As a teacher resource, see Figure 7.7, Suggestions for Using a Checklist, along with a detailed explanation and examples of revision sheets located at the end of this lesson.

1. *Connect to previous learning.* Say to students: *We have spent time reading many stories, and I have told you that you will each write your own story. In order to write the best one you can, I want you to understand clearly what I expect of each of you.*

2. *Explain group task.*
   - Explain to students that when they write their stories, they will be well aware of what you expect *before* they write. This way, there are no surprises and they can work hard to meet clear expectations. Use the analogy that when they bake chocolate chip cookies or order a pizza, they have a clear sense of what these food items taste and look like before they actually eat.
   - To set students up for success in writing, properly orient them to Figure 3.8, the Short Story Student Checklist, before passing it out. You will give them the opportunity to discuss what they think might be included in this writing type and compare a student-generated list of criteria with the checklist you will give them. To do this, tell students they will brainstorm a list in groups about possible criteria. You might say:

     *We have been studying elements of literature and have read literature in class. Think about what makes a strong short story that you enjoy reading. You will talk in your groups and make a list of those features that contribute to an interesting story and a strong piece of writing in general.*

   - Tell students to write a list of what is important to include in a story. It's important to make it clear you want a list of *both* features specific to a story (e.g., setting, character, plot, etc.) and those for strong writing in general (e.g., proper spelling and grammar, neat handwriting, etc.). Note: I have done this activity with second through eighth graders. For younger students, you might conduct this activity together as a class instead of in groups.

3. *Brainstorm list.*
   - Tell students that in their groups they will create a brainstormed list in response to this question: *What are the expectations for my finished story?* Use the roundtable strategy for students to generate this list. See directions in Figure 7.8 to see how this strategy is conducted. (Note: You can use this strategy for another lesson when students need to generate a list. To do so, merely change the prompt.)
   - To help students begin brainstorming, merely remind them of what they learned so far during this unit. While students brainstorm, casually visit each group and gently guide them. Their lists will probably contain features of short story. You also want line items about what makes *all* writing strong. Provide additional hints by saying, *Your list impressively includes elements of literature that you learned. But what if I can't read your work? Remember what all good writing includes and put it on your list.* Typically, the student who is a weak speller writes down "spelling," and then it opens it up to a new burst of energy.

# Suggestions for Using a Checklist

1. **Frequency and familiarity.** Orient students to the notion that checklists are a way of doing business in your classroom. They will sometimes help create checklists and sometimes they will be given one to use. Either way, they use these checklists as a guide. You might create a checklist as a one-shot deal for a specific assignment, and you might have one checklist that is used repeatedly. For example, you might create a checklist for a quick write to use each time they respond to an impromptu prompt.

2. **Present a checklist to students.** Avoid passing out a checklist. That will undoubtedly overwhelm kids. Instead, engender ownership by having them brainstorm what they think might be included in a checklist before you pass out your prepared checklist. Chances are they will have a pretty good idea as to what you are expecting before the formal assignment is issued since you have conducted lessons all along. In groups, have students compare what they collectively generated in brainstorming with the checklist you passed out and highlight what is missing from their brainstormed list. Students might even add to your prepared checklist because they have brainstormed something pertinent that needs to be added.

3. **Use the checklist to state objectives and find or create lessons.** Make sure you teach to most elements on the checklist. That means that you constantly refer to the checklist as you state the day's or week's objective. To do so, make an overhead of the checklist or feature it on a document camera. Also, copy it for students on colored paper so it's easily found and accessible. And certainly make sure that you have lessons for each point on the checklist or refer to past lessons for some items, like grammar or conventions.

4. **Way of doing business.** Remind students frequently that they will use the checklist to guide them while writing. This means it needs to be visible as they write. They will also use the checklist in the editing and revision stages.

5. **Revision sheet.** Make an accompanying revision sheet so students are led through the process of systematically tending to each line item on the checklist. Once they become more experienced writers, they will hopefully not need such a detailed method of utilizing a checklist. Through a prepared revision sheet, students see that every item on the checklist needs to be satisfied as a way of policy in your class.

6. **Final thoughts.** Use the checklists routinely. If you use a checklist once in a while, it won't have the same effect and impact as if you use it frequently and follow these suggestions. Teachers who use checklists wisely and effectively get improved student results. A caveat, though, is that you do not need to follow each of these suggestions every time you issue a writing assignment. You will undoubtedly have short assignments in which a brief checklist is needed. If kids are familiar with these suggestions, they will use the checklist successfully for these small assignments since they have been used and introduced properly before.

**FIGURE 7.7**

# Let's Review

1. Take out one piece of paper per group.

2. Each group member is to have a pen or pencil.

3. Raise your hand if your birthday is closest to George Washington's birthday. You are first. The person on your left is second so that the paper moves clockwise.

4. Starting with the first person, write down one word or phrase that answers this question: *What do strong short stories include?*

5. Continue to pass the paper clockwise entering one word or phrase that answers the prompt. Write a bulleted or numbered list instead of sentences.

6. No duplications are allowed, so read all the previous entries before writing yours. You may say "pass" when the paper comes to you.

7. Time limit:_____

**FIGURE 7.8**

4. ***Create a class list.***
   - Once the brainstorming is complete, have groups report out to the whole class. Write down their responses on butcher paper or the whiteboard so you have a *comprehensive* class list. Remind students to avoid duplications by looking at what was recorded before contributing new items to the list.
   - Then, make a transparency of Figure 3.8, the Short Story Student Checklist, or show it on the document camera. Have students match what they brainstormed with what you have on the checklist item by item. Applaud them for the points that are similar; there will undoubtedly be overlap and that's good. Seeing this overlap reminds students that what they thought you planned to assess them on is something they knew. It reinforces what they have learned about this genre's features.
   - Let students know that as they write their stories, their checklist should be visible constantly. It is a vehicle to guide them *while* writing and not something to use when the paper is done so they can randomly check each box. Remind students that you will assess them against each point on the checklist; hence, you will teach many lessons to assist them in satisfying most line items. Review which items you have introduced so far in the unit.
   - Distribute a checklist to each student. Students can store the checklists in a writing folder for easy reference. As you teach specific lessons, have students retrieve their checklists so you can highlight a particular line item that is the basis for that lesson. This keeps the purpose for learning center stage.

## ASSESSMENTS

- Participation in brainstorming
- Group brainstormed list

## TEACHER RESOURCE: SUGGESTIONS FOR USING A REVISION SHEET

Figure 7.7, Suggestions for Using a Checklist (teacher resource), refers to a revision sheet that is an effective instrument to assist students in producing their best work. It works in tandem with a checklist because oftentimes a checklist alone won't be an altogether successful tool in supporting students to work to their potential. After students write a first draft, they self- and peer assess using an appropriate revision sheet. There are three versions included: Figure 7.9 accompanies a personal narrative piece of writing for primary students. Figure 7.10 is for elementary students and also for a personal narrative. Figure 7.11 is appropriate for upper-elementary students writing a short story. Teachers make two copies of the revision sheet they are going to use. One is for self-assessment, and the other is for a peer to review once students have made revisions. You may also make three copies and send one home with parents to use. For primary, teachers or an aide use the revision sheet together with the student one-on-one. In this regard, the revision sheet provides the talking points for discussion and revision. Note that Figures 7.10 and 7.11 focus on revision and not editing (i.e., grammar and conventions). Conduct the lesson like this for age-appropriate students:

- Say the following: *You will carefully review your rough drafts and make sure that each item on the checklist is satisfied. To do this, you will look at your paper and fill in boxes on a revision sheet.* Show students a copy of the revision sheet on the overhead or document camera. *This revision sheet contains items from the checklist so what is on it is not a surprise.*

- Tell students that they will use this revision sheet to look at their own work, so they know what revisions to make. Once they have a second draft, a classmate will give them comments. Explain that they will be given time to make the necessary revisions based on their own and others' comments.

- Model how to use the revision sheet by filling one out using a student sample from a previous year (or from another teacher's classroom). Explain that there are three choices for completing the revision sheet, so show how this works: (1) Some spaces on the revision sheet cannot be filled in because the paper doesn't include a particular expectation(s). If this is the case, leave these spaces blank so the writer knows where to revise. (2) If a portion of the paper is weak, students fill in the appropriate spaces on the revision sheet and mark these spots with a highlighter as an indication to spend time revising these areas. (3) For great examples of something in the paper, enter these words or phrases on the revision sheet and put an asterisk.

- Let students know that they will follow this revision process: (1) self-assess using the revision sheet, (2) revise their papers based on their self-assessment, (3) give their papers to a peer who will read their second drafts and complete a clean copy of the revision sheet, and (4) revise again based on peer comments. Also, look at students' papers and give comments with or without the revision sheet. Another option is to have students take their papers home with a note to parents to complete the revision sheet with students. Make it clear to parents that they are not to mark on the student's paper at all; all comments are to be on the revision sheet in response to student work. Let students know they might use these comments to revise again as part of the writing process before it gets to the publishing step.

# Personal Narrative Revision Sheet 1

| Ideas/Content and Organization | Circle | |
|---|---|---|
| I write a personal narrative about **something true** that happened to me. | Yes | No |
| I include an **original title**. | Yes | No |
| I **begin** with a description of a **setting**. | Yes | No |
| I **begin** with a description of a **character**. | Yes | No |
| I **begin** with a **telling sentence about what happened**. | Yes | No |
| In the **middle** of my paper, I explain **how it happened in a logical order.** | Yes | No |
| I **end** by telling why it is **important** or how I **feel** about what happened. | Yes | No |
| I make sure I **stay on topic**. | Yes | No |
| **Voice** | | |
| I know **why I am writing** (purpose) and **who will read this paper** (audience). | Yes | No |
| I write in first-person point of view using the **pronoun I** because I write what happened to me. | Yes | No |
| **Sentence Fluency** | | |
| I write **complete sentences**. | Yes | No |
| I have **no run-on sentences**. | Yes | No |
| My **sentences begin in different ways.** | Yes | No |
| I use **order words** to connect my sentences. | Yes | No |
| **Word Choice** | | |
| I include **sensory details** so my reader can picture what I am writing. | Yes | No |
| I use interesting **adjectives and verbs**. | Yes | No |
| **Conventions** | | |
| I use the sounds I know to **spell**. I use tools to help me. | Yes | No |
| I use correct **end marks** at the end of each sentence. | Yes | No |
| I **capitalize** appropriate letters. | Yes | No |
| I read my paper aloud and it **makes sense**. | Yes | No |
| My writing is **easy to read**, and my paper is **neat**. | Yes | No |
| I **properly space** my words and sentences. | Yes | No |

**Figure 7.9**

# Personal Narrative Revision Sheet 2

| Ideas/Content and Organization | |
|---|---|
| This is a **personal narrative** about something **true** that happened. | What is the event? |
| There is an **original title.** | What is the original title? |
| There is a description of a **setting.** | What is the setting and one adjective to describe it? |
| There is a description of a **character.** | Who is a character and one adjective to describe this person? |
| There is a **logical order** to explain **what happened.** | How did it happen in order? <br> 1. <br> 2. <br> 3. |
| The writer tells why it is **important** or how the writer **feels** about what happened. | Why is it important or how does the writer feel? |
| **Sentence Fluency** | |
| **Sentences** begin in **different ways.** | Write a sentence: <br><br> Write another sentence that begins in a different way: |
| There are **order words** to connect sentences. | Write the order words that connect different sentences: |
| **Word Choice** | |
| There are interesting **adjectives.** | Write interesting adjectives: |
| There are interesting **verbs.** | Write interesting verbs: |

**FIGURE 7.10**

# Revision Sheet: Short Story

| Descriptors | Circle | |
|---|---|---|
| The writing is **a short story**. | Yes | No |
| The story **stays on topic and has a main idea**. | Yes | No |
| There are no **grammar or conventions** errors and the **paper uses proper formatting**. | Yes | No |
| Proper **indentation** is used for each paragraph. | Yes | No |
| The story is told in a **logical sequence** so it makes sense. | Yes | No |
| There is an original **title**. | Yes | No |
| The paper stays in **first or third person** all throughout the story. Which point of view is it? | Yes | No |

| Descriptors | Ideas/Organization |
|---|---|
| The **beginning** is **interesting** and gets the reader's attention. | Write what is interesting about the beginning: |
| The beginning provides information about the **setting** using descriptive words or figurative language. | Write adjectives, adverbs, verbs, or figurative language used for the setting: |
| The beginning provides information about the **main character** using descriptive words or figurative language. | Write adjectives, adverbs, verbs, or figurative language used for the character: |
| The beginning includes the **central conflict** (problem). | Briefly explain the central conflict: |
| The **middle** of the story **explains events** that happen. | What is one strong event that happens? |
| | What is a suspenseful event that happens? |
| The ending **resolves** the central conflict. | Briefly state the ending of the story that resolves the conflict. |

**FIGURE 7.11** *(Continued)*

| Descriptors | Word Choice | |
|---|---|---|
| **Dialogue tags** include strong verbs and are punctuated properly. | Write three different sentences with dialogue properly punctuated. **Also,** underline the strong verbs that are used in the dialogue tags:<br>1. | |
| | 2. | |
| | 3. | |
| The **dialogue** is meaningful and moves the plot forward. | Write one sentence of meaningful dialogue. Explain why it is important to the plot. | |
| The paper includes **descriptive words** for events, setting, and characters used in the middle and end of the story. | Write two sentences that use descriptive adjectives, adverbs, or verbs to describe events:<br>1. | |
| | 2. | |
| | Write descriptive words for setting:<br>1. | Write descriptive words for character:<br>1. |
| | 2. | 2. |
| | 3. | 3. |

| Descriptors | Sentence Fluency |
|---|---|
| **Sentences** begin in different ways. | Write two sentences that each begin in a different way:<br>1. |
| | 2. |

**FIGURE 7.11**

# Resource

*A Brief Primer on the ELA Common Core Standards*

This part of the book provides selected information relating to the Common Core (CC) Standards for English Language Arts & Literacy in History/Social Studies, Science, and Technical Subjects. It is primarily an overview from pages 3 to 8 of the original document's Introduction (NGA, 2010), with specific emphasis on Grades K–5. If you are familiar with the standards and their genesis, reading this Resource section may not be necessary.

## CREATION AND PURPOSE OF THE COMMON CORE STANDARDS

### Who Led the Standards Initiative, and What Is the Goal?

The effort to establish the Common Core Standards was led by the Council of Chief State School Officers (CCSSO) and the National Governors Association (NGA). They didn't start from scratch to identify grade-level standards, but rather capitalized upon the work states performed in their pursuit of creating rigorous standards. The CCSSO and NGA also looked to seminal international models and research, and they gathered input from a variety of sources: state departments of education, scholars in the field, assessment developers, professional organizations, kindergarten through college educators, parents, students, and others.

The goal of this seminal work is to "create the next generation of K–12 standards in order to help ensure that all students are college and career ready in literacy no later than the end of high school" (NGA, 2010, Introduction, p. 3). In creating these Standards, the CCSSO and NGA affirm that the standards are as follows:

1. Evidence and/or research based

2. Aligned with college and work expectations

3. Infused with rigorous content and requiring application of knowledge through high-order skills

4. Internationally benchmarked, so all students are prepared to succeed in our global economy and society

5. Built upon strengths and lessons of current state standards

### Who Are the CCSSO and NGA?

The CCSSO is a nationwide, nonpartisan, and nonprofit membership organization comprised of educational leaders from every state in the country. As stated on their website, this organization "leads and facilitates collective state action to transform our public education system in the four strategic areas of Educator Workforce; Information Systems and Research; Next Generation Learners; and Standards, Assessment, and Accountability" (CCSSO, 2011).

The NGA, according to their website, is a bipartisan national organization founded in 1908 and is the collective voice of the nation's governors. It promotes itself as one of Washington, D.C.'s most respected public policy organizations. It is comprised of governors from the fifty states, three territories, and two commonwealths. "NGA provides governors and their senior staff members with services ranging from representing states on Capitol Hill and before the Administration on key federal issues to developing and implementing innovative solutions to public policy challenges through the NGA Center for Best Practices" (NGA, 2011).

## CONTENT AND STRUCTURE OF THE COMMON CORE STANDARDS

### What Is Included in the Standards?

The CC Standards are composed of the College and Career Readiness (CCR) Anchor Standards and grade-specific standards. The CCR Anchor Standards are general, cross-disciplinary literacy expectations that students must meet to be prepared to enter college and careers (i.e., workforce training programs) ready to succeed. In the CC Standards document, these appear on the first page prior to the grade-level standards expectations of each of the four strands: (1) reading, (2) writing, (3) speaking and listening, and (4) language. Following each page of the CCR Anchor Standards are grade-specific standards of what students should know and be able to do at the end of each year in these strands, and they show progression year to year. Students are expected not only to meet each standard by the end of the specified school year, but also to retain the knowledge or further develop skills and understandings going forward. In addition, they are expected to meet the more general expectations described by the CCR Anchor Standards by the end of high school, too. These two sets of standards complement each other and together define the skills and understandings that all students must demonstrate:

- **CCR Anchor Standards** correspond to the grade-specific standards but represent broader, more general standards.
- **Grade-specific standards** expressly define what students should know and be able to do by the end of each grade level.

### What Is the Organizational Structure of the Common Core Standards?

Here is the basic organizational structure of the CC Standards with terminology and key components (NGA, 2010). See Chapter 1 of this book, "Standards and Knowledge," for more detailed information on the content.

## Sections

The ELA Common Core Standards are divided into three major sections:

1. K–5 English Language Arts

2. 6–12 English Language Arts

3. 6–12 Literacy in History/Social Studies, Science, and Technical Subjects

## Strands and Categories

The sections are divided by strands—reading, writing, speaking and listening, and language—and then further divided by categories. The key features of each strand are briefly highlighted here (NGA, 2010).

- **Reading**—text complexity and the growth of comprehension; includes *three* parts—Reading Standards for Literature, Reading Standards for Informational Text, and Reading Standards: Foundation Skills
- **Writing**—text types, responding to reading, and research
- **Speaking and Listening**—flexible communication and collaboration
- **Language**—conventions, effective use, and vocabulary

Figure R.1 lists the strands and their categories, plus the amount of standards. Each standard is assigned a number within each category. For example, the category "Key Ideas and Details" has three standards (1, 2, and 3), "Craft and Structure" includes three standards (4, 5, and 6), "Range of Reading and Level of Text Complexity" has one standard (10), and so forth (NGA, 2010). Note, though, that although some categories have one standard there might be subsets in specific grades. For example, Writing Standard 1 for Grade 3 includes four subsets (a–d): *Write opinion pieces on topics or texts, supporting a point of view with reasons. (a) Introduce the topic or text they are writing about, state an opinion, and create an organizational structure that lists reasons. (b) Provide reasons that support the opinion. (c) Use linking words and phrases (e.g., because, therefore, since, for example) to connect opinion and reasons. (d) Provide a concluding statement or section* (NGA, 2010, W.3.1).

Each strand begins with broader College and Career Readiness (CCR) Anchor Standards that were discussed previously. Each CCR Anchor Standard has an accompanying grade-specific standard translating the broader CCR statement into grade-appropriate, end-of-the-year expectations. There is a number associated with each CCR anchor standard that corresponds to the grade-specific standard so it is easy to see the connection. See the example in Figure R.2.

## Appendices

In addition, there are three appendices (NGA, 2010):

*Appendix A: Research Supporting Key Elements of the Standards* and *Glossary of Terms*. This appendix has extensive supplementary material on reading, writing, speaking and listening, and language, plus a glossary of key terms. Chapter 1 of this book includes comprehensive treatment of text types culled from the "Writing" section of Appendix A in the Common Core document. Later in this Resource section, I highlight some key research findings about reading and speaking/listening.

## Strands, Categories, and Number of Standards

**Strands** →

| Reading K–5 | | | Writing | Speaking and Listening | Language |
|---|---|---|---|---|---|
| Literature | Informational Text | Foundational Skills | | | |
| **Key Ideas and Details:** Standards 1, 2, 3<br><br>**Craft and Structure:** Standards 4, 5, 6<br><br>**Integration of Knowledge and Ideas:** Standards 7, 9 (8 not applicable for literature)<br><br>**Range and Level of Text Complexity:** Standard 10 | | **Print Concepts (K–1):** Standard 1<br><br>**Phonological Awareness (K–1):** Standard 2<br><br>**Phonics and Word Recognition (K–5):** Standard 3<br><br>**Fluency (K–5):** Standard 4 | **Text Types and Purposes:** Standards 1, 2, 3<br><br>**Production and Distribution of Writing:** Standards 4, 5, 6<br><br>**Research to Build and Present Knowledge:** Standards 7, 8, 9<br><br>**Range of Writing:** Standard 10 | **Comprehension and Collaboration:** Standards 1, 2, 3<br><br>**Presentation of Knowledge and Ideas:** Standards 4, 5, 6 | **Conventions of Standard English:** Standards 1, 2<br><br>**Knowledge of Language:** Standard 3 (begins in Grade 2)<br><br>**Vocabulary Acquisition and Use:** Standard 4, 5, 6 |

↑ **Categories**

### Total Number of Standards

- Reading Standards for Literature: *9 standards*
- Reading Standards for Informational Text: *10*
- Reading Standards, Foundational Skills: *4 (Grades K–1)*
- Reading Standards, Foundational Skills: *2 (Grades 2–5)*
- Writing: *10*
- Speaking and Listening: *6*
- Language: *5 (Grades K–1)*
- Language: *6 (Grades 2–5)*

- Grades K–1: *44 standards\**
- Grades 2–5: *43 standards\**

\**see subsets in some standards; e.g., Writing Standard 3 for Grades 3–5; Language Standards 1–5*

**FIGURE R.1**

| CCR Anchor Standard 3 for Reading |
| --- |
| 3. Analyze how and why individuals, events, and ideas develop and interact over the course of a text (NGA, 2010, R.CCR.3). |

*broad*

*more specific*

| CC Grade-Level Reading Standard 3 for Literature K–5 | | | | | |
| --- | --- | --- | --- | --- | --- |
| **Kindergarten** | **Grade 1** | **Grade 2** | **Grade 3** | **Grade 4** | **Grade 5** |
| 3. With prompting and support, identify characters, settings, and major events in a story (NGA, 2010, RL.K.3). | 3. Describe characters, settings, and major events in a story, using key details (RL.1.3). | 3. Describe how characters in a story respond to major events and challenges (RL.2.3). | 3. Describe characters in a story (e.g., their traits, motivations, or feelings) and explain how their actions contribute to the sequence of events (RL.3.3). | 3. Describe in depth a character, setting, or event in a story or drama, drawing on specific details in the text (e.g., a character's thoughts, words, or actions) (RL.4.3). | 3. Compare and contrast two or more characters, settings, or events in a story or drama, drawing on specific details in the text (e.g., how characters interact) (RL.5.3). |

**FIGURE R.2**   CCR Anchor and CC Standard Alignment Example

*Appendix B: Text Exemplars and Sample Performance Tasks.* This appendix has text exemplars that show complexity, quality, and a range of reading appropriate for various grade levels with accompanying sample performance tasks. The materials are divided into grade bands: K–1, 2–3, 4–5, 6–8, 9–10, and 11–CCR. Each band's exemplars are divided into text types matching those required in the standards. K–5 exemplars are separated into stories, poetry, and informational texts, plus read-aloud texts for K–3. Within each grade band and after each text type, brief sample performance tasks are included that reference selected published works.

*Appendix C: Samples of Student Writing.* Here are annotated samples to reflect the criteria required to meet the standards for specific writing types—opinion/argument, informative/explanatory text, and narrative—in selected grades. Each sample illustrates at least the level of quality required to meet the writing standards for that grade. Each writing sample indicates the conditions under which students produced a given piece (e.g., in-class assignments, homework, on-demand assessments, etc.). Samples were compiled from students across the country's states and districts.

## RESEARCH HIGHLIGHTS FOR THE READING AND SPEAKING/LISTENING STRANDS

### What Are the Research Findings and Key Points for the Reading Standards?

As stated earlier and shown in Figure R.1, the reading standards are divided into three categories: (1) Reading Standards for Literature, (2) Reading Standards for Informational Text, and (3) Reading Standards: Foundational Skills (NGA, 2010). The reading standards were designed with the overarching goal for all students to read and comprehend material of steadily increasing difficulty and complexity throughout the grades. When they complete the Common Core Standards, students must be able to read and understand college and career texts independently and proficiently so they can be successful post–high school. Appendix A's section of the Common Core document on reading is divided into three parts to help educators realize this critical goal: research findings as it relates to complexity, a model for measuring text complexity, and annotated examples of how educators can use this model to assess text complexity (NGA, 2010).

When I first heard the buzz about the new Common Core Standards, I repeatedly heard and read that there was more an emphasis on informational reading than on narrative to better prepare students for college and careers. After reading the research in Appendix A, I understand the rationale for their push toward more informational reading and writing. However, rest assured that narrative still has its place.

The Common Core cites extensive research to support the fact that students today are not prepared enough for the complexity of reading college or workplace texts. The authors mention with sound support that the rigor of textbooks has diminished in the last decades (NGA, 2010). As I read it, the term "dummying down" reverberated in my ears as I recall reading repeatedly that the textbooks of today do not contain the length or depth that they once had. When I taught school, I would grab a class set of old social studies textbooks before they were sent off to be recycled because I appreciated the extensive treatment and rigor of textbooks from years ago. In differentiating for students, I would offer sections of old textbooks to challenge my more able readers and use the current day's textbook for others who could not grasp the complexity of these former works. Anyone who has been in education a long period of time can probably relate.

This quote most aptly seems to synthesize the compilation of research for me: "while the reading demands of college, workforce training programs, and citizenship have held steady or risen over the past fifty years or so, K–12 texts have, if anything, become less demanding" (NGA, 2010, Appendix A, p. 2). In addition, I believe it's important that educators are aware of these other associated findings (see Appendix A, p. 3):

- Students are not given enough of an opportunity to independently read complex informational texts which comprise a majority of required college and career material.
- Students are provided too much scaffolding in reading information text which is already less complicated than it was prior to 1962, such as teacher or adult support in reading, class discussions, or summaries and glossaries that textbooks provide.

- Students are not expected to read as much expository text even though this type of reading is much more difficult than narrative. As such, they should have more exposure to informational texts and be taught targeted lessons on reading strategies tied to this genre.
- When students are asked to read expository text, oftentimes they are skimming and scanning it rather than immersing themselves in the cognitive exercises required to truly grasp the complex text.

In the K–5 classroom, the CC Standards include equity between literature and informational text. Since most elementary classrooms are self-contained and teachers address a variety of subject areas, this balance between reading types is expected across content areas. In the middle and high school grades, informational text is given greater attention as literacy is expected in other classrooms besides English language arts. In the Common Core, Figure R.3 shows the distribution between literature and informational text.

| Grade | Literary | Informational |
|:---:|:---:|:---:|
| 4 | 50% | 50% |
| 8 | 45% | 55% |
| 12 | 30% | 70% |

**FIGURE R.3**   Percentage Distribution of Literary and Informational Passages

*Source:* National Assessment Governing Board. (2008). *Reading framework for the 2009 National Assessment of Educational Progress.* Washington, DC: U.S. Government Printing Office.

Besides the research findings, Appendix A of the Common Core features a measurement model for assessing text complexity so educators can select appropriate reading for individual students across the grades. Along with thorough explanations, there are extensive annotated examples of how to use a three-part model for measurement which includes (1) qualitative dimensions of text complexity, (2) quantitative dimensions of text complexity, and (3) reader and task considerations (NGA, 2010, Appendix A, p. 4). There is a disclaimer in the section that the qualitative and quantitative measures that are described represent the best tools currently available. The authors admit that more precise, accurate, and user-friendly tools are in great demand for helping make text complexity a vital, everyday part of curriculum and instruction. What might be useful for educators, as well, is the Reading Foundational Skills section that supplements the Common Core Standards. This section, beginning on page 17 of Appendix A, features phoneme-grapheme correspondences, phonological awareness, and orthography.

## What Are the Research Findings for Speaking and Listening?

Speaking and listening are foundational building blocks to reading and writing. As such, they are a particularly integral part in the earlier years of the English language arts classroom and a predominant factor in improving literacy. Primary teachers spend dedicated time fostering oral skills as they realize this is a critical contributing factor and a prerequisite to students mastering reading and writing. Research shows "children's oral language competence is strongly predictive of their facility in learning to read and write" (NGA, 2010, Appendix A, p. 26).

It might seem like common sense, but the research supports the findings that preschoolers who hear more words have increased vocabulary when they are in kindergarten. What is interesting, as well, is that in third grade this early language proficiency correctly determines their language and reading comprehension. When children hear and learn more words orally, it contributes to better readership (Hart & Risley, as cited in NGA, 2010). As you can imagine, this has particular implications for children where English is not their first language or for those who are not exposed to rich language in their home environment. Extending the research beyond primary grades, Sticht and James report that "children's listening comprehension outpaces reading comprehension until the middle school years" (as cited in NGA, 2010, Appendix A, p. 26). That indicates a strong argument for reading aloud to students, which is why Appendix B lists not only stories, poetry, and informational texts, but read-alouds as well in the early grades. Read-alouds afford students the opportunity to absorb the content without the struggle of decoding the language, which is especially required for informational text. It is important to balance between read-alouds and the gradual support needed to enable students to read independently. Each is important in improving literacy. The progression of speaking and listening standards responds to the research connecting oral and written language in addition to the emphasis delineated in the other strands.

## LOGISTICS

### Can States Add to the Standards?

States that have adopted the Common Core Standards in their entirety have the option of adding up to 15 percent of their own standards to augment the Common Core. Here are salient quotes from Achieve (2010) to educate you on this guideline: "While states will not be considered to have adopted the common core if any individual standard is left out, states are allowed to augment the standards with an additional 15% of content that a state feels is imperative. . . . [T]he 15% guideline should be considered primarily as a *common-sense guideline* to meet specific state needs. States should be judicious about adding content and keep in mind the possible implications of doing so. Remember, a central driver in the creation of the CCSS was to develop standards that were common across states lines—and clear and focused—the opposite of the 'mile wide, inch deep' standards so prevalent in many current state standards. A literal interpretation by states of the 15% guideline (that is 15% added at every grade level and in each subject) would undermine the very reason the states developed the Common Core State Standards in the first place" (p. 1). Some states, such as New York and California, have augmented the Common Core Standards using this rule. Check with your State Department of Education or district personnel to learn if your state has done so.

For example, in first grade, the Common Core Standard 9 for literature states: "Compare and contrast the adventures and experiences of characters in stories" (NGA, 2010, RL.1.9). New York added this to the standard: "a. With prompting and support, students will make cultural connections to text and self" (New York State P-12, 2011,

RL.1.9a). A fifth-grade Common Core Standard 4 for writing reads: "Produce clear and coherent writing in which the development and organization are appropriate to task, purpose, and audience" (NGA, 2010, W.5.4). New York added the following to the original standard: "a. Produce text (print or nonprint) that explores a variety of cultures and perspectives" (W.5.4a).

### How Can Standards Be Identified?

Each CCR Anchor Standard can be identified by its strand, CCR status, and number. For example, R.CCR.6 would signify the reading strand for CCR Anchor Standard 6: "Assess how point of view shapes the content and style of a text" (NGA, 2010). For individual grade-specific standards, you may identify them by their strand, grade, and number and associated letters, as applicable. For example, RL.4.2 stands for Reading for Literature, Grade 4, Standard 2: "Determine a theme of a story, drama, or poem from details in the text; summarize the text" (NGA, 2010). The identification SL.1.1c stands for Speaking and Listening, Grade 1, Standard 1c: "Ask questions to clear up any confusion about the topics and texts under discussion" (NGA, 2010). Sometimes you will see a forward slash: RL/RI.K.1. This means that the same standard (1) appears in both Reading for Literature and Reading for Informational Text. W.1/2.6 indicates that both first and second grade have the same Writing Standard 6.

# COLLABORATION, LIMITATIONS, AND ASSESSMENT

### Who Uses These Standards Besides the ELA Teacher?

The Common Core specifically dictates a shared responsibility for students' literacy development. The K–5 standards include expectations for reading, writing, speaking, listening, and language incorporated within a range of subjects. In middle and high school, where subjects are more departmentalized, teachers will continue to teach their content-specific curriculum but will also embed literacy in history/social studies, science, and technical subjects as explicitly stated in the standards. Thus, teachers in other disciplines will share a responsibility in developing the role of literacy.

### What Aspects Are Not Covered in the Common Core Standards Document?

*Curriculum/Instruction.* The designers of the Common Core explicitly state that the CC Standards are not the curriculum. Rather, they are a clear set of shared goals and expectations that define what all students are expected to know and be able to do. They are not instructions in *how* to teach. The Common Core does not dictate to teachers, curriculum developers, or states how to reach the goals of achieving the CC Standards or what additional topics they might want to address. It is incumbent upon teachers to devise lesson plans and provide students with whatever content-rich curriculum and sound instructional strategies their professional judgment and experience tells them is most helpful in meeting the goals delineated in the standards. In short, there is a focus on results rather than means.

*Going Beyond.* The Common Core Standards do not describe everything that can or should be taught. As such, much is left to curriculum designers' and teachers' discretion using the CC Standards as a guide. Therefore, teachers may choose to go beyond what is stated in the CC Standards.

*Differentiation.* The Common Core Standards are grade specific but do not define the intervention methods or materials necessary to support students who are well below or above grade-level expectations. Teachers need to take into account their students' needs, readiness levels, and learning rates in any given classroom. Additionally, it is beyond the scope of the CC Standards to fully define the spectrum of supports appropriate for English language learners and special needs students. "The standards should be read as allowing for the widest possible range of students to participate fully from the outset and as permitting appropriate accommodations to ensure maximum participation of students with special education needs" (NGA, 2010, Introduction, p. 6).

*The Whole Child.* As far as content, the Common Core Standards do not necessarily define entirely what is required for college and career readiness. Attention to social, emotional, and physical development and approaches to learning need to augment the CC Standards. It is also strongly recommended that teachers incorporate literacy standards in other content areas not mentioned in the Common Core document, such as math and health education.

### What About Assessments?

Currently, two consortia are working on common assessments tied to the Math and ELA standards: Partnership for Assessment of Readiness for Colleges and Careers (PARCC) and the Smarter Balanced Assessment Consortium (SBAC). Each state that has adopted the Common Core has chosen which consortium it would like to use. This next generation of assessments is slated to be fully operational and administered during the 2014–2015 school year for students in third to twelfth grades.

Funding for the consortium came from United States Department of Education Race to the Top funds. Each consortium is planning optional interim and required summative assessments. The summative assessments will be a combination of computer-based and performance tasks.

Check the following websites for detailed information about the assessments and their test types; implementation timeline including pilot and field testing; available resources to prepare teachers, parents, and students for the assessments; accommodations for a range of students; up-to-date information and current status; and more:

- Center for K–12 Assessment & Performance Management at ETS (www.k12center.org)
- Partnership for Assessment of Readiness for Colleges and Careers (PARCC) (www.parcconline.org/)
- The Smarter Balanced Assessment Consortium (SBAC) (www.smarterbalanced.org/)

## CLOSING

This Resources section provides a closer look at the Common Core Standards including information about the designers and their purpose, the organizational structure and what is included in the standards, notations for each standard, responsibility of teachers across the content areas, what these standards do not address, and where to obtain more information on next generation assessments. For more in-depth information, certainly go to the source itself: the Common Core websites. Here are some useful links to access and read on your own, or use as the basis for collaborative discussion with colleagues:

- This main website address links to the Common Core Standards and the appendices: www.corestandards.org/the-standards.
- At these addresses—www.corestandards.org/about-the-standards and http://www .corestandards.org/resources—you will find links to "Key Points in English Language Arts," "Statements of Support," "Myths vs. Facts," "Presentations," "Joint International Benchmarking Report," "Summary of Public Feedback for K–12 Schools," and other resources including a PowerPoint presentation and videos. If you need to present information to a school board or parent community, or want more detailed information, you may want to access pertinent links and segments of this book, as appropriate.
- The standards are featured grade by grade at www.corestandards.org/the-standards/ english-language-arts-standards. The only caveat is that it is in PDF format and each strand is available separately. You can also access my website at www .kathyglassconsulting.com for Microsoft Word formats of each grade-level standard K–8. Once these are downloaded onto your computer, it is easier to cut and paste for curriculum mapping and lesson design.

# References

Achieve. (2010). *On the road to implementation: Adding to the Common Core: Addressing the "15%" guideline.* Retrieved from http://www.achieve.org/files/15PercentGuideline.pdf

Anderson, L. W., Krathwohl, D. R., et al. (Eds.). (2001). *A taxonomy for learning, teaching, and assessing: A revision of Bloom's taxonomy of educational objectives.* Boston: Allyn & Bacon.

Aronson, E., Blaney, N., Stephan, C., Silkes, J., & Snapp, M. (1978). *The jigsaw classroom.* Beverly Hills, CA: Sage.

Avi. (2005). *Poppy.* New York: HarperCollins.

Babbitt, N. (2007). *Tuck everlasting.* New York: Farrar, Straus and Giroux.

Bennett, K. (2005). *Not Norman: A goldfish story.* Cambridge, MA: Candlewick Press.

Black, P., & William, D. (1998, March). Assessment and classroom learning. *Assessment in Education,* 7–74.

Blau, S., Elbow, P., Killgallon, D., & Caplan, R. (1995). *The writer's craft.* Evanston, IL: McDougal, Littell & Company.

Bloom, B. S., & Krathwohl, D. R. (1956). *Taxonomy of educational objectives: The classification of educational goals, by a committee of college and university examiners. Handbook I: Cognitive Domain.* New York: Longmans, Green.

Bruner, J. S., Goodnow, J. J., & Austin, G. A. (1956). *A study of thinking.* London: Chapman & Hall, Limited.

California Department of Education. (2000). *History-social science content standards for California public schools, kindergarten through Grade 12.* Sacramento: Author.

Carmichael, S. B., Martino, G., Porter-Magee, K., & Wilson, W. S. (2010). *The state of state standards—and the Common Core—in 2010.* Retrieved from http://www.edexcellence.net/publications-issues/publications/the-state-of-state.html

Council of Chief State School Officers. (2011). "What we do." Washington, DC: Author. Retrieved from http://www.ccsso.org/What_We_Do.html

Daniels, H. (1994). *Literature circles: Voice and choice in the student-centered classroom.* Portland, ME: Stenhouse Publishers.

DuFour, R. (2004). What is a "professional learning community"? *Schools as Learning Communities, 61*(8), 6–11.

Duke, N. K., & Bennett-Armistead, V. S. (2003). *Reading and writing informational text in the primary grades.* New York: Scholastic.

Dunn, R., & Dunn, K. (1978). *Teaching students through their individual learning styles: A practical approach.* Reston, VA: Reston Publishing Group.

Erickson, H. L. (2002). *Concept-based curriculum and instruction: Teaching beyond the facts.* Thousand Oaks, CA: Corwin.

Erickson, H. L. (2007). *Concept-based curriculum and instruction for the thinking classroom.* Thousand Oaks, CA: Corwin.

Finn, C. E., Jr., & Petrilli, M. J. (2010). *Foreword.* In S. B. Carmichael, G. Martino, K. Porter-Magee, & W. S. Wilson (Eds.), *The state of state standards—and the Common Core—in 2010* (p.1). Retrieved from http://www.edexcellence.net/publications-issues/publications/the-state-of-state.html

Forbes, E. (2003). *Johnny Tremain.* Saint Paul, MN: EMC/Paradigm.

Gardner, H. (1993). *Multiple intelligences: The theory in practice.* New York: Basic Books.

Glass, K. (2007). *Curriculum mapping: A step-by-step guide for creating curriculum year overviews.* Thousand Oaks, CA: Corwin.

Glass, K. (2009). *Lesson design for differentiated instruction, Grades 4–9.* Thousand Oaks, CA: Corwin.

Kemper, D., Nathan, R., & Sabranek, P. (1995). *Writer's express: A handbook for young writers, thinkers, and learners.* Wilmington, MA: Great Source Education Group.

Kendall, J. (2011). *Content knowledge: A compendium of standards and benchmarks for K–12 education* [Online edition]. Retrieved from http://www.mcrel.org/standards-benchmarks

Kober, N., & Renter, D. S. (2011). *Common Core State Standards: Progress and challenges in school districts' implementation.* Washington, DC: Author.

Marzano, R., & Kendall, J. (2000). *Content knowledge: A compendium of standards and benchmarks for K–12 Education* (3rd ed.). Aurora, CO: McREL.

McLerran, A. (1992). *Roxaboxen.* New York: Puffin Books.

National Governors Association (NGA) Center for Best Practices, & the Council of Chief State School Officers (CCSSO). (2010). *Common Core State Standards for English language arts & literacy in history/ social studies, science, and technical subjects.* Washington, DC: Author. Retrieved from http://www .corestandards.org/assets/CCSSI_ELA%20Standards.pdf

National Governors Association (NGA). (2011). "Who we are." Washington, DC: Author. Retrieved from http://www.nga.org/cms/about

New York State P–12. (2011). *Common Core State Standards for English language arts and literacy.* Retrieved from http://www.p12.nysed.gov/ciai/common_core_standards/pdfdocs/nysp12 cclsela.pdf

Otsuka, J. (2002). *When the emperor was divine.* New York: Random House.

Robb, L., Richek, M. A., & Spandel, V. (2002). *Reader's handbook: A student guide for reading and learning.* Wilmington, MA: Great Source Education Group.

Sachar, L. (1998). *Holes.* New York: Dell Yearling.

Spandel, V. (2001). *Creating writers: Through 6-trait writing assessment and instruction* (3rd ed.). New York: Addison, Wesley, Longman.

Spandel, V. (forthcoming). *Creating writers: Through 6-trait writing assessment and instruction* (6th ed.). New York: Addison, Wesley, Longman.

Sternberg, R. J. (1996). *Successful intelligence: How practice and creative intelligence determine success in life.* New York: Simon & Schuster.

Strickland, C. A. (2009). Tools for high quality differentiated instruction: An ASCD toolkit. In C. A. Strickland (Ed.), *Professional development for differentiated instruction: An ASCD toolkit.* Alexandria, VA: Association for Supervision and Curriculum Development.

Strickland, C. A., & Glass, K. T. (2009). *Staff development guide for the parallel curriculum.* Thousand Oaks, CA: Corwin.

Tomlinson, C. (2001). *How to differentiate instruction in mixed-ability classrooms* (2nd ed.). Alexandria, VA: Association for Supervision and Curriculum Development.

Tomlinson, C., & Eidson, C. (2003). *Differentiation in practice: A resource guide for differentiating curriculum.* Alexandria, VA: Association for Supervision and Curriculum Development.

Tomlinson, C., & McTighe, J. (2006). *Integrating differentiated instruction + understanding by design.* Alexandria, VA: Association for Supervision and Curriculum Development.

Tomlinson, C. A., et al. (2002). *The parallel curriculum: A design to develop high potential and challenge high-ability learners.* Thousand Oaks, CA: Corwin.

Wandberg, R., & Rohwer, J. (2010). *Teaching health education in language diverse classrooms.* Burlington, MA: Jones and Bartlett Learning.

White, E. B. (1952). *Charlotte's web.* New York: Harper.

Wiggins, G., & McTighe, J. (1998). *Understanding by design.* Alexandria, VA: Association for Supervision and Curriculum Development.

Wiggins, G., & McTighe, J. (2005). *Understanding by design* (2nd ed.). Alexandria, VA: Association for Supervision and Curriculum Development.

Willems, M. (2003). *Don't let the pigeon drive the bus!* New York: Hyperion Books.

# Index

# CORWIN
A SAGE Company

The Corwin logo—a raven striding across an open book—represents the union of courage and learning. Corwin is committed to improving education for all learners by publishing books and other professional development resources for those serving the field of PreK–12 education. By providing practical, hands-on materials, Corwin continues to carry out the promise of its motto: **"Helping Educators Do Their Work Better."**